Mari. K........ova was bor........ .....was ....
States. Her first book, Ma.........., was a *New York Ti........*....... .he
is a contributing writer for *The New Yorker*, where she writes a regular
column with a focus on psychology and culture, and her writing has
appeared in *The Atlantic*, *The New York Times*, *Scientific American MIND*
and *The Smithsonian*, among numerous other publications.

www.mariakonnikova.com
Follow @mkonnikova on Twitter

'A gripping examination of exactly why so many of us are
such suckers for schemes that shut down our saner instincts' *Vice*

'A thrilling psychological detective story . . . What makes the book
especially pleasurable is that Konnikova's intellectual rigor comes
with a side of warm wit' *Brainpickings*

'An engaging read . . . Konnikova threads her examination with rich
narratives of historical swindles' *Los Angeles Review of Books*

'Maria Konnikova breaks down the psychology of schemes, scams,
tricks and frauds across the centuries in *The Confidence Game* an
unnerving manual for conning and getting conned . . . fortunately, the
cons are usually entertaining and the studies revealing'
Washington Post

'Konnikova covers wide-ranging studies in social psychology and
illustrates them with colorful stories about real-life con men
and wo........................ *Magazine*

'Exception.................................he ways these skilled
tricksters ....n ends' *Boston Globe*

'A compell...................................nd of the con . . . *The
Confidence Game* will teach you how confidence artists operate –
and how to outwit them'
Charles Duhigg, author of *The Power of Habit*

'An enthralling read about why we're all vulnerable to deception, by
one of the truly gifted social science writers of our time'
Adam Grant, author of *Give and Take* and *Originals*

ALSO BY MARIA KONNIKOVA

Mastermind

The Confidence Game

The Psychology of the Con and Why We Fall for It Every Time

Maria Konnikova

CANONGATE

This paperback edition published by Canongate Books in 2016

First published in Great Britain in 2016 by Canongate Books Ltd, 14
High Street, Edinburgh EH1 1TE

www.canongate.tv

1

British Library Cataloguing-in-Publication Data
A catalogue record for this book is available on
request from the British Library

ISBN 978 78211 391 1

Printed and bound in Great Britain by Clays Ltd, St Ives plc

MIX
Paper from
responsible sources
FSC® C020471

For my parents, Jane and Vitaly,
who taught me that life is never fair, nothing comes for free,
and there's no such thing as the exception to the rule

How cheerfully he seems to grin,
How neatly spreads his claws,
And welcomes little fishes in
With gently smiling jaws!

—LEWIS CARROLL,
ALICE'S ADVENTURES IN WONDERLAND

We aren't robbers, you and I.
To rob a fool, you don't need knives:
Just flatter him, tell him sweet lies,
And he is yours for life.

—BULAT OKUDZHAVA, "OF GLUTTONS, BRAGGARTS,
AND FOOLS (THE CON ARTISTS' DUET)"

CONTENTS

INTRODUCTION

The aristocrats of crime.   —DAVID MAURER

D r. Joseph Cyr, a surgeon lieutenant of the Royal Canadian Navy, walked onto the deck of the HMCS *Cayuga*. It was September 1951, the second year of the Korean War, and the *Cayuga* was making her way north of the thirty-eighth parallel, just off the shore of North Korea. The morning had gone smoothly enough; no sickness, no injuries to report. But just as the afternoon was getting on, the lookouts spotted something that didn't quite fit with the watery landscape: a small, cramped Korean junk that was waving a flag and frantically making its way toward the ship.

Within the hour, the rickety boat had pulled up alongside the *Cayuga*. Inside was a mess of bodies, nineteen in all, piled together in obvious filth. They looked close to death. Mangled torsos, bloody, bleeding heads, limbs that turned the wrong way or failed to turn at all. Most of them were no more than boys. They had been caught in an ambush, a Korean liaison officer soon explained to the *Cayuga*'s crew; the messy bullet and shrapnel wounds were the result. That's why Dr. Cyr had been summoned from below deck: he was the only man with any medical qualification on board. He would have to operate—and soon. Without his intervention, all nineteen men would very likely die. Dr. Cyr began to prepare his kit.

There was only one problem. Dr. Cyr didn't hold a medical degree, let alone the proper qualifications required to undertake complex surgery aboard a moving ship. In fact, he'd never even graduated high school. And his real name wasn't Cyr. It was Ferdinand Waldo Demara, or, as he would eventually become known, the Great Impostor—one of the most successful confidence artists of all time, memorialized, in part, in Robert Crichton's 1959 account *The Great Impostor.* His career would span decades, his disguises the full gamut of professional life. But nowhere was he more at home than in the guise of the master of human life, the doctor.

Over the next forty-eight hours, Demara would somehow fake his way through the surgeries, with the help of a medical textbook, a field guide he had persuaded a fellow physician back in Ontario to create "for the troops" in the event a doctor wasn't readily available, copious antibiotics (for the patients) and alcohol (for himself), and a healthy dose of supreme confidence in his own abilities. After all, he'd been a doctor before. Not to mention a psychologist. And a professor. And a monk (many monks, in fact). And the founder of a religious college. Why couldn't he be a surgeon?

As Demara performed his medical miracles on the high seas, makeshift operating table tied down to protect the patients from the roll of the waves, a zealous young press officer wandered the decks in search of a story. The home office was getting on his back. They needed good copy. *He* needed good copy. Little of note had been happening for weeks. He was, he joked to his shipmates, practically starving for news. When word of the Korean rescue spread among the crew, it was all he could do to hide his excitement. Dr. Cyr's story was fantastic. It was, indeed, perfect. Cyr hadn't been required to help the enemy, but his honorable nature had compelled him to do so. And with what results. Nineteen surgeries. And nineteen men departing the *Cayuga* in far better shape than they'd arrived. Would the good doctor agree to a profile, to commemorate the momentous events of the week?

Who was Demara to resist? He had grown so sure of his invulnerability, so confident in the borrowed skin of Joseph Cyr, MD, that no amount of media attention was too much. And he had performed some pretty masterful operations, if he might say so himself. Dispatches about the great feats of Dr. Cyr soon spread throughout Canada.

Dr. Joseph Cyr, original version, felt his patience running out. It was October 23, and there he was, sitting quietly in Edmunston, trying his damnedest to read a book in peace. But they simply wouldn't leave him alone. The phone was going crazy, ringing the second he replaced the receiver. Was he the doctor in Korea? the well-intentioned callers wanted to know. Was it his son? Or another relative? No, no, he told anyone who bothered to listen. No relation. There were many Cyrs out there, and many Joseph Cyrs. It was not he.

A few hours later, Cyr received another call, this time from a good friend who now read aloud the "miracle doctor's" credentials. There may be many Joseph Cyrs, but this particular one boasted a background identical to his own. At some point, coincidence just didn't cut it. Cyr asked his friend for a photograph.

Surely there was some mistake. He knew precisely who this was. "Wait, this is my friend, Brother John Payne of the Brothers of Christian Instruction," he said, the surprise evident in his voice. Brother Payne had been a novice when Cyr knew him. He'd taken the name after shedding his secular life—and that life, Cyr well recalled, was a medical one much like his own. Dr. Cecil B. Hamann, he believed the man's original name was. But why, even if he had returned once more to medicine, would he ever use Cyr's name instead? Surely his own medical credentials were enough. Demara's deception rapidly began to unravel.

And unravel it did. But his eventual dismissal from the navy was far from signaling the end of his career. Profoundly embarrassed—the future of the nation's defense was on its shoulders, and it couldn't even manage the security of its own personnel?—the navy did not press charges. Demara-alias-Cyr was quietly dismissed and asked to leave the country. He was only too happy to oblige, and despite his newfound, and short-lived, notoriety, he would go on to successfully impersonate an entire panoply of humanity, from prison warden to instructor at a school for "mentally retarded" children to humble English teacher to civil engineer who was almost awarded a contract to build a large bridge in Mexico. By the time he died, over thirty years later, Dr. Cyr would be but one of the dozens of aliases that peppered Demara's history. Among them: that of his own biographer, Robert Crichton, an alias he assumed soon after the book's publication, and long before the end of his career as an impostor.

Time and time again, Demara—Fred to those who knew him undisguised—found himself in positions of the highest authority, in charge of human minds in the classroom, bodies in the prison system, lives on the decks of the *Cayuga*. Time and time again, he would be exposed, only to go back and succeed, yet again, at inveigling those around him.

How was he so effective? Was it that he preyed on particularly soft, credulous targets? I'm not sure the Texas prison system, one of the toughest in the United States, could be described as such. Was it that he presented an especially compelling, trustworthy figure? Not likely, at six foot one and over 250 pounds, square linebacker's jaw framed by small eyes that seemed to sit on the border between amusement and chicanery, an expression that made Crichton's four-year-old daughter Sarah cry and shrink in fear the first time she ever saw it. Or was it something else, something deeper and more fundamental—something that says more about ourselves and how we see the world?

It's the oldest story ever told. The story of belief—of the basic, irresistible, universal human need to believe in something that gives life meaning, something that reaffirms our view of ourselves, the world, and our place in it. "Religion," Voltaire is said to have remarked, "began when the first scoundrel met the first fool." It certainly sounds like something he would have said. Voltaire was no fan of the religious establishment. But versions of the exact same words have been attributed to Mark Twain, to Carl Sagan, to Geoffrey Chaucer. It seems so accurate that someone, somewhere, sometime, must certainly have said it.

And it seems so accurate, most of all, because it touches on a profound truth. The truth of our absolute and total need for belief from our earliest moments of consciousness, from an infant's unwavering knowledge that she will be fed and comforted to an adult's need to see some sort of justness and fairness in the surrounding world. In some ways, confidence artists like Demara have it easy. We've done most of the work for them; we want to believe in what they're telling us. Their genius lies in figuring out what, precisely, it is we want, and how they can present themselves as the perfect vehicle for delivering on that desire.

The impostors, like Demara, showing up where they are needed, in the guise they are most needed: a qualified doctor volunteering for the navy when there is a severe shortage of physicians; a prison warden eager to take on the most difficult inmates where no one wants to step in. The Ponzi schemer who arrives with the perfect investment at a time when money is short and the markets shaky. The academic who creates just the cloning breakthrough everyone has been awaiting. The art dealer with the perfect Rothko that the collector simply hasn't been able to locate anywhere else. The politician with the long-awaited solution to a thorny issue that's been plaguing the town for years. The healer with just the right remedy, just the right tincture, just the right touch. The journalist with the perfect story to illustrate an important point. And, long before any of these are born, the religious leader who promises hope and salvation when everything seems to have hit a low point, who swears that, somewhere, sometime, the world will be just.

In the 1950s, the linguist David Maurer began to delve more deeply into the world of confidence men than any had before him. He called them, simply, "aristocrats of crime." Hard crime—outright theft or burglary, violence, threats—is not what the confidence artist is about. The confidence game—the con—is an exercise in soft skills. Trust, sympathy, persuasion. The true con artist doesn't force us to do anything; he makes us complicit in our own undoing. He doesn't steal. We give. He doesn't have to threaten us. We supply the story ourselves. We believe because we want to, not because anyone made us. And so we offer up whatever they want—money, reputation, trust, fame, legitimacy, support—and we don't realize what is happening until it is too late. Our need to believe, to embrace things that explain our world, is as pervasive as it is strong. Given the right cues, we're willing to go along with just about anything and put our confidence in just about anyone. Conspiracy theories, supernatural phenomena, psychics: we have a seemingly bottomless capacity for credulity. Or, as one psychologist put it, "Gullibility may be deeply engrained in the human behavioral repertoire." For our minds are built for stories. We crave them, and, when there aren't ready ones available, we create them. Stories about our origins. Our purpose. The reasons the world is the way it is. Human beings don't like to exist in a state of uncertainty or ambiguity. When something doesn't make sense, we want to supply the missing link. When we don't understand what or why or how something happened, we want to find the explanation. A confidence artist is only too happy to comply—and the well-crafted narrative is his absolute forte.

There's a likely apocryphal story about the French poet Jacques Prévert. One day he was walking past a blind man who held up a sign: "Blind man without a pension." He stopped to chat. How was it going? Were people helpful? "Not great," the man replied. "Some people give, but not a lot—and most just keep walking."

"Could I borrow your sign?" Prévert asked. The blind man nodded. The poet took the sign, flipped it over, and wrote a message.

The next day, he again walked past the blind man. "How is it going now?" he asked. "Incredible," the man replied. "I've never received so much money in my life."

On the sign, Prévert had written: "Spring is coming, but I won't see it."

Give us a compelling story, and we open up. Skepticism gives way to belief. The same approach that makes a blind man's cup overflow with donations can make us more receptive to most any persuasive message, for good or for ill.

When we step into a magic show, we come in actively wanting to be fooled. We want deception to cover our eyes and make our world a tiny bit more fantastical, more awesome than it was before. And the magician, in many ways, uses the exact same approaches as the confidence man—only without the destruction of the con's end game. "Magic is a kind of a conscious, willing con," Michael Shermer, a science historian and writer who has devoted many decades to debunking claims about the supernatural and the pseudoscientific, told me one December afternoon. "You're not being foolish to fall for it. If you don't fall for it, the magician is doing something wrong."

Shermer, the founder of the Skeptics Society and *Skeptic* magazine, has thought extensively about how the desire to embrace magic so often translates into susceptibility to its less savory forms. "Take the Penn and Teller cups and balls routine. They use clear plastic cups so you can see exactly what's happening, but it still works." At their root, magic tricks and confidence games share the same fundamental principle: a manipulation of our beliefs. Magic operates at the most basic level of visual perception, manipulating how we see and experience reality. It changes for an instant what we think possible, quite literally taking advantage of our eyes' and brains' foibles to create an alternative version of the world. The con does the same thing, but can go much deeper. Quick tricks like three-card monte are identical to a magician's routine—except the intent is more nefarious. But long cons, the kind that take weeks, months, or even years to unfold, manipulate reality at a higher level, playing with our most basic beliefs about humanity and the world.

The real confidence game feeds on the desire for magic, exploiting our endless taste for an existence that is more extraordinary and somehow more meaningful. But when we're falling for a con, we aren't actively seeking deception—or at least we don't think we are. As long as the desire for magic, for a reality that is somehow greater than our everyday existence, remains, the confidence game will thrive.

The confidence game has existed long before the term itself was first used, likely in 1849, during the trial of William Thompson. The elegant Thompson, according to the *New York Herald*, would approach passersby on the streets of Manhattan, start up a conversation, and then come forward with a unique request. "Have you confidence in me to trust me with your watch until tomorrow?" Faced with such a quixotic question, and one that hinged directly on respectability, many a stranger proceeded to part with his timepiece. And so, the "confidence man" was born: the person who uses others' trust in him for his own private purposes. Have you confidence in me? What will you give me to prove it?

Cons come in all guises. Short cons like the infamous three-card monte or shell game: feats of sleight of hand and theatrics still played avidly on the streets of Manhattan. Long cons that take time and ingenuity to build up, from impostor schemes to Ponzis to the building of outright new realities—a new country, a new technology, a new cure— that have found a comfortable home in the world of the Internet, and remain, as well, safely ensconced in their old, offline guises. Many come with fanciful names. Pig in a poke, dating back at least to 1530, when Richard Hill's "Common-place book" suggested that "When ye proffer the pigge open the poke," lest what comes out of the bag is not a pig at all. The Spanish Prisoner, called by the *New York Times*, in 1898, "one of the oldest and most attractive and probably most successful swindles known to the police," dates back at least to the 1500s. The magic wallet.

The gold brick. The green goods. Banco. The big store. The wire. The payoff. The rag. The names are as colorful as they are plentiful.

The con is the oldest game there is. But it's also one that is remarkably well suited to the modern age. If anything, the whirlwind advance of technology heralds a new golden age of the grift. Cons thrive in times of transition and fast change, when new things are happening and old ways of looking at the world no longer suffice. That's why they flourished during the gold rush and spread with manic fury in the days of westward expansion. That's why they thrive during revolutions, wars, and political upheavals. Transition is the confidence game's great ally, because transition breeds uncertainty. There's nothing a con artist likes better than exploiting the sense of unease we feel when it appears that the world as we know it is about to change. We may cling cautiously to the past, but we also find ourselves open to things that are new and not quite expected. Who's to say this new way of doing business isn't the wave of the future?

In the nineteenth century, we had the industrial revolution, and many present-day scam techniques developed in its wake. Today, we have the technological revolution. And this one, in some ways, is best suited to the con of all. With the Internet, everything is shifting at once, from the most basic things (how we meet people and make meaningful connections) to the diurnal rhythms of our lives (how we shop, how we eat, how we schedule meetings, make dates, plan vacations). Shy away from everything, you're a technophobe or worse. (You met *how*? *Online*? And you're . . . getting *married*?) Embrace it too openly, though, and the risks that used to come your way only in certain circumscribed situations—a walk down Canal Street past a three-card monte table, an "investment opportunity" from the man in your club, and so forth—are a constant presence anytime you open your iPad.

That's why no amount of technological sophistication or growing scientific knowledge or other markers we like to point to as signs of societal progress will—or can—make cons any less likely. The same schemes that were playing out in the big stores of the Wild West are now being run via your in-box; the same demands that were being made over the wire are hitting your cell phone. A text from a family member. A frantic call from the hospital. A Facebook message from a cousin who seems to have been stranded in a foreign country. When *Catch Me If You Can* hero Frank Abagnale, who, as a teen, conned his way through most any organization you can imagine, from airlines to hospitals, was recently asked if his escapades could happen in the modern world—a world of technology and seemingly ever-growing sophistication—he laughed. Far, far simpler now, he said. "What I did fifty years ago as a teenage boy is four thousand times easier to do today because of technology. Technology breeds crime. It always has, and always will."

Technology doesn't make us more worldly or knowledgeable. It doesn't protect us. It's just a change of venue for the same old principles of confidence. What are *you* confident in? The con artist will find those things where your belief is unshakeable and will build on that foundation to subtly change the world around you. But you will be so confident in the starting point that you won't even notice what's happened.

Since 2008, consumer fraud in the United States has gone up by more than 60 percent. Online scams have more than doubled. Back in 2007, they made up one fifth of all fraud cases; in 2011, they were 40 percent. In 2012 alone, the Internet Crime Complaint Center reported almost three hundred thousand complaints of online fraud. The total money lost: $525 million.

For the total U.S. population, between 2011 and 2012—the last period surveyed by the Federal Trade Commission—a little over 10 percent of adults, or 25.6 million, had fallen victim to fraud. The total number of fraudulent incidents was even higher, topping 37.8 million. The majority of the cases, affecting just over 5 million adults, involved one scheme: fake weight-loss products. In second place, at 2.4 million adults: prize promotions. Coming in third, at 1.9 million: buyers' clubs (those annoying offers you usually toss out with the recycling, where what seems like a free deal suddenly translates to endless unwanted, and far from free, charges for memberships you didn't even know you signed up for), followed by unauthorized Internet billing (1.9 million) and work-at-home programs (1.8 million). About a third of the incidents were initiated online.

Last year in the UK, an estimated 58 percent of households received fraudulent calls, seemingly from banks, police, computer companies, or other credible-sounding businesses. Some call recipients were wise to the scam. But somehow, close to £24 million was lost to the scammers—up from £7 million the year prior.

Countless more cases go unreported—most cases, in fact, by some estimates. According to a recent study from the AARP, only 37 percent of victims older than fifty-five will admit to having fallen for a con; just over half of those under fifty-five do so. No one wants to admit to having been duped. Most con artists don't ever come to trial: they simply aren't brought to the authorities to begin with.

No matter the medium or the guise, cons, at their core, are united by the same basic principles—principles that rest on the manipulation of belief. Cons go unreported—indeed, undetected—because none of us want to admit that our basic beliefs could be wrong. It matters little if we're dealing with a Ponzi scheme or falsified data, fake quotes or misleading information, fraudulent art or doubtful health claims, a false version of history or a less than honest version of the future. At a fundamental, psychological level, it's all about confidence—or, rather, the taking advantage of somebody else's.

This book is not a history of the con. Nor is it an exhaustive look at every con there ever was. It is, rather, an exploration of the psychological principles that underlie each and every game, from the most elementary to the most involved, step by step, from the moment the endeavor is conceived to the aftermath of its execution.

The confidence game starts with basic human psychology. From the artist's perspective, it's a question of identifying the victim (the put-up): who is he, what does he want, and how can I play on that desire to achieve what I want? It requires the creation of empathy and rapport (the play): an emotional foundation must be laid before any scheme is proposed, any game set in motion. Only then does it move to logic and persuasion (the rope): the scheme (the tale), the evidence and the way it will work to your benefit (the convincer), the show of actual profits. And like a fly caught in a spider's web, the more we struggle, the less able to extricate ourselves we become (the breakdown). By the time things begin to look dicey, we tend to be so invested, emotionally and often physically, that we do most of the persuasion ourselves. We may even choose to up our involvement ourselves, even as things turn south (the send), so that by the time we're completely fleeced (the touch), we don't quite know what hit us. The con artist may not even need to convince us to stay quiet (the blow-off and fix); we are more likely than not to do so ourselves. We are, after all, the best deceivers of our own minds. At each step of the game, con artists draw from a seemingly endless toolbox of ways to manipulate our belief. And as we become more committed, with every step we give them more psychological material to work with.

Everyone has heard the saying "If it seems too good to be true, it probably is." Or its close relative "There's no such thing as a free lunch." But when it comes to our own selves, we tend to latch on to that "probably." If it seems too good to be true, it is—unless it's happening to me. We deserve our good fortune. I deserve the big art break; I've worked in galleries all my life and I had this coming. I deserve true love; I've been in bad relationships long enough. I deserve good returns on my money, at long last; I've gotten quite the experience over the years. The mentalities of "too good to be true" and "I deserve" are, unfortunately, at odds, but we remain blind to the tension when it comes to our own actions and decisions. When we see other people talking about their unbelievable deal or crazy good fortune, we realize at once that they've been taken for a sucker. But when it happens to us, well, I am just lucky and deserving of a good turn.

We get, too, a unique satisfaction from thinking ourselves invulnerable. Who doesn't enjoy the illicit glimpse into the life of the underworld—and the satisfaction of knowing that clever old you would be smarter than all that, that you can laugh at the poor sap who fell for something so obvious and still be safe in the knowledge that you are keener, savvier, more cynical and skeptical? *They* may fall for it. You? Never.

And yet, when it comes to the con, everyone is a potential victim. Despite our deep certainty in our own immunity—or, rather, because of it—we *all* fall for it. That's the genius of the great confidence artists: they are, truly, artists—able to affect even the most discerning connoisseurs with their persuasive charm. A theoretical-particle physicist or the CEO of a major Hollywood studio is no more exempt than an eighty-year-old Florida retiree who guilelessly signs away his retirement savings for a not-to-miss investment that never materializes. A savvy Wall Street investor is just as likely to fall for a con as a market neophyte, a prosecutor who questions motives for a living as likely to succumb as your gullible next-door neighbor who thinks *The Onion* prints real news.

So how do they do it? What makes us believe—and how do people take advantage of that process for their own ends? At some point, everyone will be deceived. Everyone will fall victim to a confidence artist of one stripe or another. Everyone will fall for it. The real question is why. And can you ever understand your own mind well enough that you learn to extricate yourself before it's too late?

CHAPTER 1
THE GRIFTER
AND THE MARK

He does not answer questions, or gives evasive answers; he speaks nonsense, rubs the great toe along the ground, and shivers; his face is discolored; he rubs the roots of his hair with his fingers.

—PROFILE OF A LIAR, 900 BCE

Whenever people ask me if I've ever been conned, I tell them the truth: I have no idea. I've never given money to a Ponzi scheme or gotten tripped up on an unwinnable game of three-card monte—that much I know. And there have been some smaller deceptions I've certainly fallen for—though whether they qualify as full-fledged cons is a matter of dispute. But here's the thing about cons: the best of them are never discovered. We don't ever realize we've fallen; we simply write our loss off as a matter of bad luck.

Magicians often resist showing the same trick twice. Once the element of surprise is gone, the audience becomes free to pay attention to everything else—and is thus much more likely to discern the ruse. But the best tricks can be repeated ad infinitum. They are so well honed that there is practically no deception to spot. Harry Houdini, the magician and famed exposer of frauds, boasted that he could figure out any trick once he'd thrice seen it. One evening at Chicago's Great Northern Hotel, the story goes, a fellow conjurer, Dai Vernon, approached him with a card trick. Vernon removed a card from the top of the deck and asked Houdini to initial it—an "H.H." in the corner. The card was then placed in the middle of the deck. Vernon snapped his fingers. It was a miracle. The top card in the deck was now Houdini's. It was, as the name of the routine suggests, an "ambitious card." No matter where you put it, it rose to the top. Seven times Vernon demonstrated, and seven times Houdini was stumped. The truly clever trick needs no hiding. (In this case, it was a sleight-of-hand effect that is often performed by skilled magicians today but was, back then, a novelty.)

When it comes to cons, the exact same principle holds. The best confidence games remain below the radar. They are never prosecuted because they are never detected. Or, as in Demara's case, they are detected, but the embarrassment is too great. I wouldn't be surprised if Houdini had kept quiet about his inability to spot Vernon's trick, had the two men met in a less public setting. It's not uncommon, in fact, for the same person to fall for the exact same con multiple times. James Franklin Norfleet, a Texas rancher you'll meet again later on, lost first $20,000, and then, in short order, $25,000, to the exact same racket and the exact same gang. He'd never realized the first go-around was a scam. David Maurer describes one victim who, several years after falling for a well-known wire con—the grifter pretends to have a way of getting race results seconds before they are announced, allowing the mark to place a sure-win bet—spotted his deceivers on the street. He ran toward them. Their hearts sank. Surely, he was going to turn them in. Not at all. He was wondering if he could once more play that game he'd lost at way back when. He was certain that, this time, his luck had turned. The men were only too happy to comply.

Even someone like Bernie Madoff went undetected for at least twenty years. He was seventy when his scheme crumbled. What if he'd died before it blew up? One can imagine a future where his victims would be none the wiser—as long as new investments kept coming in.

In June 2007, *Slate* writer Justin Peters decided to be creative about his airfare to Italy. Short on money, he was nevertheless eager to spend a few months out of the country. And he had what he considered a pretty damn brilliant plan for solving the dilemma. He'd buy airline miles from someone willing to part with them, and then use them to purchase a reduced fare. He promptly started scouring the Internet for anyone with a mile surplus. He was lucky. Soon after he began his search, he found Captain Chris Hansen, a pilot with countless unused miles he'd put up for purchase on Craigslist. Peters quickly replied to his posting—god forbid the miles went to someone else. They talked on the phone. Captain Chris seemed knowledgeable and friendly. "Our conversation convinced me that he was on the level," Peters writes. A deal was promptly arranged: $650. A hundred thousand miles. PayPal. Simple.

Except PayPal rejected the transaction. How odd, Peters thought. He followed up with the captain about the error. The pilot was strangely silent.

Peters, however, was desperate. His scheduled departure date loomed ever closer, and still no tickets. So he returned to the hunt. Bingo. Franco Borga, ready seller of miles. Borga responded promptly and, of all things, included his driver's license in the reply. He was who he said he was, not some Craigslist scammer. A phone call later—a "very nice conversation"—and they were in business. Seven hundred dollars on a Green Dot card, and the miles would be his. (Green Dot cards, a favorite of the con artist, are gift cards that you can easily buy at any supermarket or drugstore. You can recharge them, and anyone with the account number can access the balance—a way to move funds without the hassle of a wire transfer.)

Four days later, still no miles. It was finally dawning on Peters that he might have been scammed. But then, lo and behold, his long-lost pilot resurfaced. He'd been abroad, he explained, with limited e-mail access. But he still had the miles for Peters's use. Victory. Of course Peters still wanted them—especially, he told the captain, after he'd been so callously scammed. Captain Chris sympathized completely. The Internet was a predatory place. To put Peters's mind at ease, the captain then sent him a contract; he was, as Peters had always known, on the level.

PayPal still on the fritz, Peters quickly wired the promised $650.

By this point, everyone but Peters can see how the story will end. Three days, no miles. Four, five, six days. No miles, no e-mails. He had fallen for the exact same scam twice in one week. In this case, he had clear proof of the deception: no miles. But imagine a situation where chance plays a bigger role. A stock market. A race. An investment. Who's to say it wasn't just bad luck?

P. T. Barnum may never have said, "There's a sucker born every minute." (He very likely did not.) But among the con men of the early twentieth century, there was another saying. "There's a sucker born every minute, and one to trim 'em and one to knock 'em." There's always something to fall for, and always someone to do the falling.

Who is the victim and who, the con man? What kinds of people are the Bernie Madoffs and Captain Hansens of the world? And do a Norfleet and a Peters share some underlying traits that bind them together? Is there a quintessential grifter—and a quintessential mark?

* * *

Eighteen State Street. A small, two-window-wide cream house. Teal-and-white trimmed shutters. Grass sprouting in between slabs of surrounding concrete. A small teal-and-cream garage, a basketball hoop affixed to the top. This is where the Great Impostor once made his home. Although he would do his best to have you forget it.

Ferdinand Waldo Demara, Jr.—our old Korean naval surgeon friend, Dr. Cyr—was born on December 12, 1921, in Lawrence, Massachusetts, the first son and second child of a prosperous local family. His mother, Mary McNelly, was an Irish girl from Salem, Massachusetts, a product of the strictest of Catholic upbringings. His father, Ferdinand Senior, was French Canadian, the first generation to have made it south of the border. He'd come in search of wealth, and, by the time young

Fred was born, had found some semblance of it, from the movie business. He'd started as a simple projectionist in Providence, Rhode Island, but over the years he'd saved enough that he dreamed of owning his own theater. In Lawrence, he'd met a local backer, and before long, the Toomey-Demara Amusement Company was running its first cinema: The Palace. It was a success, and Fred Senior seemed born to it. He was, Demara's mother later recalled, "one of the few men who could carry a cane and sport spats and not look foolish doing it."

Fred wasn't born in that modest State Street house. No, sir. He was a product of the fashionable Jackson Street. Where his classmates at the Emily G. Wetherbee School were mostly the sons of mill workers, he stood out. He was a class above. And a head above, too; even then, Fred was a giant.

Fred wasn't particularly popular, what with his constant better-than-thou-ness. But nor was he particularly disliked. That is, until another boy thought that he'd ratted him out to the teacher. "We're going to get you at lunch," he and a newly formed posse promised. Fred promptly went home at recess. But before lunch, he returned. When the boys surrounded him, he pulled out a dueling pistol. "I'm going to shoot your guts out," he threatened. Two more guns were found in his bag, and Fred was suspended.

His behavior soon grew so out of control that he was placed in a Catholic school, St. Augustine's. And it was there that he swapped flat-out violence for a slier sort of approach.

St. Augustine's had a Valentine's Day tradition. Each eighth grader would give a seventh-grade boy a small gift. It was a simple ceremonial exchange to symbolize a "turning over" of the class to the rising eighth graders. By the time Fred was in eighth grade, though, the family's fortunes had taken a sharp downward turn. Shortly after his eleventh birthday, the Toomey-Demara Amusement Company went bankrupt. Good-bye, Jackson Street. In its stead, an old carriage house on the outskirts of town. State Street.

Demara desperately didn't want to be poor. "Please, Little Jesus and

Mother Mary," he would pray. "Please don't make us poor. If you don't I'll say a rosary every night of my life." His prayer went unanswered.

That February morning, he wanted to be sure to make an impression, show those poor Catholic kids how a real gentleman behaves. And so, he made his way to the bakery and candy shop off Jackson Street, close to the house that was no longer theirs. The family, he knew, still had an account there. He arranged for the largest heart-shaped box of chocolates to be delivered to the school at three sharp.

The box never came. Somehow the order had gotten lost in the mix—or perhaps the confectioner had grown suspicious that the Demaras' account wasn't what it once was. Whatever the holdup, if there was one thing Fred hated more than being poor, it was the humiliation of being called a liar. He'd promised the biggest gift the school had ever seen, and he had come up empty-handed. He vowed to make it right. He returned to the store in a huff. This time, he ordered not only the large heart but smaller boxes for every child in the grade. To put on his account.

This time, there was no mix-up. If the boy had the nerve to order up such a storm, clearly the family could pay. You wouldn't do something like that, and do it so confidently, unless you could back it up. The boxes promptly arrived, wheeled to St. Augustine's in a large cart overflowing with chocolate. The Demara family, of course, had no way of paying for them.

From then on, until, at fifteen, he dropped out to join the first of a string of religious orders, Fred Demara was known as the Candy Butcher. And from there, it was a stone's throw to his first full-on con: stealing an unsuspecting student's credentials to try to get a commission in the navy.

Was the life of an impostor always his destiny? Was he born to be a grifter?

* * *

Con artists are evil human beings, with malicious intentions and no conscience. Would that it were so. It would make the world a much easier place to be in. We'd ferret out the bad guys and be on our merry way. The reality, however, is far messier.

In his essay "Diddling," Edgar Allan Poe describes the features of the swindler: "minuteness, interest, perseverance, ingenuity, audacity, *nonchalance*, originality, impertinence, and *grin*." Modern psychology agrees with him on one particular point: the nonchalance. For the most part, humans have evolved as cooperative animals. We can trust one another, rely on one another, walk around with a wallet full of cash not worrying that every single stranger will rob us, and go to bed with the certainty that we won't be killed in our sleep. Over time, our emotions have evolved to support that status quo. We feel warm and fuzzy when we've helped someone. We feel shame and guilt when we've lied or cheated or otherwise harmed someone. Sure, all of us deviate now and then, but for the most part we've grown to be quite decent—or, the opposite of nonchalant. For the most part, we care about others and know that they care to some extent about us. Otherwise, much of society would collapse.

But there's an exception. A very small number of people may have evolved to take advantage of the general good of others, fueled by the nonchalance that makes many a con artist what he is. These people don't care; they remain perfectly indifferent to the pain they cause, as long as they end up on top. It makes perfect sense. If the vast majority of the people who surround you are basically decent, you can lie, cheat, and steal all you want and get on famously. But the approach only works if few take advantage of it—if everyone did the same, the system would self-destruct and we would all end up doing worse. Calculated nonchalance is only an adaptive strategy when it's a minority one. Or, as Adrian Raine, a psychologist at the University of Pennsylvania whose research centers on antisocial behavior, puts it, "Persistent immoral behavior can be thought of as an alternative evolutionary strategy that can be beneficial at low rates in society. By lacking the emotional experiences that serve to deter immoral behavior, and by using deception and manipulation, individuals may be able to successfully cheat their way through life."

There's another word for this calculated—inbred, even—nonchalance. Psychopathy, or the basic absence of empathetic feelings for your fellow human beings. It's nonchalance brought to a biological extreme. But do con artists actually fit that bill? Is it fair to say that the Demara-like grifters of the world are more likely than not clinical psychopaths—or are they just slightly more devious versions of our more conniving selves? Is it a qualitative difference between our small daily deceptions and the wiles of the confidence man, or is it just a simple matter of degree?

Robert Hare's Psychopathy Checklist–Revised, the most common assessment tool for antisocial, psychopathic behavior, looks for things like responsibility, remorse, pathological lying, manipulativeness, cunning, promiscuity and general impulsiveness, superficial charm, grandiosity, and the like. Score high enough, and you are labeled psychopathic, or "suffering soul," for the many such you leave in your wake. One of the defining marks of the psychopath is the inability to process emotion like other people. To a true psychopath, your suffering means nothing. There's no empathy. There's no remorse. There's no guilt. When psychopaths experience something that would shock most people—disturbing images, for instance—their pulse stays steady, their sweat glands normal, their heart rates low. In one study of clinical psychopathy, psychopaths failed to engage the same emotional areas as non-psychopaths when making difficult moral decisions—for instance, whether or not to smother a crying baby if doing so would save the entire village while a failure to do so would condemn everyone, baby included. For the overwhelming majority of people, it's a draining choice. The emotional areas of the brain fight it out with the more utilitarian ones for an answer. In psychopaths, the battle is absent: they exhibit nonchalance in its most extreme form.

Psychopaths, according to Hare, make up an estimated 1 percent of the male population; among women, they are almost nonexistent (though still present). That means that out of every hundred men you meet, one will be clinically diagnosable as a psychopath. But will he also be a born con man?

On one level, the data seem to suggest a direct affinity between the two, grifter and psychopath developing hand in hand. One tantalizing piece of evidence: when people acquire the neural deficits associated with psychopathy later in life, they start behaving remarkably, well, psychopathically—and remarkably like a con artist. In lesion studies, people who experienced early life lesions in the polar and ventromedial cortex—areas implicated in psychopathy—begin to show behaviors and personality changes that very closely mimic both psychopathy and the grift. Two such patients, for instance, showed a newfound tendency to lie, manipulate, and break the rules. Others described them as "lacking empathy, guilt, remorse, and fear, and . . . unconcerned with their behavioral transgressions." Psychopathy, then, is a sort of biological predisposition that leads to many of the behaviors we expect from the confidence artist.

But that's not exactly the whole story. Psychopathy is part of the so-called dark triad of traits. And as it turns out, the other two, narcissism and Machiavellianism, also seem to describe many of the traits we associate with the grifter.

Narcissism entails a sense of grandiosity, entitlement, self-enhancement, an overly inflated sense of worth, and manipulativeness. It sounds, in short, like someone much akin to our Fred Demara, someone who can't stand to be seen as inferior, who needs to be the center of attention, and who will do what it takes to get there. A narcissist will do everything necessary to preserve his image. It's Fred lying to the candy store to avoid embarrassment—not the greatest of cons, but one driven by that kind of self-centric tendency.

But perhaps even more relevant is Machiavellianism—a characteristic that is almost predicated on the ability to deceive, as ruthlessly and effectively as Machiavelli's most ideal of princes and the most famed of confidence artists, both.

In the psychology literature, "Machiavellian" has come to mean a specific set of traits that allows one to manipulate others to accomplish one's own objectives—almost a textbook definition of the con. Writing in 1969, Richard Calhoon, a marketing professor at the University of North Carolina, described the Machiavellian as someone who "employs aggressive, manipulative, exploiting, and devious moves in order to achieve personal and organizational objectives." And, indeed, the so-called high Machs—people high on the Machiavellianism scale, a measure first developed in 1970 by two psychologists who wanted to capture leaders' manipulative tendencies, Richard Christie and Florence Geis—tend to be among the most successful manipulators in society. In one series of studies, when a high Mach was placed in a situation with a low Mach, he tended to emerge ahead in most any scenario. The low Mach would let emotions get in the way. The high Mach, however, wouldn't be as easily disturbed.

In one early review, the Machiavellians among eleven distinct samples, including students, academic faculty, parents, children, athletes, the staff of a mental hospital, and business employees, were more likely to attempt to bluff, cheat, bargain, and ingratiate themselves with others. They were also more successful at doing so. In another study, the Machiavellian-minded among us made for more convincing liars than the rest: when people were taped while denying that they had stolen something (half were being honest, and half lying), those scoring higher on the Machiavellianism scale were believed significantly more than anyone else. In a third, business school students had to decide whether or not to pay someone a kickback, a behavior that is largely considered unethical (and is against the law). They were all given a rationale for why, in this case, the kickback made sense. Those who scored higher in Machiavellianism were more likely to take the bait when the rationale made it more cost-effective to do so.

Machiavellianism, it seems then, may, like psychopathy, predispose people toward con-like behaviors and make them better able to deliver on them. Delroy Paulhus, a psychologist at the University of British

Columbia who specializes in the dark triad traits, goes as far as to suggest that "Machiavellian" is a better descriptor of the con artist than "psychopath." "It seems clear that malevolent stockbrokers such as Bernie Madoff do not qualify as psychopaths," he writes. "They are corporate Machiavellians who use deliberate, strategic procedures for exploiting others."

So wherein lies the truth: is the con artist psychopath, narcissist, Machiavellian? A little bit of all? Demara seems to be proof of the "all of the above" choice. Doctors are often accused of playing God. Demara took that criticism to a grotesque extreme. What ego, what blithe disregard for the lives of others and overconfidence in oneself, can lead someone to not only pose as a surgeon but perform multiple surgeries without any of the requisite qualifications to do so? To place oneself in a position where one is the only medical recourse for hundreds of men? It seems not only the height of narcissism, but, too, the most psychopathic of behaviors: the power to kill who knows how many others. And what a dose of Machiavellianism that must entail, to convince a nation's army and manipulate other doctors, a captain, soldiers, the whole lot that you're the real deal.

Demara wasn't humbled by his stint in Korea. Quite the contrary. He was emboldened. When Robert Crichton set out to write his biography, the impostor spent days convincing him to let him deliver his pregnant wife's baby. He could, he assured him, do it better than anyone else. Why rely on a hack when you could get a real medical expert? Crichton, of course, knew, rationally, that Demara had no training to speak of. But he had saved those soldiers. And he had read all those textbooks— probably more closely than your average doctor. The more Demara cajoled, the more Crichton's resolve to tell him, once and for all, that his wife was off-limits weakened. It took Crichton's wife, Judy, to put a lid on the plan: he had put the proposal before her in all earnestness.

Now that's a true artist.

Actually, here's the true artistry: even after this mishap, as we'll call it, when Judy told Bob that Fred wasn't to set foot in their house again, her resolve, too, eventually melted away. It was only a few years after the Great Impostor went away—and after he'd sued Crichton and Random House for allegedly withholding funds—that that same Judy let him babysit their toddler daughter.

Now *that's* a true artist.

***

But the Demaras of this world are only part of the picture. It is possible, it turns out, to possess all the tenets of the dark triad, and then some, and still not turn to con artistry. Psychopaths, narcissists, and Machs may be overrepresented in the grift, but they are also overrepresented in a number of other professions that line the legitimate world. As Maurer puts it, "If confidence men operate outside the law, it must be remembered that they are not much further outside than many of our pillars of society who go under names less sinister." Leadership and high-profile roles. Wall Street. Politics. Law. Test most any of them, and you'll find a percentage of psychopaths and dark-triadists that makes Hare's 1 percent estimate look naïvely low.

When Shelby Hunt and Lawrence Chonko gave the Machiavellianism scale to one thousand professional marketers, they found that over 10 percent scored in the highest possible range—and far, far above the population average. In other words, they were among the highest possessors of traits that hinged on manipulation and deception. And yet, they engaged in a legitimate business. None of them were criminals. None of them were even aristocrats of crime.

The dark triad pushes people in the direction of manipulation—Christie and Geis found that the highest Mach scorers among doctors had consistently chosen to be psychiatrists, a field where manipulation and mental control are central, while, in a separate study, Machiavellian students were more likely to specialize in business and law than any other areas—but it does not compel them to push that manipulation beyond a point that's generally socially accepted.

And while some would doubtless argue that I've just made my own point—what are politicians, lawyers, businessmen, admen, and market-ers but thinly veiled con artists?—the truth is that real con artists aren't simply born. They are, as is usually the case, made as well. As the pop-ular saying among scientists goes: genes load the gun; the environment pulls the trigger. The exact same traits could easily be put to use in more or less devious ways. The choice is not predetermined. And the presence of Machiavellianism or psychopathy or narcissism no more marks someone as a grifter than the presence of charisma or nonchalance.

James Fallon discovered he was a psychopath by accident. He'd been running two projects simultaneously: a large imaging study of Alzhei-mer's patients, where his own family served as "normal" control brains, and a small side project on the brains of psychopaths. As he was going through the Alzheimer's scans, one brain popped out. It had all the mark-ings of the psychopath. Hmm. Clearly, someone had made a mistake and mixed one of the psychopathic scans in with the Alzheimer's data.

Normally, results in typical lab studies are anonymized so that nothing tips the experimenter off to the identity of the subject. In this case, Fallon decided to make an exception. The scan would need to be deanonymized so that they could determine where the data belonged. He asked one of his technicians to run the numbers and find the identity of the scan owner.

The end of the story is the subject of Fallon's subsequent book, *The Psychopath Inside*. There was no mistake. The scan was in fact his own.

Fallon had been a vocal proponent of the genetics of psychopathy. It, and many other conditions, he'd argued, were largely determined by the luck of the draw. If your brain was psychopathic, you'd simply drawn the short straw. Now that his own brain was at stake, however, he decided to dig deeper. Was it as predetermined as he'd always assumed?

Today, Fallon believes that the genetics are there, true, but that cer-tain critical periods in your childhood can nudge you more or less toward full-blown clinical psychopathy, so you exhibit some signs, for instance, but not the whole arsenal. Luck out, you become a high-functioning psychopath, like Fallon, and, perhaps, some of the con artists in this book. Get the bad draw, you become a violent psychopath, like the ones who fill up jails and sit on death row.

Apart from the period in utero, a time that we now know is crucial for the development of your genome's epigenetic markers—that is, the methylation patterns that will determine how, precisely, your genes will be expressed—Fallon believes that the first three years of life play a crucial role in determining your psychopathic future. In that period, a child naturally develops so-called complex adaptive behaviors, like the ability to deal with fear, to smile, to react to those around her. But sometimes that process is interrupted, usually by something particularly stressful. A single traumatic event or a baseline of stress at home or in school could both, in theory, interrupt normal development and make the psychopathic traits you were genetically predisposed to more likely to assert themselves—perhaps in much the same way as they surfaced in Demara after his family's sudden fall from grace and the total uprooting of his childhood home. But in its absence, a would-be cunning deceiver becomes a respected neuroscientist instead.

For most people to go from legitimacy to con artistry, three things need to align: not just the motivation—that is, your underlying predisposition, created by elements like psychopathy, narcissism, and Machiavellianism—but alongside it, opportunity and a plausible rationale. In corporate fraud, for instance, few people choose to con in a vacuum. Instead, according to one study, about a third of perpetrators aren't simply willing to go one step beyond what's technically legal (predisposition); they also perceive an aggressive sales environment (opportunity) and feel they must do something to stand out (rationale)—a question of company culture and atmosphere meeting a willingness to cut corners and the chance to rationalize away that cutting as a matter of necessity.

Grifters are made when predisposition and opportunity meet. That's one of the reasons, according to some sources, that insider trading—when businessmen turn con artist—flourished at Steven Cohen's now infamous hedge fund, SAC Capital Advisors, for as long and as widely as it did. "You self-justify that it's not so bad because everybody is trying to get an edge," a source close to the fund explained over lunch one day. "And it's less likely that I'm going to get caught because, clearly, somebody would've been caught by now." At SAC, he continued, "There was no evidence that people ever stood up at the top of the firm and said in words that a third grader would understand, 'By the way, don't break the law. Don't cheat, don't steal—we don't do that here.'" Take the indictment of the hedge fund itself. "One prospective employee was rumored to have engaged in insider trading at his prior place of employment. And he was hired. Over the objection of the compliance officer. And, shockingly, he started engaging in insider trading within a couple of weeks of joining."

The experimental literature could have predicted that outcome. One study of marketers found that the ethical structure of the organization where they worked affected whether or not those high in certain con-like skills (specifically, Machiavellianism) would act on their propensities. Those who worked in more highly ethical organizations, with greater structure and less flexibility for making decisions according to one's own whims, were significantly less likely to act in con-like ways than those who worked in more loosely structured organizations with less of a clear-cut ethical direction.

The behavioral norms of a company, culture, or setting—how it is and isn't acceptable to act—must be communicated clearly and unequivocally. When they aren't, it becomes too easy for those on the cusp of fraud to take the next step. "It's a cliché to say this," says Preet Bharara, a U.S. attorney for the Southern District of New York, who has gained a reputation for aggressive pursuit of fraud. "But it's true. The tone at the top really does matter." While at the extremes, people create the opportunity themselves—they will con their way through life no matter where you place them—for a significant percentage of the conning population, the surroundings matter. The same trader who commits fraud at a fund that looks the other way might be a straight shooter elsewhere.

We care how we're perceived, and if we think that most people will frown upon our actions, we become less likely to contravene the norm. It's not so much "monkey see, monkey do" as "monkey *think* someone might see, so acts accordingly."

The pattern isn't altogether uncommon. USIS, the contractor that used to supply two thirds of the security clearances for much of the intelligence community, appears to have spiraled from a few faulty checks to thousands. At first, it seemed like one rogue employee had submitted sixteen hundred falsified credit reports; one bad apple does not a rotten tree make. But by January 2014, it had become clear that it wasn't a bad apple. According to the Department of Justice's suit, that was but the tip of a much larger scandal: the company had faked well over half a million background checks between 2008 and 2012—or 40 percent of total background checks. (The extent makes the Royal Canadian Navy's hire of Demara pale in comparison.) It wasn't one bad apple. It was a tree that allowed such apples to flourish.

The grifter's rationale for what he does, in a way, is the culmination of predisposition and opportunity: if you have the predisposing traits, and you sense a good opportunity, you will find a way to rationalize it. About half of those who commit fraud also cite intolerable competitive conditions, be they market or corporate; they want to somehow level the playing field and convince themselves that a bit of deception is one of the only avenues open to them.

Time and time again, Demara explained away his deceptions as good intentions gone astray. He wasn't a grifter; he was someone caught up in bad circumstances, but who would always try to make good. He didn't con hapless members of various religious orders by pretending to be a high-achieving academic in search of life's meaning; he wanted to spread teachings of the faith. Donning the identity of Ben W. Jones to be a prison warden in Texas? It was because the prisoners needed some-one like him. And the stint in the Canadian navy as surgeon? They needed professionals. He was only trying to save some lives. So good was he at rationalizing away his escapades that Crichton ended up de-picting him as more victim than perpetrator, someone to whom the grift just happened because of a bad twist of fate.

It's not just opportunity that breeds rationalization and actions. Globally, some cultures may also be more accepting of the types of behaviors and rationales that we would consider con-like. In one study, foreign students were more likely to pay a kickback than American ones, no matter the incentives. They had simply grown up in societies with different norms and different resulting standards of behaviors. What to Americans seems ethically dubious may seem to others a fact of how the world works. In Russia, a plagiarist wouldn't get a second look—and even a data falsifier might get a free pass, as long as the data was falsified in the appropriate direction.

For some people, the rationalization might seem almost benign. Just over 20 percent of fraudsters say they simply want to hide bad news: their performance isn't what it ought to be, they feel ashamed, and they truly believe that, with just a little wiggle room, they can get back on their feet and no one ever needs to know. Of course, that doesn't usually happen.

At the beginning of his career in private practice, one local lawyer represented the CFO of a small computer start-up. It was the late nine-ties. The economy was seeing a bit of a downturn. And the CFO decided to "cook the books" one quarter. "He was a very decent guy, a little bit of an ingénue," he recalls. "He was the guy that went to his kids' basket-ball games, and when he started being investigated, he was the guy that would sit in the conference room—I felt bad for him—looking like he was going to cry. He was very upset." The CFO had reasoned that he'd only cheat that one time. And then the next quarter would be better, and he would go back and fix his misstatement. "And then it didn't get better. And then the third quarter didn't get better. And now you're in, in a major way." One bad statement led to the next. It wasn't inevitable. But it happened just as inevitably.

Is he a con artist? Most people would likely say not. He is just someone who made a bad choice, whose luck ran out, who made an ethical misstep, true, but without some greater malice. Many might, like his lawyer, even sympathize. Bad break. But he's a fundamentally decent guy. He just wanted to make it work.

And yet, the exact same case shows the opposite side of the story: that no con is ever as innocent as it might appear. The company had gone over everything in minute detail to try to determine the extent of the CFO's malfeasance. "It showed that he had used the company credit card for his own personal use to the tune of hundreds of thousands of dollars starting some point after he first started cooking the books," the CFO's lawyer says. "My opinion of him changed a little bit. Here's a guy that's trying to do a better job, and doesn't want to lose his job, and then, well, once he made that first mistake, then it was just easier to make the next mistakes."

Thus is a grifter born. There's no such thing as an innocent cutting of the ethical corner. Once you've decided to get on the sled, and have eased yourself over the edge of the hill, it's too late to break. It starts with a small thing. A credit in a candy store. A fudged line in a financial statement. A rogue quote massaged ever so slightly to make your case more compelling. And lo and behold, nobody notices. And even though you thought it was just the once, because the circumstances were so extreme and you were in such a tight corner, those circumstances somehow never get any better. You're always pressed for time, for money, for energy, for mental space. Always needing to do just a bit too much with a bit too little. And once you do it once, and successfully at that, the temptation to do it again, do it more, do it differently, grows. Rather than a cut corner, it becomes another tool in your arsenal. It's like in the Mafia movies: the only one that matters is the first one you kill. After that, piece of cake.

———

Who, then, is the con artist? He displays a dark triad–influenced bent, and he acts when the opportunity arises, for unlike other, less sinister-minded counterparts, he can rationalize away just about any behavior as necessary. And yet, despite this seeming underlying commonality, con artists can still surprise us and resist easy classification. Some conform to expectations, others do not, and there may be significant divergence from the profile that emerges from one study to the next. One review of just under six hundred cases of company fraud in seventy-eight countries between 2011 and 2013 managed to capture some of the personality characteristics of the perpetrators—and not all of them, it turns out, fit the dark triad mold. Some did, it's true—one fifth admitted to having committed fraud, they said, "Just because I can," a pure dark triad response if ever there were one. Over 40 percent were motivated by greed—but even more, just under half, by a sense of superiority, the hallmark of narcissism. They were simply better, they felt, and so they deserved more. Many reported being motivated by a sense of anger, of being underpaid and undervalued. Who are you not to appreciate me? I'll show you.

But others seemed both less sinister and less cold-mindedly rational in pursuit of profit. A third were seen as extroverted, and 35 percent as quite friendly. About 40 percent were also highly respected by their colleagues—though only one in five had impressed anyone as a great intellectual or substantive businessman.

And then there are those who are downright compassionate. In March 2015, Sarah Carr received a phone call from the IRS informing her she was liable for payments on one of her businesses. She broke down crying. She was nine months' pregnant, she explained, and didn't know how she could get the money. "Calm down," the voice said, now seeming agitated himself. It was all a scam, he bluntly explained. In fact, as we know, this is one of the most common scams come springtime: the fake IRS agent. People are scared, they panic, and they hand over the cash. This time, however, the mark's sob story was enough to make the grifter veer from the script. Since she was pregnant, she was off the hook. She'd chanced upon a con artist with a conscience.

* * *

The truth is, the grifter may be more difficult to capture accurately because, to some extent, we all have the capacity for deception: if you're a sentient being, you've almost certainly deceived at some point in your life. From reptiles to humans, the animal kingdom is full of liars. Some snakes can even fake their own death for their own sinister purposes. Or take the cuckoo finch—a venerable brood parasite that tries to pawn off its own eggs on hapless mothers about to do the heavy labor of incubating. One egg would be a simple swindle, someone trying to pull one over on you. But the cuckoo finch is a true con artist, leaving multiple eggs in a nest. That way, the mother can't tell the parasites from her own.

In 2009, a group of scientists at the University of Turin, led by Francesca Barbero, found that a certain interloper caterpillar reliably received more food, better care, and more thorough protection than the ants whose home it invaded. The caterpillars simply pretended to be queen ants: they had learned the distinction between worker and queen sounds, and now their pupae and larvae had evolved to make queen-like noises. Even when the ant colonies were low on food, the impostors would receive preferential treatment. After all, they were potential queens. Since then, the researchers have learned that at least twelve other species of butterfly employ the same technique. Mimic a queen, and let yourself be carried into the ants' nest without raising so much as a foot or a wing in labor.

Impostors permeate the animal kingdom. The stick insects that look like twigs you wouldn't think twice about; the leaf insects that take on the contours of a flowering plant: phasmids, or what the Greeks called "apparitions." Now you see them, now you don't. Disappearing acts are as old as nature.

And in the human world, deception is no less common. According to psychologist Robert Feldman, who has spent more than four decades

studying the phenomenon, we lie, on average, three times during a routine ten-minute conversation with a stranger or casual acquaintance.
Hardly anyone refrains from lying altogether, and some people report
lying up to twelve times within that time span. I might open a conversation, for instance, by saying how nice it is to meet someone—when I'm
really not at all happy about it. I might go on to say that I grew up in
Boston—a lie, technically, since I really grew up in a small town about
forty minutes outside the city. I could say that the person's work sounds
fascinating, when it's no such thing, or compliment him on his (drab) tie
or his (awful) shirt. And if the person mentions loving a certain downtown restaurant where I've had a terrible experience? I'm likely to just
smile and nod and say, Yep, great place. Trust me: we often lie without
giving it so much as a second thought. Or in the words of Paul Ekman, a
psychologist who studies emotional expression broadly and lying in
particular, "Lies are everywhere."

We lie in most any context—Feldman's work has turned up frequent
lies in relationships ranging from the most intimate (marriage) to the
completely casual. Some lies are small ("You look like you've lost a bit of
weight") and some bigger ("I did not have sex with that woman"). Sometimes they are harmless, and sometimes they are not.

And we lie from a very young age. In a series of studies with three-
year-olds, developmental psychologists asked each child to stay in a
room with a new toy, by herself, without turning around to peek at what
that toy might be. Hardly any child could resist the temptation to look
(four out of thirty-three, to be precise), and over half proceeded to lie
about having done so. In a follow-up with slightly older children, the
five-year-olds fared even worse: all of them looked, and all of them lied.

As we reach adulthood, many of the same habits remain, and at
times they take on a more pernicious guise than "You look great in that
dress!" According to the Insurance Research Council, a quarter of adults
feel that it's fine to increase an insurance claim when they felt they were
making up for the deductible. It may seem fine, but it's actually fraud—
soft fraud. And what about a slight fudge here or there on a tax return?

sticking it to the man, and you're certain others do
ok at those corporate tax loopholes!—but each time
misreport so much as a dollar, you've committed fraud.

legitimate professions find it difficult to escape the image of being a bit loose with the truth. Each November, Santon Bridge, a small rural town in Cumbria, England, holds a contest: the world's biggest liar. From all over the UK and beyond, people gather in a tavern in the center of town to try their hand at the tallest, yet still somehow believable, tall tale they can muster within a five-minute time span. The most convincing of the lot gets the crown for the year. But there's an exception to the generally democratic enterprise: lawyers, politicians, salespeople, real estate agents, and journalists are not allowed to participate. Presumably, they would be at an unfair advantage. They are simply too well versed in the art of stretching the truth to offer a level playing field to the laypeople.

Would you be a grifter—even a mild one—if given the chance? Try this short test. Take your index finger, raise it to your forehead, and draw the letter *Q*.

Done? Which way is your *Q* facing—tail to the right, or tail to the left? The test, described in detail by Richard Wiseman, a psychologist and famed skeptic, is a way to gauge your "self-monitoring" tendency. If you drew the letter with the tail to the left, so that others could read it, you are a high self-monitor. That means you are more concerned with appearance and perception—how others see you. To achieve the desired effect, you are likely more willing to manipulate reality—even just a bit—to make a better impression. Con artists, in some sense, merely take our regular white lies to the next level. Plagiarists. Fabulists. Confabulists. Impostors. They take that desire to shine, to be the best version of something, and they fly with it.

* * *

So could you spot the grifter in a sea of faces, pick him up out of your daily interactions? Are there signs that will give the confidence artist away by virtue of who he is and what he's up to—namely, taking advantage of you? Given that we all have the capacity to deceive, and have all done so at some point in our lives, you'd think we'd be experts in spotting lies in others, at picking the grifter out from the crowd. Just as when we're little we're certain our mothers know whenever we're stretching the truth—I was sure mine could read my mind and so tried to hide behind pieces of furniture or books, so that her mentalist rays couldn't penetrate inside—so, too, do we grow up believing that we're fairly decent when it comes to spotting someone else's deceptions.

Over the years, a folklore has developed around the facial and physical cues that can give someone away—a folklore that has, in recent years, been put to the empirical test. In 2006, Charles Bond, a psychologist at Texas Christian University who has studied lying since the 1980s, assembled a team of researchers spanning seventy-five countries and forty-three languages. His goal: to determine whether there are any universal theories of lying—signs that, to most people, signal deception no matter the culture. In one study, conducted in fifty-eight countries, over twenty-three hundred people were asked to respond to a single question: "How can you tell when people are lying?" One sign stood out: in two thirds of responses, people listed gaze aversion. A liar doesn't look you in the eye. Twenty-eight percent reported that liars seemed nervous, a quarter reported incoherency, and another quarter that liars exhibited certain telltale motions. Just over a fifth thought facial expressions and narrative inconsistencies betrayed lying. And just under a fifth thought that liars used filler words like "uh" and made frequent pauses, and that their skin would flush to signal their betrayal.

A second study flipped the process around. This time, people saw a list of possible behaviors. Which of these, they were asked, did they associate with lying? Now nearly three quarters of the responses signaled gaze aversion, two thirds noted a shift in posture, another two thirds that liars scratch and touch themselves more, and 62 percent said that they tell longer stories. The answers spanned sixty-three countries.

There are universal folk beliefs, true. The only problem is, they are just as universally wrong. "The empirical literature just doesn't bear it out," says Leanne ten Brinke, a psychologist at the University of California at Berkeley whose work focuses on detecting deception. They persist because they fit our image of how a liar *should* behave. We *want* liars to exhibit signs of discomfort, like fidgeting, hemming and hawing, being inconsistent, flushing. We *want* liars to avert their gaze. They should feel shame and want to hide. Children as young as five already think that shifting your eyes away is a sign of deceit. In fact, if we are told beforehand that someone is lying, we are more likely to see them turning their eyes away from us. But that desire is not grounded in what liars actually do. Just because we want someone to feel ashamed, it doesn't mean they do—or that they aren't perfectly capable of hiding it in any event.

The mismatch between our conception of a liar and the reality—that there's no "Pinocchio's nose," as ten Brinke put it—is surely one reason that, despite our confidence, our ability to tell a lie from the truth is hardly different from chance.

Paul Ekman doesn't just study the prevalence of lying. His more central work focuses on our ability to discern deception. Over more than half a century of research, he has had over fifteen thousand subjects watch video clips of people either lying or telling the truth about topics ranging from emotional reactions to witnessing amputations to theft, from political opinions to future plans. Their success rate at identifying honesty has been approximately 55 percent. The nature of the lie—or truth—doesn't even matter.

Over time, Ekman did find that one particular characteristic could prove useful: microexpressions, or incredibly fast facial movements that last, on average, between one fifteenth and one twentieth of a second and are exceedingly difficult to control consciously. The theory behind microexpressions is relatively straightforward: lying is more difficult, theoretically, than telling the truth. And so, with the added strain on our mind, we might show "leakage," or these instantaneous behavioral tells that seep out despite our attempts to control them.

Microexpressions, though, are too fleeting and complex for any

kind of untrained expert to spot: out of Ekman's fifteen thousand subjects, only fifty people could consistently point them out. About 95 percent of us miss them—and if we're in the world of virtual con artists, or
ones that strike over the phone, no amount of microexpression reading
will do us any good. And as it turns out, even if we could read every
minute sign, we would not necessarily be any better equipped to spot
the liars among us—especially if they are as masterful at their craft as
that prince of deception, the grifter.

Last summer, I had the chance to talk to one of Ekman's original
fifty human lie detectors, so to speak. She goes by Renée; her work, she
explains, is too sensitive for any further identification. These days, she
consults for law enforcement and trains others to spot lies. But, she admits, she is not infallible when it comes to the practiced deceivers she
now deals with—not the liars of the videotapes in a psych study, but
the people who lie as part of who they are, the real masters of the game.
"Those people aren't always an open book," she told me. They don't lie
like the amateurs. They are craftsmen. For them, lying isn't uncomfortable, or cognitively draining, or in any way an anomaly from their daily
routine. It is what they do and has, over time, become who they are.
Take psychopaths, she says. "The smart, intelligent psychopath is a super liar." Someone like Ted Bundy, say. "He scares me and makes me
uncomfortable," she says with a shudder. "People like him seem to have
the ability of the truth wizard, but they have no conscience. A superin-
telligent psychopath is my match." She names a few more, among them
serial killer Richard Kuklinski, better known as Iceman. "If you watch
him in his interviews, he is cold to the core." Normally, Renée says, she
trusts herself. But the best liars are a difficult match for even the best
truth-seers.

Even then, it's not a skill that can be easily learned. "I don't think
my ability is trainable," Renée admits. "If we could, we'd be doing it already. I can give others tools, but they won't be at the same level."

What's more, Ekman says, cognitive load may come from many areas, not just deception. Even with microexpressions, there is no surefire

way of knowing whether someone is actually being untruthful. We can read signs of extreme pressure, but we don't know where that pressure necessarily comes from. We might be worried, nervous, or anxious about something else. It's one of the reasons lie detectors are also notoriously unreliable. Our physiology is just as subject to minute pressures as our physiognomy, not necessarily from the strain of deceiving. Sometimes this signals lying. Sometimes it signals other types of cognitive load, like stress, fatigue, or emotional distress. And in all cases it is impossible to be absolutely certain.

With con artists, lie detection becomes even trickier. "A lie," Ekman says, "is a deliberate choice to mislead a target without any notification." Plus, the more you lie, the fewer identifying signs, even tiny ones, you display.

Even professionals whose careers are based on detecting falsehood are not always great at what they do. In 2006, Stefano Grazioli, Karim Jamal, and Paul Johnson constructed a computer model to detect fraudulent financial statements—usually, the purview of an auditor. Their software correctly picked out the frauds 85 percent of the time. The auditors, by contrast, despite their professional confidence and solid knowledge of the typical red flags, picked out fewer than half—45 percent—of the fraudulent statements. Their emotions, it turns out, often got in the way of their accuracy. When they found a potential discrepancy, they would often recall a case where there was a perfectly reasonable explanation for it, and would then apply it there as well. Their assumptions probably gave people the benefit of the doubt more generously than they should have. Most people don't commit fraud, so chances are, this one isn't, either.

In fact, even when you know exactly what you're looking for, you may find yourself further from accuracy than you would like. In August 2014, Cornell University researchers David Markowitz and Jeffrey Hancock analyzed the papers of social psychologist Diederik Stapel. They had chosen Stapel for a very specific reason. Three years earlier, in September 2011, it was revealed that he had perpetrated academic fraud on a massive level. By the time the investigation concluded, in November 2012, it was evident that data for fifty-five papers had clear evidence of fraud; they either had been massaged or, in the egregious cases, were completely fabricated. Stapel had never even run many of the studies in question; he'd merely created the results that would support the theory that, he was sure, was accurate.

When Markowitz and Hancock tested whether the false publications differed linguistically from the genuine ones, they found one consistent tell: the deceitful papers used far more words related to the nature of the work itself—how and what you measure—and to the accuracy of the results. If there's not much substance, you "paper" more: you elaborate, you paint beautiful prose poems, and you distract from lack of substance. (Who doesn't remember doing a bit of the same on a college essay, to hide evidence of less than careful reading?) But however useful these tools of linguistic analysis may have been, they are far from perfect. Close to a third of Stapel's work eluded proper classification based on the traits Markowitz and Hancock had identified: 28 percent of papers were incorrectly flagged as falsified while 29 percent of the false papers escaped detection. A real grifter, even on paper, covers his tracks remarkably well, and as much as we may learn about his methods, when it comes to using them to ferret out his wiles, we will oftentimes find ourselves falling short.

But why would this be the case? Surely it would be phenomenally useful to have evolved to be better at spotting liars, at protecting ourselves from those who'd want to intrude on our confidence for malicious ends?

* * *

The simple truth is that most people aren't out to get you. We are so bad at spotting deception because it's better for us to be more trusting. Trust, and not adeptness at spotting deception, is the more evolutionarily beneficial path. People are trusting by nature. We have to be. As infants, we need to trust that the big person holding us will take care of our needs and desires until we're old enough to do it ourselves. And we never quite let go of that expectation. In one study, Stanford University psychologist Roderick Kramer asked students to play a game of trust. Some could just play as they wanted, but others were led to believe that the partner they were playing with might be untrustworthy. Our default, Kramer found, was trust. Those students who were specifically told that there might be some wrongdoing ended up paying more attention to possible signs of untrustworthiness than those who had no negative expectations. In reality, the partner behaved in the same way in either case, but his behavior was read differently in the two conditions: we read behavior as trustworthy unless we're explicitly told otherwise.

And that may be a better thing than not. Higher so-called generalized trust, studies show, comes with better physical health and greater emotional happiness. Countries with higher levels of trust tend to grow faster economically and have sounder public institutions. People who are more trusting are more likely to start their own business and volunteer. And the smarter you are, the more you are likely to trust: a 2014 survey by two Oxford psychologists found a strong positive relationship between generalized trust, intelligence, health, and happiness. People with higher verbal ability were 34 percent more likely to trust others; those with higher question comprehension 11 percent more likely. And people with higher levels of trust were 7 percent more likely to be in better health, and 6 percent more likely to be "very" happy rather than "pretty" happy or not happy at all.

And in some sense, this excess optimism in others' basic decency is a good thing, at least most of the time. Remaining in a state of pleasant deception is often preferable to confronting the truth. It's nice to think you look beautiful in everything you wear. That you're radiant today despite a lack of sleep. That your invitation really was turned down because your guests had an inescapable conflict. That your article or project idea or pitch was rejected because, despite being wonderful, it really just wasn't a "good fit." Or any of the other white lies we hear dozens of times a day that we don't give a second thought to, just because they smooth the flow of normal social interactions.

As well as making us feel better, not spotting lies can make us perform better. In 1991, Joanna Starek and Caroline Keating followed the progress of a Division I college swim team from upstate New York. They wanted to know if swimmers who were better at self-deception—ignoring negative stimuli about themselves and interpreting ambiguous evidence as positive—performed any differently from those who were more honest and perceptive. They had each swimmer take the Self-Deception Questionnaire, a test developed in the 1970s by psychologists Ruben Gur and Harold Sackeim, followed by a test of binocular rivalry, where each eye would see a different word and the swimmer would need to quickly report what she saw. Finally, they had the coach reveal which of the swimmers had qualified for the Eastern Seaboard Swimming and Diving Championships. The more adept a swimmer was at self-deception, the researchers found, the more likely she was to have made the cut. It wasn't the people who saw the world most clearly who did best; it was, rather, those most skilled at the art of seeing the world *as they wanted it to be*. And the world-as-we-want-it-to-be is precisely what the con artist sells.

The irony is inescapable. The same thing that can underlie success can also make you all the more vulnerable to the grifter's wares. We are predisposed to trust. Those who trust more do better. And those who trust more become the ideal, albeit unwitting, player of the confidence game: the perfect mark.

* * *

They say you can't cheat an honest man. When it comes to confidence schemes, though, that simply isn't true. Honesty has nothing to do with it. Honest men, after all, are often the most trusting, and trust, as we know, is deadly when it comes to the con.

Apple. Mr. Bates. Chump. Egg. Savage. Winchell. They say a sucker is born once a minute. There are about as many names for him. But at the end of the day, they all amount to the same thing: victim. The grifter's mark is not greedy, no more so than anyone else. Nor are marks dishonest, any more than those of us who harbor fleeting suspicions of our own worth and exceptionalism. They are, simply, human.

Robin Lloyd wasn't looking to get rich. She was just a poor college student who thought she'd finally caught a lucky break. It was 1982, and Robin was making her first ever trip to New York City. She'd grown up in the suburbs, and was in college at Smith, a small school in western Massachusetts. Spending time in urban environments was not something she'd ever given much thought to. One of her classmates, though, was a native New Yorker—she'd grown up in the Bronx—and invited her out for a weekend in the big city. Robin was excited. She had hardly any money, but the trip seemed well worth it.

On the first day of the trip, Robin and her friend made their way down from the Bronx to Broadway. It was tumultuous, exciting. It felt slightly dangerous, and that, too, was exciting in its own way. "It was the eighties, remember, and New York was not as cleaned up and cosmopolitan as it is now," Robin tells me as we share a very New York bodega coffee—she has long since become a New Yorker herself. Everything was new and full of promise, a life she'd never even known existed in parallel to her own. And there, right on the sidewalk, was a loud-talking man seated behind a cardboard box. He was doing something at lightning speed with three playing cards, shuffling them around, flipping them, turning them this way and that. And money was being made: it looked to be some sort of game, and if you were good, it seemed, you could easily double your stake. All you had to do was follow the cards and bet on the right one—*Follow the lady*, as they say. "I remember being like a kid at the circus, so fascinated by him showing us how easy it was to win this game, that if you just threw down twenty bucks, the odds were so good you could double your money," Robin says. She didn't take the decision to play lightly. She had only two precious twenty-dollar bills in her pocket—her money for the entire two-day trip. "At this time in my life, I had no winter coat," she remembers. "I didn't even have three dollars to buy a Coca-Cola." It was below freezing, and she wore a turtleneck, a sweatshirt, and a denim jacket on top. "I was getting by, but barely—I was getting through college."

But something about this man's patter seemed genuine; it was almost as if he saw her woes and wanted to help her with a quick influx of cash. And she'd just seen a lucky winner who'd doubled his money with ease and walked away elated. She decided to go for it. Hands slightly shaking—she was nervous—she put down a twenty. "Sure enough, it doubled." She couldn't believe her good fortune. But just as she was about to pick up her winnings, the man quickly interjected. Wouldn't she like to double it again? "It was so exciting, the energy there. There was a crowd around us, and you want to win and want to believe so much." And so, she acquiesced. She placed her last remaining bill on top.

The moment the cash left her hand, she regretted it. "I thought, this is not going to go well. That is much more money than I can afford to lose." But for a second there, she had really believed that she would make it all back. "Right on the very next game, I lost it." She had no more money to play with, and so, even as the sympathetic man urged her to try again and reverse her luck, she walked away, empty wallet in pocket. That evening, they were visiting a friend at Columbia. The girls ordered Chinese takeout. It would have been exciting—a real New York City thing to do—except there was only one thing Robin could think of. How was she going to come up with her three-dollar share for the food?

Three-card monte games are one of the most persistent and effective cons in history. They still line some New York City blocks over thirty years later. But we tend to dismiss the victims as rubes: who in their right mind would fall for something like that? Even Robin felt that way, calling herself a fool and admitting her embarrassment at being pulled in so easily. "I probably deserved it," she says. But that's in retrospect. In the moment, it's not nearly so simple. Robin was educated and intelligent (today, she's an editor at *Scientific American*). She was a good judge of people—she was studying sociology, after all. She was frugal and not easily swept up by spur-of-the-moment whims. She doesn't fit the typical profile of a sap. But she was up against forces far greater than she realized. Monte operators, like all good con men, are exceptional judges of character—and exceptional creators of drama, the sort of narrative sweep that can make everything seem legitimate, natural, even inevitable. They know what to say to whom, how to say it, when to create a "lucky" diversion, how to make it seem like the game is all about skill— legitimate skill, not a risky gamble. To someone who has never heard of a shell game (monte's close cousin, where instead of cards you watch shells and guess which one holds the bead) or a monte gang (a group of conspirators working together to make the game seem legitimate), it's a dangerous proposition. When I mentioned to Robin that the winner she'd seen was a shill, a part of the monte gang planted there to lure people in, she expressed surprise. To this day she hadn't realized that that was how the game worked. "The rational part of me knows I was conned. But there's still a part of me that feels like I was unlucky."

Over the years, many researchers have tried to identify what it is that separates those susceptible to cons—ideal marks—from those immune to them. It would be great, after all, to pinpoint exactly the things most likely to have you fooled, and to beat them once and for all. Wouldn't it be wonderful if there were a shot that could inoculate you against all forms of chicanery?

We certainly have some strong ideas about marks. When representatives of all Better Business Bureau offices in the United States were asked to think about what things separated scam victims from nonvictims, a few trends emerged. Some were obvious: gullibility, a trusting nature, a proneness to fantasy, and greed were perceived to be the traits that set victims apart. Victims were also seen as less intelligent and educated, poorer, more impulsive, and less knowledgeable and logical. And older: your grandmother is more likely to be fooled than you. But is the perception true?

As it turns out, a good con artist will upend all of these expectations. We think we know the typical victim profile. We think we know what makes a mark. And we think absolutely wrong.

In 2014, the AARP asked more than eleven thousand adults over the age of eighteen, from twelve states, to answer questions designed to figure out whether there were any characteristics that made people more vulnerable to online scams. Certain behaviors, they found, especially in combination with certain life circumstances, were particularly common. Victims tended to be more active in their online activities and gave out more personal information on social media—not just "No, duh" things like birth dates and phone numbers, but things like their daily activities, geo-tags and schedules, check-ins and tweets from specific restaurants or stores that made it easier to fake knowing them—or, in some cases, being them.

The behaviors to avoid, the researchers discovered, were, for the most part, fairly standard Internet best practices: clicking on pop-ups (don't); opening e-mails from senders you don't know (again, don't); using online auction sites (this one is tricky—some are legitimate); signing up for free limited-trial offers (bad idea); downloading apps (don't do it unless you know what it is and trust the source); and using online payment sites (again, tricky—many are fine, but it's the times when the secure connections go bust that you need to worry).

The problem is, not only does this best-practice list deal with only one very particular kind of con, but most of these activities apply far more broadly than is actually useful. One in five Americans who are online—about 34.1 million people—does seven or more of the fifteen things the study associated with fraud susceptibility. But the number who get conned is far lower. If one fifth of the country were falling for Internet scams, Nigerian princes would be the happiest men alive.

When it comes to predicting who will fall, personality generalities tend to go out the window. Instead, one of the factors that emerges is circumstance: it's not who you are, but where you happen to be at this particular moment in your life. If you're feeling isolated or lonely, it turns out you're particularly vulnerable. Likewise if you're going through a job loss, divorce, serious injury, or other major life change, are experiencing a downturn in personal finances, or are concerned with being in debt. People in debt, in fact, are also more likely to fall for fraud that's completely unrelated to finances, like weight-loss products.

One of the reasons that Robin Lloyd fell for a basic game of three-card monte was that she really needed the money and, on top of that, was completely out of her element. Had either of those factors not been present, she would likely have walked away with her forty dollars still in her wallet. Instead, her motivation to believe was far higher than it normally would be—I need that money so I want to believe that money is obtainable. And her usual deception radar was more off than it normally would be—it's often hard to calibrate your reading of social cues in a new environment, especially when that environment is unlike any you've previously encountered. On another day, in another town, Robin would have laughed; that day, in Manhattan, she fell.

It makes a certain kind of sense. Often, patient, levelheaded people will go a bit crazy in the wake of a major life change—we become more impulsive, less stable, riskier versions of ourselves. And our impulsivity and appetite for risk are some of the only reliable indicators of fraud susceptibility. In one study, risk takers were over six times more likely to fall victim than those whose risk tolerance was low. Given the right circumstances, just about anyone can fit that description. When we're feeling low, we want to get out of the slump. So, schemes or propositions that would look absurd in another light suddenly seem more attractive. When we're angry, we want to lash out. Suddenly, something that once seemed like a gamble looks awfully appealing. A victim isn't necessarily foolish or greedy. A victim is simply more emotionally vulnerable at the exact moment the confidence artist approaches. Risk taking and impulsivity need not be stable aspects of our personalities; they are intimately tied to where we find ourselves emotionally at any given point.

Victims may also be more prone to belief, broadly speaking. One study of con victims found that two factors seemed to play a major role in which emotionally susceptible people, in particular, fell prey to an unscrupulous actor: they were more optimistic and more religious. In other words, they believed things could get better, and they believed that greater forces could play a role in that improvement. But then again: which of us doesn't on some level, in some guise believe that might be true?

The more you look, the more you realize that, even with certain markers, like life changes, and certain tendencies in tow, a reliably stable overarching victim profile is simply not there. Marks vary as much as, and perhaps even more than, the grifters who fool them. In a 2011 study of over seven hundred fraud victims, alongside fifteen hundred non-victims, psychologists Karla Pak and Doug Shadel found that different types of people fell for different types of cons; depending on where you look, the profile of the ideal mark shifts considerably. Victims of investment frauds, like Bernie Madoff's Ponzi scheme, and business opportunity frauds, like a lucrative investment in a new oil field, were more likely to be well-educated older men who made over $50,000 a year. Lottery frauds, on the other hand—fake tickets and the like—were likely to claim victims who were less educated and earned less money. When it came to prescription drug fraud and identity theft, the typical victim was a single female who made less than $50,000 a year. Older adults were more likely to experience a different type of con: from within the family, or by someone close to them. In a 2012 survey from the Elder Investment Fraud and Financial Exploitation Program, the top two risks to older adults were theft or money diversion by family members and theft by caregivers. Strangers came in third place.

Given the right fraud, it seems anyone can be a victim—even a con artist. There's an entire subset of cons, in fact, devoted to catching the master grifter at his own game, often perpetrated by others who feel he might have gotten too big for his boots. Con artists tend to be supremely confident—how can anyone beat me at my own game?—and that confidence is often their undoing. One master flimflammer, Oscar Hartzell, whom we'll meet in detail later on, fleeced thousands of people out of millions of dollars for several decades. While he was living in London, he spotted a curious ad in the paper for a crystal ball séance that would tell you your future. Intrigued, he went. Over the promised crystal ball, Miss St. John Montague read him a wondrous prediction of his future life. Soon, he was visiting her three times a week, parting with thousands for her confidential advice. Realizing she'd found an ideal mark, Montague set a private investigator on Hartzell's trail, who quickly uncovered his own murky dealings. Over the next five years, she would use the information to extract a further $50,000—a con woman getting the better of the con man who had seen through so many traps in his day.

The distinction between ideal mark and ideal grifter can be a spotty one. In 2003, two Spanish brothers purchased what they thought was a beautiful painting by Goya. After the sale's conclusion, though, they learned the painting was in fact a fake from the nineteenth century. A 2006 court order ruled that they could keep the painting for the price of the original deposit of 20,000 euros—a good price for a work from the time. Having themselves fallen for a scam, the two brothers decided to learn from their experience: this time, they would become the con artists. In December 2014, they attempted to unload the painting on a wealthy Arab sheikh, passing it off as authentic Goya. An Italian middleman offered to broker the deal: he would act as objective guarantor for both parties for a 300,000-euro deposit. The brothers traveled to Turin, where they handed over the painting and brokerage fee in exchange for a down payment of 1.7 million Swiss francs. Thrilled with themselves, they went to deposit the haul. It was fake. The middleman and "sheikh" promptly disappeared, with painting and real euros in tow. The marks had become grifters only to once more find themselves marks.

Con artists are often the best marks because they think themselves immune. And that false sense of immunity extends to victims more broadly: the better protected you are and the less likely you think you'll be a victim, the more you're apt to lose if a con artist can find a way to earn your trust. It ends up that the more you know about something, the more likely you are to fall for a con in that specific area.

Colorado boasts one of the most fraud-savvy, well-educated retirement communities in the United States. It's not as popular a destination as sunny climes like Florida, and the people who do go there are a fairly self-selected bunch. The majority of them have instated various protections against common cons in their day-to-day lives, from protective software and e-mail filters, to fraud alerts on credit cards, to personal measures like never giving out an e-mail address or phone number. Indeed, when the AARP surveyed its Colorado members, it found significant but single-digit amounts of victimhood. About 7 percent of them had been a victim of identity theft. And just about 6.5 percent of them had been the victims of fraud—still a high number, of course, but far better than national averages. Then, however, came the twist. This was typically investment fraud, and the sums lost were far above the typical scam. A full 10 percent had lost over $100,000, and another 21 percent between $10,000 and $99,999. As for the rest: a quarter had lost a relatively modest sum below $10,000, and half had no desire to even report how far they'd been taken. They'd admit to having fallen for it, but not by how much.

They had, for the most part, thought they were very knowledgeable about investing, and over 60 percent were investors in stocks, bonds, and other securities. But investment fraud is the precise fraud they fell for. They felt protected, and their guard, predictably, went down.

Even when it comes to a con that seems as obvious as a psychic, it's not just those we tend to think of as gullible who fall for it. "Lawyers, professional athletes, college professors—people call me from all walks of life," Bob Nygaard, a former police officer turned private investigator specializing in psychic cons, told the television show *20/20*.

An increasing number of financial professionals have also turned to psychic help—especially in the wake of the 2008 crash. "It used to be always love, love, love. Now it's money, money, money," Mary T. Browne, a favored psychic of Wall Street, told the *New York Times* in 2008, just as the financial crisis hit. She's the real deal, though. She's not one of those "storefront gypsies who take advantage of people's fear." No, no. She's been psychic since she turned seven, when she saw a dead woman rearranging the flowers that surrounded her coffin. She claims to have persuaded two clients to reject higher-paying offers from Bear Stearns eighteen months before its collapse. A session with her (in 2008): $400.

Jude Deveraux, a bestselling romance novelist, handed about $17 million over seventeen years to Rose Marks, a psychic who split her time between Florida and New York. And for what? Marks had told her that she could transfer the soul of her dead son into another boy's body and reunite mother and child once more. "When I look back on it now, it was outrageous," Deveraux later testified. "I was out of my mind."

What unites all of these marks, then? They are human, and humans are fallible.

"Confidence men," David Maurer sums up, "trace upon certain weaknesses in human nature. Hence until human nature changes perceptibly there is little possibility that there will be a shortage of marks for con games."

So if anyone is a potential mark, how does the con artist choose the mark to begin with? How to pick out the best one for this particular game, the one most likely to fall quickly and profoundly? That's what grifters are particularly good at: looking at a sea of faces and finding the one who, at this point in time, would be the perfect mark. It's the first step of the confidence game, the put-up, and no one is better at it than Apollo Robbins, the so-called Gentleman Thief famed for his sleights of hand in even the tightest of circumstances. (Two career highlights: stealing the president's top secret itinerary from a Secret Service man and removing the cartridge from a pen belonging to Penn of Penn and Teller fame.) As Robbins told me over dinner one evening, he never just steals willy-nilly. First, he cases. He observes. He profiles. Only then does he begin his act.

CHAPTER 2
THE PUT-UP

I can spot someone's weakness a mile away. In any room I can
pick out the best target.

—SIMON LOVELL, FORMER CON ARTIST

Debra Saalfield was heartbroken. A professional dancer and
ballroom dance instructor, she had been working at what she
saw as a dream job: marketing for a Times Square dance company. But in July 2008, within a two-day stretch, she had lost job and
boyfriend both.

Debra had been splitting her time between Florida and New York.
Florida was home, where she had her house and her three children, but
New York would be soon, she'd hoped. There was the job, and, well, her
boyfriend was going to propose any day. Now, however, she was in
the West Village not to move the rest of her things permanently up to the
city, but to move whatever she'd left out of her now ex's apartment. The
next day, she was scheduled to fly back to Florida.

The packing was emotionally grueling, each item a reminder of a
life she'd no longer have. Debra walked down the stairs. She needed to
clear her head. A walk would do her good.

It was then that she saw it. A sleek triangle of a building on the corner of Seventh Avenue South and Bleecker Street, immediately familiar to anyone in the neighborhood: the home of Zena the Clairvoyant. Deep blue awnings, adorned by a single gold *Z*. A heavy gold frame by the entrance, offering everything from palm readings to horoscope charts. Crimson and gold curtains with thick tassels—also gold—cover the windows, inviting you to peer inside another world. Come in, the whole façade seems to beckon, and all your troubles will be over. "Walk ins welcome!" the sign brightly declares.

Debra had walked past it many times. Her boyfriend—ex-boyfriend—had warned her to stay far away. It wasn't a good place. Now, though, she slowed her step. It couldn't hurt, could it?

Almost out of rebellion—he couldn't tell her what to do—she opened the door. Inside, it was even more opulent than she'd envisioned. Beaded curtains. Hanging plants. Ornate lanterns adorning the ceiling. A sign advertising Zena's second office, in Cannes. Could Zena see her? she inquired.

Sylvia Mitchell sat upstairs, awaiting her next customer. She lived in Mystic, Connecticut (the irony of her hometown surely inescapable even to her), and she'd been working as a, well, mystic for over a decade. In most every way, "Zena" was her home. The door opened. There was Debra. Tall, thin and elegant, long strawberry blond hair streaming down her back. She moved with a smooth grace—a dancer, perhaps? She looked to be older than Sylvia herself—the clairvoyant had just turned thirty-six—and she appeared a bit lost.

Debra, in turn, saw an attractive thirtysomething with a welcoming face. "Very charming, very comforting, very pretty. Dressed nicely," she would later recall. She was here, she told her, for a basic psychic reading, one of Zena's entry options, at a mere seventy-five dollars.

Sylvia Mitchell carefully took Debra's palm and began to talk. Almost immediately it was as if a greater force took over. A pained look came over her face. There was something else there. She had "very important information that could help her change and better her life, but it would cost her $1,000," she told Debra, according to one detective's statement.

A thousand dollars was a lot of money. But Sylvia seemed open and sincere. And her time was, of course, valuable. Maybe this was the thing she needed to make everything better—the job loss, the ruined love life. "My heart was pounding out of my chest," Debra later remembered. She handed over a check.

All of a sudden, Mitchell's flash of insight crystallized. In her past life, she told Debra, she'd been an Egyptian princess. As a royal, she had grown rather too attached to material possessions. "She told me I was part of a ruling city, a good doer, but I had a problem," Saalfield later told jurors. That materialistic attachment was creating negative energy in her life—and that energy, in turn, was bubbling over into her love and professional lives. But, Mitchell told her, there was a solution. "In order to get my life back in order, there was something I needed to do," Debra said. She could hand over $27,000, as an exercise in letting go of wealth. Sylvia would keep it for her in a jar. And she could have it back any time she so desired.

Saalfield had recently divorced. She knew she would need a financial cushion, what with three children, so she had taken out a line of credit on her house for "emergency money." She decided to tap into the supply. It seemed like emergency enough: "At the time, it felt like it was an emergency because I was very unstable," she says. Anyway, Sylvia had promised she could have it back. Debra gave Mitchell a check for $27,000.

"I needed some direction and guidance, and she said she was pretty confident that she could help me. I don't know that I thoroughly trusted her, but I wanted to listen to words of comfort," she told jurors. "I had a meltdown. I lost it. I was unable to keep myself together."

The next morning, however, she regretted her haste. Her "judgment had been clouded," she said. Thinking quickly, she went to her bank. Could she stop the check? Too late, she was told. It had already been cashed. So Debra called Zena. Could she have a refund? she asked

Mitchell. She'd parted with her money, just as she'd been ordered to do, but now she wanted to reconnect with it. "I called her immediately and told her I made a mistake and needed my money back," she says. Not possible, Mitchell told her. She was sorry, but the money simply wasn't available.

Saalfield was adamant. By this time, she was back in Florida. But the loss was too great. She couldn't afford it, and neither could her children. It was worth an extra flight. She returned to the city, anxious for the return of her $27,000. Her calls went unanswered. So she went in person. One time, she recalls, she stood in front of the parlor for the better part of a day, ringing the buzzer some fifteen times. No one answered.

Debra alerted the police, and in short order hired a lawyer and private investigator. If she couldn't get her money back herself, maybe they would be more persuasive.

* * *

"Most people are intuitive psychologists in their daily lives—wondering why people think or behave as they do," says Nicholas Epley, a University of Chicago psychologist who studies how we perceive others and what can make some of us more accurate than others in those perceptions. From the moment we see someone, we form impressions of who they are, what they're like, whether we're likely to get along with them or not. The process happens almost instantaneously—some research shows that we make certain judgments, like trustworthiness or likely level of power, within fractions of a second, and that those judgments then endure no matter how much longer our conversation lasts—and it happens unconsciously. Unless we're actively people-watching and trying to make predictions about strangers' backgrounds, lives, and desires—a vaunted pastime—we don't do this for any particular reason except that it's the perfectly natural thing to do. We're curious. And who knows when we might have to use the insight we've gleaned. Whether we mean to be or not, we are all of us intuitive psychologists.

For con artists, though, intuitive psychology, the process of sizing up who someone is, what they're made of, what they desire, isn't a nice evolutionary by-product or a fun way to pass the time. It's their livelihood. One of their great skills is to discern details of a victim's life without her knowledge, so that she doesn't even realize how much she's given away—and then, to use those very details to impress the victim with their insight. That ability is, indeed, the first step of a con: the put-up. The moment when a confidence artist investigates and chooses his prey. And it is, in more senses than one, the most crucial step of the entire operation. Size someone up well, and you can sell them anything. A magic crystal. An Egyptian curse. The Eiffel Tower. Fail to do so, and the most elaborate or attractive master plan will fall on deaf ears.

Since the late 1990s, Epley has been exploring the underpinnings of intuitive judgment. We come up with instinctive explanations for other people's appearance, actions, and words all the time—but how are we actually doing it? he wondered. And how accurate is our intuition? The process, he posits, is twofold. There's person perception—being able to tell who someone is, or what psychologist Daniel Gilbert terms "ordinary personology." We look at basic physical features, like gender, age, and height, at facial structure, at skin tone, at body language (standing tall? hunched? leisurely? hurried?), and, of course, at clothing. And then, there's what Epley terms, borrowing from Daniel Wegner, mind perception—being able to tell what others feel, what they desire, what drives and motivates them. We listen to their words and their voice, read their gestures and their tone, infer between the lines to get a sense of their inner world.

When someone gestures with her hand, we can almost immediately tell whether it means, "I don't care," versus "I'm angry," versus "I'm thrilled." When someone activates her zygomatic major, a muscle on either side of the mouth that is almost impossible to control consciously, we can tell she is genuinely happy. When someone moves quickly, expansively, and with determination, we can tell that she's either angry or exceptionally thrilled, depending on context; if she's more lethargic and closed, it could signal boredom. Our faces are capable of some three thousand expressions, according to Paul Ekman's estimates. And we can reliably read at least seven of the basic contours (and multiple permutations of them). From our posture to how we hold a glass of water, from our choice of outfit to how we've styled our hair and how we open the door, we throw off cues about ourselves and our minds with every step, every flicker of the eye, every choice of phrase.

That is, if, like the grifter scanning the room for his prey, you're ready to catch them. While we laypeople are good at the broad strokes basics, we tend to fare worse when it comes to reading nuance. While we're good at the overt bodily cues, we are not so great at the cues of the mind. We infer entire belief systems from one rogue statement, craft personalities and backstories with no bearing on reality from one surface clue. We simplify when we should caveat and gloss where we should elaborate. Often, we use snap judgments—what Daniel Kahneman calls heuristics—when we meet someone new, and end up with a superficial, highly stereotyped version of what they are like. Take Saalfield's impression of Mitchell: charming, comforting, pretty. And indeed, Mitchell is always elegant, impeccably dressed, well coiffed and manicured, with an enticing, open smile. She relies in part on those surface cues to inspire the type of trust she will need to lure her fortune-seekers.

We know, theoretically, that we should pay more heed and exercise caution, that we should incorporate other people's perspectives into our own, walk a mile in their shoes, or whatever other cliché we want to invoke. But practically, we remain superbly egocentric in all our judgments. In his book *Human Knowledge: Its Scope and Its Limits*, the philosopher Bertrand Russell observed, "The behavior of other people is in many ways analogous to our own, and we suppose that it must have analogous causes." We are our own prototype of being, of motivation, of behavior. People, however, are far from being a homogeneous mass. And so, when we depart from our own perspective, as we inevitably must, we often make errors, sometimes significant ones. In one series of studies, Epley and his colleagues found that people were far slower to discern a different perspective from their own, and that under time pressure they were unlikely to do so at all. He called it "egocentric anchoring": we are our own point of departure. We assume that others know what we know, believe what we believe, and like what we like.

For the layperson for whom conning is far from mind, the frequent inaccuracy in judgment isn't silly or stupid. It is, quite often, adaptive. As with white lies, it is not always helpful to our sense of self and well-being to correctly discern someone else's negative feelings or nasty thoughts. It's likewise not helpful to think their views at opposing ends from our own: we like people who are more similar to us more than those who differ, and isn't it better that the world be filled with friends rather than strangers? In a study of married couples, psychologists Jeffry Simpson, William Ickes, and Minda Oriña videotaped married couples as they addressed a problem point in their marriage. After, each spouse viewed the interaction, recorded her own feelings, and tried to decipher her partner's at each point in the conversation. Accuracy, it turns out, was overrated. Those who were better at reading threatening cues also felt worse about their partners and marriages by the end of the study. The less accurate actually came out ahead—as did their relationship satisfaction. We never learn to be expert people-readers because that expertise can backfire spectacularly. Why form accurate judgments when the inaccurate ones make our lives far more pleasant and easy?

For a con artist, however, accuracy is paramount, and feelings of self-worth, far less so: for him, self-worth is ingrained in his very ability to ferret out social nuance and personal vagaries better than anyone else. And there is one central factor that can override most shortcomings and make us far more accurate at figuring out who someone is and what makes her tick: motivation. People who are motivated to be accurate, whether financially or personally, suddenly become far more adept at reading faces, bodies, and minds alike. In one set of studies, people in powerful roles failed spectacularly at reading others. But when the researchers, Jennifer Overbeck and Bernadette Park, gave them a motivation for accuracy—make your subordinates feel engaged and included—they were suddenly far better at person-reading than they'd ever been. They were more accurate in judging employees' personalities and abilities than their counterparts who'd been instructed to pay attention to efficiency and productivity.

Con artists are motivated, always. They are us, as our best, most perceptive selves—who've also had years of practice. They are masters of the put-up: they can read our background, our beliefs, our emotions and their shifts, even the desires we thought we'd hidden so well. When Saalfield walked into Zena, Mitchell likely knew before she even opened her mouth that she was emotionally vulnerable. She was attuned to her every gesture, from the way she moved to the way she shook her hand. Saalfield didn't even need to mention a troubled love or work situation. To a discerning eye, it was all written on her face.

On a winter evening, I made my way to a mind reading of my very own, this one from tarot cards. I knew all about the cold read—the signs that I would be giving out that would tip the reader of my future off about my inner life. And I agonized over how much to leave in the open and how much to omit. Should I take off my wedding band? Arrive without a purse? What should I wear? In the end, I opted for looking like myself (minus my name), to give the experiment an air of authenticity. Did I have any one question I wanted to focus on? my reader asked. I opted for a take on my career. Soon, the man was busy telling me all about the woes of the publishing industry, the instability, the career uncertainty, the changes that the digital world had brought with it. He was discussing my job insecurities—but made sure to temper them with optimistic interludes: somehow, despite all the uncertainty, it would all work out. He even knew that at moments of deep panic, I thought about dropping it altogether. If the industry was crumbling, would I be able to get out in time?

Of course, Mr. Tarot wasn't actually talking about publishing. He had no idea I was a writer. He was using lines that would fit most any job description, and dilemmas that most any youngish woman in the earlier stages of her career would likely ask herself. Who *doesn't* worry about the future of their career path? Who *doesn't* think these days that their industry is in a state of flux? Who *hasn't* thought about leaving it all behind? Each statement could have applied just as easily to any number of jobs, but to me it seemed as if he actually had an insight into what, precisely, I did. He left me with a reassuring message. It would work out, and I didn't have to panic about losing my ability to make a living—as long as I didn't let my self-doubt get the better of me. I was my own worst enemy, and I could at any moment sabotage my own success. I had to stop those corrosive thought patterns and think instead in a more constructive, positive light. Then the world would be mine for the taking. Not bad advice. I nodded appreciatively as I walked back out to the street. Maybe there was something to this after all.

The psychic—and the con artist more broadly—isn't just a master cold reader and psychologist. He is someone who has endless practice getting things right, and is endlessly motivated to avoid making a glaring error. An error in the put-up, after all, is a costly one indeed; it could render the entire con ineffective. As it turns out, our best, practiced selves can tell quite a bit about others, even things that might seem unbelievable. In 1988, psychologist Linda Albright and her colleagues at the University of Connecticut ran three studies to test how well motivated individuals could read one another in what she termed zero acquaintance conditions—that is, the first time they ever met. She found considerable accuracy in judgments of both extroversion and conscientiousness: not only did observers tend to agree, but the people they were judging thought the impression representative of themselves. In another series of studies, highly motivated individuals were better at discerning the facial emotions and tone of voice of a stranger. They were, as well, more accurate at determining the stranger's internal emotional state.

In 2010, Nicholas Epley and Tal Eyal of Ben-Gurion University published the results of a series of experiments aimed at improving our person and mind perception skills. The title of their paper: "How to Seem

Telepathic." Many of our errors, the researchers found, stem from a basic mismatch between how we analyze ourselves and how we analyze others. When it comes to ourselves, we employ a fine-grained, highly contextualized level of detail. When we think about others, however, we operate at a much higher, more generalized and abstract level. For instance, when answering the same question about ourselves or others—how attractive are you?—we use very different cues. For our own appearance, we think about how our hair is looking that morning, whether we got enough sleep, how well that shirt matches our complexion. For that of others, we form a surface judgment based on overall gist. So, there are two mismatches: we aren't quite sure how others are seeing us, and we are incorrectly judging how they see themselves.

If, however, we can adjust our level of analysis, we suddenly appear much more intuitive and accurate. In one study, people became more accurate at discerning how others see them when they thought their photograph was going to be evaluated a few months later, as opposed to the same day, while in another, the same accuracy shift happened if they thought a recording they'd made describing themselves would be heard a few months later. Suddenly, they were using the same abstract lens that others are likely to use naturally—and so, they were much more perceptive about how they came off in reality, and not just in their own minds.

For an enterprising mind reader—that is, the grifter mid-put-up—this skill is crucial: you have to know what cues others are using to judge you, and what cues simply don't matter. If you think you look tired that day, your confidence might go down, and your persuasiveness along with it, but if you realize that no one else will notice and instead your overall demeanor will make a much bigger difference, you can focus on the big picture, confidence fully intact.

In a second series of studies, Epley and Eyal looked at the opposite effect: do we become better at reading other people when we approach them at the same intimate level of construal as we naturally do ourselves? This time, they gave photographs of other students to their subjects, telling them that the picture had been taken either earlier that day or a few months prior. Sure enough, those who thought the photographs had been taken hours earlier became much more nuanced in their judgments than those who thought they were a few months old—they were looking at others for the same fine level of detail they did in themselves. It was a relatively simple change in thought, but one that came with a high payoff. A con artist looks at everyone at that fine level. When it comes to the put-up, accuracy matters—and con men don't just want to know how someone looks to them. They want to correctly reflect how they want to be seen.

What's more, confidence artists can use what they're learning as they go in order to get us to give up even more. We are more trusting of people who seem more familiar and more similar to us, and we open up to them in ways we don't to strangers: those like us and those we know or recognize are unlikely to want to hurt us. And they're more likely to understand us. If your new acquaintance shares your taste for comedy clubs and favors the same everyday style of dress, it's a good indication that you may also be compatible in other respects. After all, tastes, habits, and lifestyle choices have to come from somewhere. Those who are very different from us, however, may have motives that aren't quite as friendly. My own psychic dropped a seemingly unrelated "You're not originally from New York, are you?" early in our reading. No, I'm not, I told him. Neither was he, he assured me, but he wouldn't live anywhere else. I nodded in agreement. Throughout the reading, many more such "similarities" came to light—he, too, had been uncertain about his career; he wanted to make some changes; he was actually far more artistic and felt, at times, that he was selling out, but he had to pay the bills. By the end, I thought him a kindred spirit. (As I'm sure do most of those who emerge from his readings—much like Sylvia Mitchell's clients saw her as a friend, someone quite like them, with problems and aspirations similar to their own.)

In one study, psychologist Lisa DeBruine asked people to play a sequential trust game, a game where the way you act depends on how you think your partner will act. (The most famous example of the genre is the prisoner's dilemma, where everyone benefits from staying silent but if someone talks and you don't, you fare worst of all.) No player's partner, however, actually existed. What she thought was a virtual teammate was in fact a photograph that had been subtly altered in one of two ways: it was morphed to resemble either a stranger or the player herself. The more similar to her own face the picture became, the more trustworthy a player judged it to be. Look at that face; how can someone not trust and respect it? Even more surface similarities, like shared birthdays (even birth months) or names, create an effect of greater liking—and greater willingness to help and comply.

But both similarity and familiarity can be faked, as the con artist can easily tell you—and the more you can fake it, the more real information will be forthcoming. Similarity is easy enough. When we like someone or feel an affinity for them, we tend to mimic their behavior, facial expressions, and gestures, a phenomenon known as the chameleon effect. But the effect works the other way, too. If we mimic someone else, *they* will feel closer and more similar to *us*; we can fake the natural liking process quite well. We perpetuate minor cons every day, often without realizing it, and sometimes knowing what we do all too well, when we mirror back someone's words or interests, feign a shared affinity for a sports team or a mutual hatred of a brand. The signs that usually serve us reliably can easily be massaged, especially in the short term—all a good con artist needs.

"Try honestly to see things from the other person's point of view," Dale Carnegie advised in his treatise on winning friends and influencing people, a sort of unwitting bible for cons in training. And if you're having trouble? "Talk in terms of the other person's interests." Someone mentions something in passing? Latch on to it and mirror it back multifold. Did you read one cue correctly—a Floridian address, perhaps, from an unseasonable tan? Seize on it. Do so masterfully, and you become better liked and seem more interesting yourself. Our defenses drop away. And suddenly you have all the interests and beliefs you can work with, making the put-up a matter of a moment.

Familiarity, too, can be faked, so that trust and affection—and thus, a con's successful progression—follow smoothly in its wake. In April 2005, Tom Jagatic and his colleagues at Indiana State University set out to gauge who might be vulnerable to phishing attacks, or attempts to gain sensitive personal information from someone by posing as a legitimate third party, like a bank or phone company. Their targets: students at their own university. Their aim was to find out what it would take to get someone to trust you and open up.

First, they looked at publicly available information on social networks: Facebook, LinkedIn, MySpace, Friendster (2005, remember), and LiveJournal's Friend of a Friend project. Next they sent their victims an e-mail that seemed to come from one of their friends at the university. When they clicked on the provided link, though, it brought them to a Web site that was clearly not affiliated with ISU, but that still asked them for their university login credentials.

An attack was considered a "success" if someone clicked on an e-mail link and proceeded to enter their university username and password. Over 70 percent of the students entered their login information. It had, after all, come from a friend. It was, in other words, nice and . . . familiar.

It's not just typical college students. In an earlier study on West Point cadets, four out of five students followed a fictitious embedded link from a "colonel" who didn't actually exist, to view their grade reports.

One of Fred Demara's preferred tactics on his many impostor adventures was something he termed "papering." Before he made a request for someone's credentials, in the run-up to assuming their identity, he would "paper" the trail with letters, calls, and conversations, posing as various people with a tie to his assumed identity who were all reaching out to the institution in question with queries and spontaneous-seeming recommendations. That way, by the time the request came around, he was a familiar presence. People were expecting him, he seemed more trust-worthy, and thus he became much more successful at attaining the precise certification he needed. His "friends" were only too happy to help.

With time, he could also rely on some "extras" who made the job all the simpler—people who had, over the years, met him, been taken in, and remained willing to vouch for him, certain that this time would be different and would mark his return to legitimacy. Indeed, many times he convinced Robert Crichton that he'd gone straight—for real and for good, this time—forcing Crichton to play an inadvertent shill in the pa-pering game. "I have been really trying to get a job!" he wrote in one letter, in November 1960. And of course, after their deep relationship, he'd given Crichton as a reference. Would Crichton oblige? "If they write to you please give me a real good buildup and sign any name that strikes your fancy . . . on good stationery natch."

Whether in the world of college or business, virtual or physical, the most effective way of creating an illusion of familiarity, to lull the mark into revealing ever more about himself and thus make the put-up that much more successful, remains the same: personal contact. Moran Cerf, now a neuroscientist, used to work as a hacker of sorts: a member of a team that helped companies determine their security vulnerabilities. The most important part of the job, he told me, is to first gather the hu-man intelligence, or HumInt—no technical skills as such; merely skills at reading people and latching on to what they've already shared freely, albeit, at times, unwittingly. The more specific the information, the bet-ter and more believable it would be.

Even though the attack itself was technical, the put-up remained supremely human. One woman on their team had no real technical savvy. Instead, her unique role was as head of the HumInt effort. She'd make friends. Check schedules. Research locations. Gain trust. And then the team could commence their hacking efforts. All they needed, Cerf says, was one single entry point.

And gaining a single entry point is quite simple if you know what you're doing. For instance, just having a brief conversation with someone, however meaningless—a simple exchange of hellos—is enough to gain their trust later on. The person you spoke with feels more familiar and thus more friendly—so you become more likely to trust her later on. In one study, seeing someone once, however briefly, even with no further interaction, made people more likely to agree to something later asked of them—just what Cerf's teammate was angling for. You're no longer a stranger; you're that girl who had coffee at my favorite coffee place just down the street from the office. What a coincidence. Of course I'll help.

Cerf's accomplice was a researcher who would report back on her findings rather than use them for nefarious purposes, but she did precisely what the confidence man does each time he begins the put-up: profile the likely candidates to target, and then use that profile to ingratiate herself before she's made a single demand. The ease with which she was able to succeed should frighten us.

It's an effect that can be achieved with even less of an effort than a casual chat over coffee. In the winter of 1967, Robert Zajonc (pronounced *ZYE-unts*), a social psychologist at Stanford University, came across an intriguing story from a Corvallis, Oregon, newspaper. For two months, the article said, a mysterious figure had been attending a course at Oregon State University, called Speech 113: Basic Persuasion. The figure had an odd appearance: it was draped entirely in a black bag. The only visible part of his—or maybe it was a her?—body was the feet. They were bare. Each class, the hooded figure sat, silently, on a table in the back of the room. The professor, Charles Goetzinger, was the only one who knew its identity. The students, meanwhile, referred to the presence as the Black Bag.

But, strange as it was, that wasn't what intrigued Zajonc about the story. Instead, he found himself drawn to Goetzinger's description of the students' reactions to the Black Bag. They had changed, according to the professor, "from hostility to the Black Bag to curiosity and finally to friendship." The Black Bag hadn't done anything, said a single word, or interacted with a single student. But their views of him changed all the same. Could it be, Zajonc wondered, that they'd gotten used to his presence (it was a he, after all)—and did that mere fact make them somehow friendlier toward him?

It wasn't a new idea. In 1903, Max Meyer had played Oriental music to his students repeatedly, from twelve to fifteen times. The more they heard it, the more they liked it. The effect was later replicated for classical music, unusual combination in colors in art, and even seats in a classroom. (Ever wonder why people usually stick to the same seat, even if there's no assigned seating?) It's a matter of things "growing on you." But these were all consciously retained. What Zajonc was interested in was that word "mere": could exposure without conscious processing accomplish the same thing?

In 1968, Zajonc published the results of his research—results that are, perhaps, one of the most important insights that advertisers, marketers, and their less scrupulous colleagues in the con have taken to heart in executing the put-up. First he showed people series of images— Turkish nonsense words, Chinese-like characters, or photographs, depending on the study. Then he tested their liking for them. The more times they had seen them, he found, the more they liked them. He later reproduced the effect with random shapes projected onto a screen that appeared and disappeared so quickly that it was difficult to tell what exactly was being shown and, crucially, how many times it had appeared. Over and over, people chose the shapes they had seen earlier as more pleasing—even though they had no conscious memory of ever having seen them and couldn't distinguish old from new at above-chance levels. Zajonc called it the mere exposure effect: familiarity breeds affection. And affection is a fount of the personal information so essential to the successful put-up.

Mere exposure has real evolutionary value. If we've seen something before, and it didn't kill us, well, our chances are probably better than with something we can't predict. The better-the-devil-you-know type of reasoning. Konrad Lorenz, the Nobel-winning ethologist, showed that a raven would react with an immediate escape response in the presence of any new object, be it a camera, a stuffed polecat, or anything else. But after a few hours and repeated exposure, the bird began to approach. Infants do the same thing. In one early study, babies cried when they heard a new sound for the first time. By the fourth time, they were more curious than anything else. Alas, like many normally adaptive tendencies, our reaction to mere exposure is all too easy to co-opt.

It certainly doesn't hurt when we go beyond mere exposure to the level of conversation—and not only have a conversation, but then have accurate recall for the details when we make our next bid for trust. We like it when we feel someone knows the "real" us. Something as simple as remembering our name can instantly turn a confidence artist from persona non grata to someone we like, admire even, and certainly someone we're willing to help. In one series of experiments, people were more likely to buy something from a relative stranger if that relative stranger happened to recall their name. They viewed the mere recall as a compliment; clearly they were important enough to note, and if that person thought so, then it was a very discerning person indeed. As that masterful manipulator Dale Carnegie put it, "Remember that a person's name is to that person the sweetest and most important sound in any language." "Knowing" us is the con man's bread and butter.

In fact, some cons are based *entirely* on false knowledge. A seasoned technique: pretend you're someone's relative and that you met at a wedding. All you need to know is the name of the wedding party in question, and you're golden. We would much rather fake knowledge than appear ungracious. Herman Melville hit upon the power of such false familiarity in his novel of the con, *The Confidence-Man*. Aboard a steamship, a con artist in various guises approaches select passengers. As he learns something about one from talking to another, or from simple observation, he uses it in his next conversation, pretending to be an old business acquaintance or social associate. It works like a charm.

In February 1960, Mr. and Mrs. Alan James Blau of Pittsfield, Massachusetts, placed an official announcement in the *New York Times*. Their son, Andrew, had become engaged to a girl from California, a Miss Kelly Smith Hines. The date was set for June. The family was flooded with well-meaning congratulations; what a happy life event. Some days later, Mrs. Blau received a phone call. It was Kelly's aunt, Nancy. She was passing through Pittsfield and wanted to meet Andrew's parents. Mrs. Blau was a bit miffed—why hadn't anyone warned her?—but happy to oblige. She met Aunt Nancy at the bus station, took her to lunch, had a wonderful conversation. Aunt Nancy told her about her house in Carmel, inviting her to stay when it came time for the wedding. They talked about wedding gifts—Spode china, Aunt Nancy suggested; a wonderful choice, Mrs. Blau concurred. At the end of the afternoon, it was time to drive the visiting guest back to the bus station. Alas, Aunt Nancy was absentminded. She only had traveler's checks with her. Would Mrs. Blau kindly loan her fifty dollars for the remaining trip? Well, of course. She was almost family.

Later that evening, Mrs. Blau called her son in New York. Why hadn't he told her about Aunt Nancy? she demanded, slightly annoyed. Andrew was surprised. Aunt who? He called Kelly. Kelly drew a blank. Kelly called her mother. Her mother was perplexed. Mrs. Hines called *her* mother, Kelly's grandmother. The mystery only deepened. Aunt Nancy, it turned out, was a professional wedding impostor. She would read announcements in newspapers, visit parents, and come away with meals, housing, and "small loans" in the process. Thus she made her modest living. (Today, Kelly is of a more forgiving bent. She feels that "the poor woman was single and bored and just looking to be part of other people's lives for a little while.")

Aunt Nancy is the perfect embodiment of faked familiarity: do your homework, and the put-up falls rapidly into place. You don't have to expend much effort on the groundwork that forms the basis of real familiarity, and instead, reap the same psychological benefits by simply appearing to be closer than you are and to know more than you do.

Cerf has been out of the hacking-for-hire business for over a decade. But recently, he said, he checked in with some of his old teammates. Hadn't their jobs, he wondered, gotten far more difficult over time, as companies and people alike became more tech savvy? Quite the contrary. They'd grown easier. Now the HumInt effort didn't even require all that much physical legwork. All you needed to do was successfully friend someone on Facebook or connect with them socially on some other network—and if you could get them to see you as friendly long enough to click on just one link or download just one file, the whole system would eventually be yours. One entry point is all that is required.

We reveal a great deal about ourselves without necessarily realizing it. And everything we reveal becomes the perfect fodder for the well-executed put-up, to then be used to gain our trust. Even a novice could find out, say, our bidding history or shopping preferences on eBay—and any public gift list, be it on Amazon or a wedding or baby registry, can give further color to not only our desires but our important life events. Security questions like mother's maiden name, too, can be easily hacked by a quick search through public records. All a con artist needs is to do his homework.

And to a con artist, that legwork is always worth it, no matter how difficult or devious the process. The put-up, after all, is the the foundation of his livelihood. On July 14, 1975, Sandip Madan lost his younger brother, Gunish, known as Chuchu to the family. He was only thirteen, and his death came as an utter shock. Their mother, understandably, was devastated. "She was distraught with grief that lasted for decades," Madan told me, "and sought spiritual comfort." In the spring of 1978, her depression still acute, she was offered a brief glimmer of hope. A close friend of the family's told them that a famous sadhu, a Hindu ascetic purported to have divine powers, was visiting New Delhi. His name was Bhootnath. And he could bring the whole family to see him.

The Madan family arrived in Bhootnath's temporary residence. Outside his audience chamber, the anteroom was filled with followers and would-be supplicants. The excitement was palpable. Some exchanged confidences about their hopes for the visit. Others extolled his past exploits. This was a true holy man.

After a brief wait, they were shown into the presence of Bhootnath himself. "We met him as strangers he knew nothing about," Madan says. But somehow, he was soon sharing insights that there was no apparent way he could have known. "He had an uncanny knowledge about my mother having lost her child and being in torment about it." He saw, he said, the boy's soul. He was in the afterlife. He was happy. And he wanted his mother to be happy, too. At peace, at last. She was unnerved—who wouldn't be? She hadn't shared any of this. But she was also relieved. Maybe they had found a holy man after all.

Bhootnath suddenly shifted his attention. He looked straight at Sandip. He had just glimpsed a slice of his future, he said. He would be joining the IAS, India's civil service. Sandip was shocked. It was indeed his aspiration. How had he known?

The audience was over. Bhootnath waved his arms and, out of thin air, *prasad* appeared before them—holy food, some nuts and raisins. He gave them his blessing and sent them on their way.

Had they just been in the presence of divinity? Something about the visit didn't sit quite right. At the last minute, Sandip's new wife, Anita, and an aunt, Ranjit, his mother's younger sister, had decided to join in the excursion. And about the two of them, Bhootnath had been both wrong and clueless. How could he have been so right about some things and so completely off base about others?

The answer was far less holy. The same family friend who had set up the visit had also been giving Bhootnath information to prepare him for the meeting. And the details he hadn't been able to glean—well, those anteroom supplicants weren't quite what they seemed, either. They were his associates, posing as guileless hangers-on to pick what crumbs of knowledge might fall from the actual visitors.

For several months, Madan recalls, Bhootnath was the toast of New Delhi. Everyone was excited. Magazines and newspapers wrote about him. Wealthy donors flocked to his side. But then he made one slip too many, and fell as quickly as he rose, to be replaced, in short order, by the next miracle worker.

Even if there's no Facebook and no willing friend—well, con artists are enterprising. No piece of data is too small for the put-up, and no amount of effort to obtain it too large. In 1898, Mollie Burns, a schoolteacher and typist, fell ill on a trolley car in uptown Manhattan. Luckily, a Good Samaritan was there to help. Elizabeth Fitzgerald took pity on the sick girl and walked her to her hotel room. Was she not from around here? she asked as she led her down the sidewalk. Actually, she was, Burns admitted. It was just that she'd had a fight with her mother and had left home in a huff. Hence the hotel room. Fitzgerald sympathized—mothers were tough—and, after checking to make sure that Mollie had what she needed, took her leave. She had to get on with her day.

Except her day, oddly enough, would now center on her chance acquaintance. In Harlem, where she lived, Fitzgerald was known as Madame Zingara, the famed clairvoyant of Harlem. And she couldn't let an opportunity like this pass her by. It was the thing of a moment for a practiced hand like herself to track down Burns's mother. And from there, over a nice cup of sympathetic tea, to learn that the topic of the fight had been an affair that Burns was having with a married man, one E. T. Harlow.

Madame Zingara promptly called on Burns. She'd had a vision, she told her. And that vision included "shocking details" of her personal life—which, for a small fee, she would keep to herself. Burns, eager to preserve her reputation, parted with several hundred dollars, almost everything she had.

A week later, Madame Zingara called again. She now knew that Burns was going to be named as a correspondent in a divorce suit. But, again, for a small fee she could keep that from coming to pass. Burns promptly gave up the rest of her savings. She wasn't the only one. The clairvoyant was very good at what she did. She had convinced the entire family that they would all be ruined by a disgraceful divorce. They were lucky, though. For $1,000, she managed to keep ruination at bay.

But she went one step too far when she tracked down Harlow himself. She had had a revelation, she told him. He was having an affair with Mollie Burns, and "evil spirits" were working against him. The cost of an exorcism (at a special rate): $500. Unlike the Burnses, Harlow went to the police. And Madame Zingara went to jail.

Not for long, though. One of her clients, Henry Straus, whom she'd convinced she could help find gold, supplied her bail, and she didn't lose any time in fleeing to Chicago. She was arrested again in the winter of 1899, escaped again, and was finally caught and sentenced for fraud in 1900.

In the hands of an artist, the mind reading game comes full circle. The more familiar and similar someone seems, the more you like them, the more you share with them, the more information the con artist has to feed back to you. And the circle begins anew.

But heaven forbid the mark himself should make use of the same approach and see through game and artist both. To avoid that happening, the confidence man becomes an expert in tripping us up: even as he perfects the put-up, he knows how to make us even worse at reading social cues than we normally are. Call it the anti-put-up: put up the mark all the while making sure he can't do the same thing right back. Things that trip us up, Epley has found, include pressure—time, emotional, situational—and power. When we're feeling pressure, we grow far less able to think logically and deliberately. When we're feeling more powerful, we tend to feel as if we don't need others quite as much, and our ability to read their minds and the cues they throw off falters. In a version of the self-monitoring task (the Q on the forehead), Adam Galinsky and his colleagues asked people to draw an E on their foreheads. If you'd just thought about a time when you were in a high-powered position, you drew the E from your own perspective (prongs facing right). If, however, you'd just been reflecting on times when you had relatively little power, the letter flipped toward your conversation partner's point of view. A flipped letter, in turn, signals a greater willingness and ability to take others' point of view into account, and a better ability to read the social signs they throw off. There's nothing a con artist likes to do more than make us feel powerful and in control: we are the ones calling the shots, making the choices, doing the thinking. They are merely there to do our bidding. And so as we throw off ever more clues, we ourselves become increasingly blind to the clues being thrown off by others.

Take Demara's stint in the Royal Canadian Navy. Part of his success—that is, the reason he wasn't unmasked at once and managed to slip by with what seemed like a semblance of medical knowledge—was that he'd mastered the power dynamic perfectly and loved to make those around him feel like the experts in control. He'd deferred to another doctor's expertise in drafting the "field guide" for soldiers who didn't have ready medical attention. The fellow doctor was so much more knowledgeable, he'd told him, and he felt like a neophyte in comparison. The ploy worked like a charm, and Demara received all the free medical advice he could want. Later, on the ship, he did much the same thing with the captain and senior officers, always deferring to their power and seniority—even though he, too, had a claim to an elevated status. That way, he could glean all he could from them, and they, in turn, would be too flattered to scrutinize him too closely.

Another thing that detracts from our mind reading prowess: money. Specifically, thoughts of it. In a series of nine studies, psychologist Kathleen Vohs, the chair of marketing at the University of Minnesota's Carlson School of Management, found that people who were reminded of money, even in passing, ended up paying less attention to others, and, indeed, wanted to put more distance between themselves and others. Con artists are well aware of this. And so they make financial woes (or windfalls) front and center of their put-up—much as Sylvia Mitchell did with her victims, bringing up financial considerations right away: they had too great an attachment to money; they were in an emotional predicament because they had an unhealthy relationship with material possessions; and so on. While they were busy thinking through the implications, she was busy reading them.

* * *

Lee Choong was a businesswoman from Singapore who had earned a master's degree in business from NYU. Her life, however, wasn't going quite as planned. Professionally, her job seemed at a standstill. It was 2007. She was working between eighty and a hundred hours a week at a high-profile investment bank. It was a good job. It paid well. So many others were out of work; she should have been happy. But her countless hours seemed wasted somehow. She missed her family, especially her mother, who had fallen ill and needed care. Romantically, too, there were some bumps. She had her eye on a coworker. She knew that was never a good idea, but she couldn't help herself. The coworker, alas, was oblivious to her affections, as these things so often go. And there was one more hitch: she was a fellow female. Choong was coming to terms with a new sexual identity, and one not particularly welcome in her home culture. She felt lonely, lost, vulnerable, and exposed.

And there it was. That warm, beckoning yellow glow from the hanging lanterns. The same beaded curtain. The same welcoming, reassuring smile that told her she wasn't only welcome here; she was safe.

Sylvia Mitchell could sense right away that Choong's energy field was all out of whack. Negative energy, she told Choong, permeated her existence. But there was hope. Sylvia could get rid of it—if only she agreed to put $18,000 in a jar for Sylvia to hold. Just as an exercise. It was a gesture of good faith that would help clarify the dark forces that surrounded her.

Then Mitchell went even further. In a past life, she told Choong, her family had somehow wronged the object of her crush; that was why she now found herself in the throngs of unrequited love. But a happy future together was possible, she assured her. She could sense it. To make it real, however, would require work. Real work. Work that couldn't be accomplished in a single visit, or even just a few.

Over the course of the next two years, the two women would med-itate together, to better focus their energy on future love-full bliss. On her own, Mitchell said she would perform various rites to help the pro-cess along. It would take time, she warned. The slight in the past life had been severe. Time—and $128,000, which, bit by bit, Choong surren-dered to her new confidante.

As their relationship deepened, perhaps unsurprisingly Choong's problems were showing no signs of abatement. Instead, they had only grown more severe. Her workplace love complained of sexual harassment—and soon after, Choong was fired.

Her mother was still sick. Choong was without love, without a job, short on funds. Mitchell had taken most of what she had.

* * *

Neither Saalfield nor Choong was a particularly gullible woman. They were professionally successful, smart, good at what they did. And, as they would both later publicly state, they were highly skeptical of Sylvia Mitchell. But they were also vulnerable emotionally—she was just what they needed, just when they needed it. And she was just so good. "I feel as an intelligent, educated woman, it is one of the most humiliating things that's ever happened to me," Saalfield later confessed.

In some sense, the role of a psychic is easier than that of many con-fidence artists when it comes to the put-up: the marks, in a certain re-spect, come preselected. Just by walking into the parlor, you've shown yourself to be open to belief and suggestion, and you're obviously search-ing for an easy answer to your problem or situation. That's true of other types of rackets as well. In the age of the Internet, it's easier than ever to clear the first hurdle of the put-up: those who respond to the false ads, e-mails, or other phishing schemes. Gone is the need to be psychologi-cally savvy from first glance. All you need is to be savvy enough to build an alluring storefront or craft a message that will hook your potential prey. (The bad grammar and seemingly implausible notes: those aren't from stupidity. They're actually well thought out beforehand. Scammers have learned the hard way that notes that sound too legitimate hook too many fish, making the weeding-out process incredibly costly. Now only the true sucker falls for the pitch.)

And yet, in another sense, the need for perceptive psychology in the put-up—to be a good person and mind reader both—never goes away. Even with the best-laid trap, you still need to be a master of the cold read to reel in the big fish. A person can, like Saalfield, walk into a psychic's lair on a vindictive lark. Had Mitchell been a lesser artist, Debra would have been out just seventy-five dollars. Not cheap, but not the end of the world. But with the right touch, despite her best skepticism, Saalfield parted with far more—and not just a lot of money. Money she didn't actually have.

A thorough put-up is essential for the con artist. You need to select your victims with care. One slip, like Madam Zingara's, and an entire career can be in ruins. Demara didn't just let Robert Crichton write his biography. He scouted him out first: background checks before he responded to his first letter, and multiple broken meetings in New York after that. As Crichton waited for Demara to arrive, the impostor would hide and observe how he acted. He wanted to make sure he wasn't getting just any writer. He wanted to get the writer who would write the story he wanted. He wanted not just a biographer but also a mark.

And he got, eventually, just that. Crichton had to write two drafts of his book. The first was more journalistically forthcoming. It told of a man who had hurt many and had, perhaps, a side even darker than that of the impostor: he was, multiple suits and complaints alleged, prone to abusive and sexually inappropriate advances toward young boys. The draft was rejected. It was too dark and pessimistic, according to the editors. An impostor needed a lighter touch, more escapades and farce, less heartbreak. Crichton gave the matter serious thought. He was a serious writer, and wanted to tell a serious story. He did not want to sugarcoat the truth.

But then he looked back on his time with Fred. The darker version might have seemed more journalistically true, but personally he felt that Fred's story was quite a different one. In his eyes, he later wrote in a private letter, Demara was indeed a "convert from sin." He was troubled, yes, but he was also capable of huge feats of strength and goodness. Many of his dark deeds were the result of alcohol—a serious, lasting drinking problem. But he overcame it "by sheer willpower" and, in the end, was unlike any alcoholic Crichton had encountered. "He never would allow himself finally to lose his sense of pride and dignity. They say all alcoholics do," he observed. "It amazed me and amazed experienced doctors at Bellevue Hospital." (Demara had been briefly admitted as a patient, with Crichton afforded sole visiting privileges. One wonders in retrospect whether that wasn't a further ploy to create a deeper base for personal sympathy.) "No matter how bad he was he made monumental and sometimes tragically pathetic efforts at dignity, pride, self-esteem. He was truly a victim, you might say, of a chemical force over his own true nature."

And that true nature, Crichton reasoned, was essentially good, regardless of what escapades may have taken place. "I early lost fear of his taking advantage of me in any way," he said. "He was decent, fair, generous, kind . . . For a so called 'bad actor' at the time I could only conclude that I would trust him and his word above almost any person I know." Demara had simply been a victim of unfortunate circumstances, which masked his fundamental decency, and even talent. "I felt he had a genuine call [to religion] but simply did not know how to respond to it. This I know, people respond to Demara. Just as he would have made a good politician, which is not to me an evil word as it unfortunately is to too many Americans, I feel he would have made a good preacher because he really loves people, enjoys them, understands them, likes to listen to them." Crichton concluded, "He's a pretty remarkable person and, this is especially true, he does remarkable work when he's trusted, when people really back him. Then he responds with real zeal."

The darker version, Crichton decided, was incorrect. The man was ready for redemption. He had hurt others almost in spite of himself. And so Crichton created a new draft of Fred, the one that eventually made it to the bestseller lists. Fred became a hero. Demara, it seems, had intuited the outcome perfectly. He was a mind reader second to none, so good at the put-up that he could manipulate almost anyone he chose to deal with. He had picked a writer who he knew would agree with the redemption story—someone optimistic and ready to see the good in poor ol' Fred.

For many years, Crichton kept believing. After *The Great Impostor* was published, Fred began to hit his biographer up for money, time and time again, and always with a perfectly legitimate excuse. May 29, 1961: "I am here without clothes or money. If anything good happens to the book, you know where I will be." February 23, 1961: "I could use some money, if any available, to return to California, I borrowed against salary to get here." No date: "As much as I dislike to ask, believe it or not, I would like to take you up on that offer of money. I am really desperate." No date: "I am absolutely without money and my clothes etc. are still in Missouri (being shipped, I hope). Any suggestions?" Each time, it was his "last chance" at redemption. Each time, he just needed a bit more.

Eventually, Crichton would buy him a new car and pay for him to attend school for ministry training. In the late 1960s, he even tried to set him up with positive media coverage at Calvary Ranch, a new venture for young troubled boys that Demara swore was to be his final, legitimate project. (He ended up absconding with funds and abandoning the ranch and boys soon after. He was then hit with another molestation suit, which his lawyer successfully parried away.) Even then, Crichton kept believing in his reformation. "It is the old Demara tragedy replayed," he wrote of his work at the ranch for boys. "He's doing his usual brilliant job but because he lacks the proper credentials his work will be sacrificed and the good it is doing dumped because he can't comply with legal formalities and bureaucratic procedures."

Crichton wasn't being daft. Demara simply had that effect on people: his intuitive psychology was second to none, and he was able to read his marks well enough to know just how to play any event to make it seem, to each one, the perfect story of redemption. "My husband and I both feel you are a godsent man," wrote one Detroit woman after learning about Demara's Korean escapades. She wanted him, she said, to perform a lung operation on her daughter. As late as February 1974, Muriel von Weiss, the president of the Long Island Writers, wrote to say that Demara had pulled yet another disappearing act and that his supposed conversion to legitimacy was a ruse. But even still, she wished him well and "agree[d] . . . he did a lot of good." "His brand of con operation," she felt, "was limited to credentials and not motivated by greed or power hunger, and he performed in each career better than some of his legitimate peers." Conveniently forgotten were the instances where he had real power to do harm.

One evening, Crichton realized he'd been taken in yet again when he inadvertently misinformed a reporter of Fred's whereabouts. "Later that night the reporter called me back and said how could I account for Rev. Hanson denying he knew Demara," he wrote to the same Robert Hanson. "From long and painful experience I knew exactly how. One was that Demara indeed was not there and had never been there, two, that one of Demara's superiors or colleagues was covering for him (that is a bad word, it should read—protecting) and the other was that Demara himself was answering the phone, announcing a name such as yours and denying that he was there or ever was there." Crichton knew exactly what Demara was up to, yet he kept believing in him all the same.

In the face of accumulating evidence, though, Crichton's goodwill eventually evaporated. Twice Demara had sued him. And one time too many he had made a fool of him for relying on his goodness. He had made Fred a hero, but Fred, in the end, deserved none of it. "Your reputation, as you well know, really far outruns many of your actual accomplishments," he wrote in one letter. And later: "I have made a hero out of a bag of guts. If you don't think I won't, if need be, destroy the image, I will."

In his notes for *The Great Impostor*, Crichton had summed up Fred's techniques—and their success—in Fred's own words, the essence of the put-up in the telling of the confidence man himself. "Americans would rather be liked than right. (This fact allowed you to operate after reasonable suspicion was aroused.) Americans are amazingly forgiving to the errant sinner (almost everywhere you went they would have you back). Americans are among the most trusting people in the world. Accept you at your word and at your face value until proven otherwise. (They don't stand and watch you or question you but wait for you to volunteer your own information. This, of course, is a great asset to the impostor.) The test of the freedom of this country. Where else but in America could a guy like me operate? On ability of famed impostor to circulate: If they aren't looking for you, they don't see you." What Crichton didn't realize was how closely those words captured his own experience. Fred had profiled him just as he had all of his other victims and had played out the precise drama that Crichton both wanted and expected to see—the perfect put-up, perfectly tailored. But because Crichton was himself a character, he failed to see the ruse with the detachment he reserved for the great impostor's other marks.

* * *

The put-up is all about mind reading, learning to elicit the personal from the seemingly impersonal, to convince your mark to open up without realizing she's doing it. And so it's no surprise that actual "mind readers" are oftentimes the most dangerous type of confidence artist there is: their technique, at its best, is so perfectly honed that almost no one is immune to it. So dangerous is the effect that there are actual statutes trying to guard against it—an exception in the world of the con. In New York State, fortune-telling, powers of the "occult," and pretensions to "exorcise, influence, or affect evil spirits or curses" are classified as a misdemeanor, unless they come with a big "for entertainment or amusement only" disclaimer. (As one psychic quipped, "I call it CYA—Cover Your Aura.") Though it's been on the books since 1967, Offense

165.35—"Fortune Telling," punishable by ninety days in jail or a fine of $500—is rarely invoked. Since 2010, according to the *New York Times,* ten people have been charged under the statute. Some places, though, go further. Warren, a suburb of Detroit, requires its psychics to undergo criminal background checks and have their fingerprints taken before they can peddle their wares.

It's an attempt at protection from the power of the put-up masters— those people who can read us like a book and convince us they see the "real" us behind the mask. But no matter what we do to legally ramp up against the errant mystics, we *don't* have protection against the principles they operate on—which are the underlying principles of any successful con. Each put-up is tailored for you, so while you may understand its operation in general, in your particular case you are unlikely to see it coming.

That's why psychics are so dangerous: no matter what, it can be difficult to convince people that they aren't real. One former mentalist I spoke with—a magician who performs mind reading tricks instead of the usual visual illusions—ended up quitting the business. No matter her disclaimers, no matter how often she told her audience that these were all tricks, some believed even more the more she denied. In the end, she said, her conscience couldn't allow it.

Harry Houdini spent the later part of his life going after psychics and mystics; he, too, felt that they were a danger beyond the simple criminal. Earlier in his career, he'd tried his own hand at mysticism. "As a side line to my own phase of mystery shows I have associated myself with mediums, joining the rank and file and held seances as an independent medium to fathom the truth of it all," he wrote in the 1924 book that catalogued his efforts, *A Magician Among the Spirits.* "At the time I appreciated the fact that I surprised my clients, but while aware of the fact that I was deceiving them I did not see or understand the seriousness of trifling with such sacred sentimentality and the baneful result which inevitably followed," he continued. "To me it was a lark. I was a mystifier and as such my ambition was being gratified and my love for a mild sensation satisfied." But when he saw the reactions he was provoking, and stopped to think about them in greater earnest, he realized it was more than a lark. "As I advanced to riper years of experience I was brought to a realization of the seriousness of trifling with the hallowed reverence which the average human being bestows on the departed, and when I personally became afflicted with similar grief I was chagrined that I should ever have been guilty of such frivolity and for the first time realized that it bordered on crime." For the next quarter century, after he quit his own mentalism-for-entertainment efforts, he devoted his life to ferreting the practice out more broadly.

Mysticism, he argued, was a game as powerful as it was dangerous. "It is perfectly rational to suppose that I may be deceived once or twice by a new illusion," he wrote, "but if my mind, which has been so keenly trained for years to invent mysterious effects, can be deceived, how much more susceptible must the ordinary observer be."

In 1923, Houdini consulted for a panel, organized by *Scientific American* magazine, not unlike the decades-long endeavor by James Randi, known as the Amazing Randi: it offered a prize to anyone who could prove genuine psychic powers. None were able to claim it. Houdini then offered a second prize, of $10,000, available at any of his shows. If anyone could demonstrate a psychic phenomenon that he couldn't replicate, the money was theirs. Again, none could.

But as hard as he fought, just as hard the believers flocked—even when mysticism was the furthest thing from his mind. After a performance in Boston, to which he had invited Sarah Bernhardt, who was herself performing there that week, he found himself in a car with her. Apart from being one of the most acclaimed actresses of her time, Bernhardt was an amputee. "Houdini, you do such marvelous things," she told him. "Couldn't you—could you bring back my leg for me?"

Houdini was startled. "You cannot be serious," he replied. "You know my powers are limited and you are actually asking me to do the impossible."

"But you do the impossible," she answered.

Psychics, mystics, clairvoyants, mediums: they are, in some ways, the heart of the confidence game. The put-up is their fundamental building block. They don't mess with just any beliefs; they mess with the deepest beliefs we have.

And the most intelligent among us succumb all too easily. The psychologist Daryl Bem made a splash in 2011 when he decreed that psi—precognition—is real. But he is far from the first scientist to fall for the lure of the paranormal. In the 1970s, John Mack became convinced of the power of UFOs. Chairman of the Harvard Medical School's psychiatry department and Pulitzer Prize–winning author, he grew increasingly certain that alien invasions were real and that there were, at present, aliens among us. He met his first UFO survivor, Budd Hopkins, in 1989. As he later told *Psychology Today*, "Nothing in my 40 years as a psychiatrist prepared me for what he had to say. I was impressed with his sincerity, depth of knowledge, and deep concern for the abductees. But what affected me even more," he continued, "was the internal consistency of the highly detailed accounts [of abduction] by different individuals who would have had no way to communicate with one another."

And on a smaller level, we experience something similar all the time. Even if you aren't religious, for instance, your chances of falling for superstition are high. In the middle of the 2014 NFL playoffs, the Public Religion Research Institute conducted a survey to determine how many fans were seeing the hand of, well, something that wasn't the football players in the games' outcomes. Turns out, the answer was about half—or roughly fifty million Americans. A quarter thought their team had, at one point or another, been cursed. Another quarter had prayed to God for help for their team, and one fifth thought that their actions would determine whether the team won or lost.

There are, as well, the smaller gestures of faith. Twenty-one percent of fans performed a ritual prior to each game: dancing in a circle, sitting in the same seat, giving a pep talk in front of the television screen. If you don't do it, who knows. You might be the one to throw the curse.

"If there had been any real unalloyed demonstration to work on, one that did not reek of fraud, one that could not be reproduced by earthly powers," Houdini concluded, "then there would be something for a foundation, but up to the present time everything that I have investigated has been the result of deluded brains or those which were too actively and intensely willing to believe." But it's not the fault of the brains; it's the strength of the put-up. If you read someone correctly, and do your research thoroughly enough to know her deepest desires, hopes, fears, and dreams, you can make her believe most anything.

* * *

In 2011, Debra Saalfield and Lee Choong banded together to sue Sylvia Mitchell. In July of that year, she was arrested on charges of grand larceny.

As Saalfield entered the court, she wore an elegant striped skirt, black shirt with tan jacket draped on top, a single strand of pearls at her neck. She was here to see that no one else fell for Mitchell's lies.

As the trial wore on, more cases came to light. Robert Millet had borrowed $7,000 from his father, adding it to $3,000 of his own to pay Mitchell's fee. What she offered: a red thread with knots that symbolized the "karmic blocks" in his life. Go home, she instructed him, hold the string tightly, and pray for the knots to dissolve. When he opened his hand, he told the jury, the knots had seemed to disappear.

Another woman, anonymous by choice, walked in for a crystal reading ($60). She, too, had some "blockages." But if she wore white to bed every night for a week, and slept with a special jar under her pillow, the blockages would dissipate. Inside the jar: a list of goals—a "prayer list," Mitchell called it—wrapped in $900 cash, a bit of water, and a wad of spit. After a week, this time dressed all in black, the woman was to return to Mitchell, jar in hand.

When the woman came back, Mitchell took the jar and asked her to step out into the waiting room. When she was called back in, the water in the jar was red. Mitchell said the red represented the "impurities" in her life.

Mitchell's game was coming apart. Adam Brown, one of the lawyers suing her, called what they were seeing "organized psychic crime." And one anonymous juror later told the *New York Times,* "She was clearly robbing these people in a heinous way." She "is not in the business of cleansing spirits. She's in the business of cleaning out bank accounts," as Assistant District Attorney James Bergamo put it. "She finds people's weaknesses, and she exploits them to her advantage." She is, in other words, the master of the put-up: read someone's vulnerabilities well, and their confidence is yours for the taking. "You're dealing with a confidence scheme," Bob Nygaard told the AP. "It becomes clear to you the script [the psychics] are following."

At the trial's close, the jury heard two written statements, one from Choong, the other from Saalfield.

"I have always believed in compassion, but Sylvia Mitchell preyed on that to steal from me," Choong wrote in a statement. "I suffer guilt and sorrow whenever I think about this. I constantly wish I could do more for my mother." In her statement, Saalfield wrote, "She has destroyed a piece of me that I will never get back. She has taken my self-respect away from me. She has affected my health, my family relationships, and my honor."

In her defense, Mitchell said she was only trying to help. Who knows—maybe things would have been far worse without her assistance.

The trial drew to a close. For two days and six hours, the jury deliberated. On Friday, October 11, 2013, Sylvia Mitchell was found guilty of ten counts of grand larceny and one count of scheming to defraud. As the verdict was read, Mitchell appeared to scowl.

By November, the scowl was gone. She'd been in jail for a month. Her hair frizzled, outgrown roots showing dark beneath the blond. On Thursday, November 14, she received her sentence: five to fifteen years in prison and restitution of approximately $110,000 to Choong and Saalfield. Justice Gregory Carro couldn't be clearer. Mitchell had focused on people undergoing "some dramatic stress," and then she took them for all they had. Of all the bad con artists out there, she was the worst there was.

* * *

Unlike many victims, Debra Saalfield got her happy ending. Two years after she'd lost $27,000 in Mitchell's clutches, and a year before she would take her to trial, she entered the Pro/Am American Style World Ballroom Dance Competition at the Ohio Star Ball. Everyone who was anyone in dance was there. As Debra Rolquin, her stage name, she danced the night away, partnered by her instructor of seven years, Tomasz Mielnicki. And at the end of the evening, she went home with the Rising Star Award for her age group. She'd beaten out thirty-two couples.

In September 2011, two months after Mitchell's arrest, she married.

CHAPTER 3
THE PLAY

Be a patient listener (it is this, not fast talking, that gets a con man his coups).

—THE FIRST COMMANDMENT OF THE CON MAN,
FROM VICTOR LUSTIG, CON ARTIST

It was early fall 2013, October 10 for those counting. The weather that day had been unseasonably cold, hovering in the forties, the first whiffs of the chill of the season filling the air. The streets of downtown Dublin were filled with tourists ducking in and out of stores, posing with wide grins underneath the Spire of Dublin. People leaving work early, others, out for a quick cup. In their midst, one young woman stood out. She seemed dazed and distressed as she wandered down O'Connell Street, looking around timidly, a helpless-seeming terror in her eyes. It was a quarter past four in the afternoon. She stopped in front of the post office, or, as locals would have it, the GPO. In between the thick columns—it would take three of her, at least, to put her arms around one, and a good ten to stand head to head to reach its top—she looked even more forlorn. She was dressed in a purple hoodie under a gray wool sweater, tight darkly colored jeans, and flat black shoes. Underneath, her face was ashen. She was shivering. She wasn't talking.

A passerby, stunned by her appearance, asked if she needed help. She looked at him mutely, as if not quite grasping the essence of the question. Somebody called the police. An officer from the Store Street garda station, the closest to the child—she seemed so small and frail that to call her a young woman didn't feel right—answered the call. He took her to a hospital. It seemed the best thing to do.

She was a teenager—fourteen or fifteen, at most. At five feet, six inches, she weighed just over eighty-eight pounds. Her long blond hair covered a spiny, battered back. Once she did talk, some days later, it became clear she had only the most rudimentary grasp of English, a word here or there, no more. Not enough to say who she was or why she'd appeared as she had.

But the girl could draw. And what she drew made her new guardians catch their breath. One stifled a gasp. One burst out crying. There she was, a small stick-like figure, being flown to Ireland on a plane. And there she was again, lying on a bed, surrounded by multiple men. She seemed to be a victim of human trafficking. One of the lucky ones who had somehow managed to escape.

Three weeks later, the girl still wasn't talking, or nothing that made much sense, at least. The state was throwing everything it had at getting her help. Who was she? Where was she from? Into early November, the Irish authorities poured over two thousand man-hours into 115 possible lines of inquiry. Door-to-door queries. Reviews of CCTV footage. Missing-persons lists. Visits to airports, seaports, rail stations. Guesthouse bookings. Did anyone fail to turn up, or fail to return? It was costing a pretty penny—€250,000—but every cent was worth it if it brought them closer to helping a child regain her lost home and, as well, her fragile sanity. It was dubbed Operation Shepherd. Eventually, the police came up with and systematically tested over fifteen possible identities for their charge. All had come up short.

On November 5, the Garda Síochána won the right to undertake an extraordinary step. It would distribute the girl's image publicly. (The picture itself had been taken on the sly; she'd refused to be photographed and had shied away from anyone in anything resembling an official uniform.) The girl was not only a minor but in a highly vulnerable state; the decision was an unprecedented one. But nothing else had worked.

As the child's picture was broadcast across television and newspapers, the Irish National Police told the world what they knew about the teen. "She has limited English. We're unable to decipher her nationality at the moment," a sergeant told cameras. And anything anyone knew would be most welcome. "Any information is vital to the investigation, and the welfare of the child," the police implored. "Any information passed to us will of course be treated in the strictest of confidence." The girl's temporary guardian, Orla Ryan, concurred: "I am extremely concerned about the welfare circumstances of this young person. What we know about her, at present, is limited. It is in the child's best interests to be identified, and I fully support An Garda Síochána in their continuing investigation."

The media frenzy began right on cue. It was such an odd case, and everyone had a theory. The teenager was quickly dubbed "GPO Girl," for the place she'd first turned up.

And then, ten hours later, there was a lead. And it came from an unlikely source: Interpol. Could anyone in Australia, they asked, help out?

Why Australia? Wasn't the girl supposed to be Eastern European? The media grew confused. But the garda perked up. Though they hadn't yet revealed its nature, they had their first real, plausible lead.

* * *

The put-up is all about choice of victim: learning what makes someone who she is, what she holds dear, what moves her, and what leaves her cold. After the mark is chosen, it is time to set the actual con in motion: the play, the moment when you first hook a victim and begin to gain her trust. And that is accomplished, first and foremost, through emotion. Once our emotions have been captured, once the con artist has cased us closely enough to identify what it is we want, feeling, at least in the moment, takes over from thinking. As any good confidence man will tell you, someone who is emotional is someone who is vulnerable. And so, before a single element of the actual con is laid out, before a single persuasive appeal is made, before a mark knows that someone will want something, anything at all, from him, the emotional channels are opened. And as in that first rush of romantic infatuation, we abandon our reason to follow our feeling.

Governing our reality are two systems, one emotional, one rational. And the two don't follow the same rules. Or, as William James, the father of modern psychology, put it in his essay "Brute and Human Intellect," in slightly more poetic fashion, "To say that all human thinking is essentially of two kinds—reasoning on the one hand, and narrative, descriptive, contemplative thinking on the other—is to say only what every reader's experience will corroborate."

Whereas the rational concerns itself with the "right" choice, the proper impression, the correct course of action, emotions, says psychologist Seymour Epstein, cause us to think in "categorical, personal, concretive, unreflective, and action oriented" fashion. They have us thinking reflexively instead of reflectively, reacting instead of considering. They have us just where someone who may wish to take advantage wants us.

Robert Zajonc devoted much of his five-decade-long career to the study of emotion—how it affects us, how it colors our thoughts and actions, how it compels us to move in one direction or another. When he first entered psychology, the behaviorists were holding sway. These were the great minds like B. F. Skinner and John B. Watson who looked toward the environment for cues as to why we act the way we do. Behavior, they argued, could largely be accounted for by almost purely cognitive reactions to discrete, identifiable environmental stimuli. Zajonc was at the forefront of a group that begged to differ. Yes, the environment was crucially important. But so, too, was the way it made us feel. We didn't react in a predictable, logical, purely cognitive way, in the manner of a rat who presses a lever once he realizes that it leads to food. Even the rat, in fact, is likely not acting like a stereotypical rat in most cases. Shock it, fail to provide it with food, and it can bite and lash out—an emotional response rather than a cognitive one. Lashing out at the hand that feeds you, after all, isn't the best way to go about getting fed.

On September 2, 1979, Zajonc addressed the annual meeting of the American Psychological Association, held that year in New York City. He was there to receive an award for Distinguished Scientific Contribution, and his remarks on the occasion contained the culmination of his thinking and study on the nature of emotion in our lives. A year later, they were published as a paper titled "Feeling and Thinking: Preferences Need No Inferences." What he meant by that is one of the fundamental principles of the successful play. For it is during the play, first of all, that con artists appeal to the most base emotions. Our desires, our fears, our loneliness, even our physical pain. They go right for the heart.

In his work, Zajonc told his listeners, he'd found that the conventional wisdom in the psychological community—that feelings come after thought—was wrong. Our emotional reactions are often our first. They are made naturally and instinctively, before we perform any sort of evidence-based evaluation. Early psychologists had recognized that fact. Wilhelm Wundt, one of the founders of the Gestalt movement in the nineteenth century, wrote, "When any physical process rises above the threshold of consciousness, it is the affective elements which as soon as they are strong enough, first become noticeable. They begin to force themselves energetically into the fixation point of consciousness before anything is perceived of the ideational elements." In other words, any experience was, first and fundamentally, an emotional one. The ideas and cognitive processing came after. "The clear apperception of ideas in acts of cognition and recognition is always preceded by feelings," Wundt concluded.

Zajonc emphatically agreed: that was precisely what he had been attempting to prove through his research. Emotion, he had found, could be activated quite easily—the mere exposure effect that makes many a put-up a success—and, as it turned out, it also inspired great confidence.

Far more confidence, in fact, than cognitive reasoning. The process wasn't logical. Mere exposure, his studies had illustrated, often didn't breed any sort of objective sense of familiarity or recognition. You didn't remember that something had happened, that you'd seen something, heard something, felt something. Instead, it bred a simple, subjective liking. You didn't know why, but you preferred this one thing. "Which do you prefer?" had become a question of "Which do I like more?" Our quick like-dislike judgments of something or someone, Zajonc found, happened all the time, in the absence of any conscious memory or cognitive effort.

In lower animals, an affective reaction is often the only one. If you're a rat, you have to respond fearfully to a snake long before you process what the snake is. Otherwise, you'll be a very dead rat. Fundamentally, "Friend or foe?" is a more important survival question than almost anything else. If you accept that those types of instant judgments are essential to our continued survival as a species, you, in a sense, accept that feeling precedes thinking.

"Human beings are social information processors before they are processors of facts, figures, and logical arguments," writes Michael Slater, a psychologist at Ohio State University who studies how media influences beliefs and behaviors. "Every parent soon learns how effectively even a toddler with limited language skills can process information about emotions and manipulate human relations." Even without the elaborate cognitive skills of logical argument and persuasion, an effective emotional manipulator, from babies to rogues, can achieve almost limitless ends.

It's not surprising, then, that the cues of emotion predate language. They are in the voice, the posture, the eyes, the tone, the touch. We can reliably interpret the emotion in a voice even when the words are completely obscured. In one study, when people were asked to interpret a video, the tone of voice was twenty-two times more effective at predicting the variance in judgments than the content of the words themselves. Nonverbal cues had over four times the effect of verbal ones on changes in ratings. Even when electronic filtering or masking was used to make the words of a recording unintelligible—in this case, it was the audio recording of a play—people could still reliably report on the emotion those words had expressed. In fact, how we say something ourselves, even if we're asked to do so in the absence of any genuine emotion, can often boil over into how we end up feeling. Merely smiling or frowning, for instance, changes the pattern of blood flow to our brains. The result is a physiological change in our emotion that can come quite close to mimicking the genuine artifact.

Not only do we form emotional impressions long before we create any rational understanding, but those impressions, in turn, are "irrevocable." "We can readily accept that we can be wrong," Zajonc told his audience that September afternoon. "But we are never wrong about what we like or dislike." Or, in a con artist's interpretation, most any cries of foul play will fall on deaf ears if you've already decided you like the person doing the conning. They "feel" more right. We trust our feelings more than anything anyone can tell us to the contrary. Our preferences need no inferences—and activating those preferences is what the play is all about.

Joan met Greg in early 2011. From the first, she was smitten. "He was wonderful, he was brilliant, and he was kind of creative, really, really funny, and really kind and generous," she recalls as we sip coffee at a small café in New York's West Village. She doesn't seem angry or resentful. Just sad. Perhaps a bit bewildered. "He would have charmed you like he charmed everyone else, including me." They started dating. Early in their relationship, her grandmother became ill. Greg was up to the challenge, comforting her into the early hours of the morning. She was having a problem at work, or difficulty with a proposal. He'd stay up all night to help out. She demonstrated an interest in something. He'd immediately jump in with both feet. "He was kind of improbable, like where you would mention almost anything, like deep-sea diving, he'd be like, 'Oh, here's how to do this.' And then it would turn out that he's either done it or manufactured a suit for someone else who did," she says. "He knew how to set bones—he'd been a paramedic. He built me a kitchen—he knew how to make stuff. He knew how to cure things and take care of sick people." It seemed too good to be true, but in a way that was, in fact, real. They traveled together, talked about the future. Soon, they were talking about moving in together.

Joan was in love. So in love that she didn't let any minor inconsistencies bother her. He was a graduate student in an exclusive science program. But she'd never met any classmates or labmates, nor seen any degrees or evidence of ongoing research. Her friends loved him—but she'd never met anyone who had known him for longer than a few months. He accompanied her to parties, met her family, came along on her work trips. But she was never asked to do the same for him. It was as if he'd taken on her life. But it didn't seem strange. "I just kept thinking, God, I'm so lucky."

One day, she offered to introduce him to a prominent researcher in his field—a Nobel laureate. She'd known Dr. Stanley for many years and thought Greg would benefit from the acquaintance, especially since he'd mentioned that he admired his work. Greg demurred. At first, Joan was beyond surprised: why would anyone turn down an introduction? But Greg made it very clear. He wanted his career to be based on his own skill and intelligence, not networking connections from his girlfriend. She understood and didn't give it any further thought.

They moved in together. It should have been perfect, but there was something a bit off about his arrival. The types of personal effects that accompany most any move were oddly missing. No personal history. No records. Nothing of any sort to confirm the reality of his life. Even his mail was off: there simply wasn't any. He explained that he got it delivered to another address, a PO box. But Joan never saw a single envelope. One afternoon, Joan found an ID from the school where he was studying. It seemed, frankly, fake, so she confronted him. He didn't deny it. He'd lost his real one, he told her, and a replacement cost fifty dollars. So he had put together a plausible version on his own. She accepted the story.

Still, just in case, Joan started to probe further. Early in their relationship, she'd done what any modern girl does: a Google search. Greg's name was too common, though, and hardly anything came up. Now she redoubled her efforts, looking for him in the school's databases. She came up empty. He had an explanation for that, too: he'd failed a few courses and didn't want to tell her, because it was embarrassing. Now he was working at another lab.

His personality started to change. It turns out, Greg had quite a temper. "He had the ability to go from perfectly fine to extremely angry and upset and volatile within ten seconds for reasons that didn't seem logic driven." He was jealous and possessive. He flew off the handle without any seeming provocation. He became emotionally manipulative, threatening to leave if she went on a European bike trip that she'd been looking forward to. In retrospect, something was clearly off. In the moment, she found a way to explain it all away—she loved him too much. "We did play by his rules all the time," she says, but, she reasoned, "His rules were good ones. He was smart, he did things that were good for me and good for the relationship, and generally kind of maximized everyone's happiness. And every once in a while he'd pull something like that—but I knew it was bullshit, childish, but no big deal. There was so much good in this relationship, so I just let it go."

The breaking point came one afternoon when Greg was away visiting family. Joan had been fighting the nagging doubts for too long. Before he left, Greg had blown up at her yet again—this time, because she asked if she could visit his lab. She was being pushy and unreasonable, he'd screamed, before storming out for the airport. It seemed such a trivial request; his reaction set her on edge. She called her old professor friend—the same scientist she'd wanted to introduce to Greg earlier. She voiced her doubts. Yes, she was probably being paranoid, Dr. Stanley told her, but he happened to know the head of Greg's lab. Did she want Dr. Stanley to give him a call? She did.

Greg had never worked in the lab. He had never been in the program. Everything he'd told her had been a complete lie. The rest crumbled soon after: the scientific career, the college degrees, every single detail about his life—none of it was true. He had crafted an entire persona, complete with false background and family history, for her benefit. She had been in a relationship with a master manipulator, an impostor who managed to make his way into her life in the most intimate way imaginable.

Looking back on it, she realizes that all the red flags were there. But in the moment—well, she was in love. Greg had a knack for getting everyone to like him at first sight, and her friends were on his side. Joan was living a fantasy, but one that is largely condoned by society: an ideal, sweep-you-off-your-feet love that conquers all. She liked him too much to notice anything awry—and nobody told her otherwise. Preferences need no inferences.

In 1996, George Loewenstein, a psychologist at Carnegie Mellon University, enumerated the effects that such "visceral influences" could have on our behavior. "Success, in many professions, is achieved through a skillful manipulation of visceral factors," he wrote. "Automobile salespersons, realtors, and other professionals who use 'high pressure' sales tactics, for example, are skillful manipulators of emotions. Con men are likewise expert at rapidly invoking greed, pity, and other emotions that can eclipse deliberation and produce an override of normal behavioral restraints. Cults and cult-like groups such as 'EST' use food deprivation, forced incontinence, and various forms of social pressure in their efforts to recruit new members," he continued. "In all of these cases there is a strong emphasis on the importance of immediate action—presumably because influence peddlers recognize that visceral factors tend to subside over time. The car or house one is considering will be 'snapped up' if not purchased immediately, and the one-time-only deal will expire. The once-in-a-lifetime opportunity for enrichment will be lost if one doesn't entrust one's bank card to the con artist, and there is an unexplained urgency to the insistence that one signs up for EST in the introductory meeting rather than at home after careful deliberation." It is the essence of the play: the heat of emotion, as divorced as possible from the cool rationality of time, reason, and deliberation.

At the end of his life, Zajonc concluded that feeling almost always came first. Emotion was, simply, a more powerful force than logic. If you measured it for brute strength, it would be the ton-lifting muscle man to cold cognition's svelte and toned but not quite record-breaking physique. It would be the reason a young victim of human trafficking would have countless resources devoted to her cause with nary a question. For who questions a child who has been emotionally wrecked?

* * *

Samantha Lyndell Azzopardi was born in 1988 to a middle-class couple, Bruce Azzopardi and Joan Marie Campbell. Sammy to her friends, she grew up with her mother and brother, Gregory, in Campbelltown, New South Wales, just outside of Sydney, Australia. From her days at Mount Annan High School to a job waiting tables at Pancakes on the Rocks, a welcoming Campbelltown restaurant with wood floors, airy booths, and cheerful orange walls where she worked for four or five months, she was seen as "a lovely girl," but one "who had issues."

In the late summer of 2013, Sammy decided to visit her mother's ex, Joe Brennan, in Clonmel, a small town some 175 kilometers southwest of Dublin, along the banks of the River Suir. It wasn't much, but it was the largest borough in County Tipperary. For three weeks, she'd lounged about, enjoying a summer break away from it all. Then, abruptly, she left. Joe had done nothing to provoke her, as far as he could tell, but then again Sammy had always been prone to erratic behavior. He wasn't worried. She pulled this kind of thing all the time.

It came as a surprise—not a shock so much as a reminder that he should have been more vigilant, should have guessed something like this was coming—when he saw the news that November afternoon. That photograph. That poor lost girl. The horrifying story of human trafficking. That was Sammy. Brennan picked up the phone to call the police.

With the help of Brennan's tip and Interpol, the story of the GPO girl fell apart. Azzopardi had, in her twenty-five years—not fifteen, not even close—acquired over forty aliases. Emily Peet. Lindsay Coughlin. Dakota Johnson. Georgia McAuliffe. Emily-Ellen Sheahan. Emily Sciberas. Her criminal history dated back to her teens.

Was she Samantha? the police confronted her. She wouldn't speak. As more evidence poured in, she started communicating with short notes—in English. But her steadfast refusal to let the ruse go entirely prompted a second psychological evaluation. The girl might not be who she said, but she did not seem mentally all there.

But she was. Cleared for travel, Sammy was returned to Australia, her native country, with a firm injunction to stay away from Ireland. Her deception, said Justice George Birmingham as the decision came down, had come "as a shock to everybody and as a surprise."

How had it happened? Azzopardi instinctively knew how to get emotions going to the point where nothing else mattered: when it came to the play, she was brilliant. Her pictures had told a story. And what a story. A devastating one, and one that no sane person would ever lie about. Who makes up a history of human sex trafficking? What kind of person do you need to be?

* * *

Storytelling is the oldest form of entertainment there is. From campfires and pictograms—the Lascaux cave paintings may date as far back as 1700 BCE—to tribal song and epic ballads passed down from generation to generation and city to city, it is one of the most fundamental ways humans have of making sense of the world and, as well, enjoying it. And no matter how storytelling formats may change, the stories they convey never get old.

Stories bring us together. We can talk about them and bond over them (both liking them and hating them). They are shared knowledge, shared legend, shared history, and, in a sense, shared future. Stories are meant to entertain and educate, to pass the time and record it. They are so natural that we don't notice how much they permeate our lives. And we pay little attention when yet another one catches our eye or ear. After all, stories are on our side. No matter the format, they are an ever-present form of entertainment.

That's precisely why they are such a powerful tool of deception, and so vital when it comes to the play. When we're immersed in a story, we let down our guard. We focus in a way we wouldn't if someone were just trying to catch us with a random phrase or picture or interaction. And in those moments of fully immersed attention, we may absorb things under the radar, so to speak, that would normally either pass us by or put us on high alert. We may even find ourselves, later, thinking that some idea or concept is coming from within our own brilliant, fertile minds, when really it was planted there by the story we just heard or read.

Feeling is first. And the best way to activate strong feeling is simple: you tell a compelling story. The play begins, first and foremost, with that oldest of human endeavors, a dashing good yarn. Story is the quickest path to emotion. "He has a secret," after all, makes for a far more intriguing proposition than "He has a bicycle."

In his book *Actual Minds, Possible Worlds*, Jerome Bruner, a central figure in the cognitive revolution in psychology during the second part of the twentieth century, proposes that we can frame experience in two ways: propositional and narrative. Propositional is the part of thought that hinges on logic and formality. Narrative, on the other hand, is more like a story. It's concrete. It's imagistic. It's personally convincing. It's emotional. And it's strong.

In fact, Bruner argues, it's responsible for far more than its logical, systematic counterpart. It's the basis of myth and history, ritual and social relations. "Popper proposed that falsifiability is the cornerstone of the scientific method," Bruner told the American Psychological Association at their annual meeting in Toronto in the summer of 1984. "But believability is the hallmark of the well-formed narrative." Even science constructs narratives all the time. There is no scientific method without the narrative thread that holds the whole enterprise together.

For stories make things more plausible, more convincing, more, well, fundable. A proposal with a compelling narrative arc, rightly or wrongly, stands out from one that takes the essence of the project in numbers. As the economist Robert Heilbroner once confided to Bruner, "When an economic theory fails to work easily, we begin telling stories about the Japanese imports or the slowness of the Zurich 'snake.'" When a fact is plausible, we still need to test it. When a story is plausible, we often assume it's true.

Gary Lyon never tired of telling strangers of his daughter's illness; she had leukemia, and was in the hospital for treatments. Fate really must have had it in for him: he had run out of gas on his way to see her. Could they spare some cash—just ten or twenty pounds—to get him there? He would repay them, of course. And their kindness would be well rewarded. Sometimes, it would be his son in the hospital awaiting surgery when he'd run out of gas. The outlines changed depending on the day, but the story was always a deeply compelling one. Hardly anyone ever questioned him. The detail was too vivid—and you had to be heartless to leave a man desperate to see his hospitalized child stranded without a car. In February 2015, Lyon was convicted of multiple counts of theft and fraud: the money for the gas was being used to finance a fifty-pound-a-day drug habit (crack cocaine). But that wasn't what most disgusted the judge. Instead, it was that his daughter really had been sick with leukemia in the past. She had since recovered, but Lyon had continued to use her as a prop.

No one questions a cancer victim, just like no one questions an escapee from human trafficking. I could refuse money to a man whose car broke down—I can question that fact, ask to see the stalled vehicle, offer a ride to a gas station—but I can't refuse to be generous to a man who is trying to make it to a sick child. Facts are up for debate. Stories are far trickier. Emotions on high, empathy engaged, we become primed for the play. The best confidence artist makes us feel not like we're being taken for a ride but like we are genuinely wonderful human beings.

Sonya Dal Cin is a psychologist at the University of Michigan, where for the last seven years she has been working to determine how stories— the stories we hear, the stories we absorb, the stories we tell ourselves— can affect how we think and how we behave, often without our conscious awareness. What the story says, what it means, how it's told, and who has told it: all these factors, Dal Cin has found, can conspire to have a meaningful and lasting effect on our own thoughts, actions, and opin- ions. They can even overcome significant resistance in our beliefs or attitudes: so strong is narrative that it has been shown to be one of the few successful ways of getting someone to change her mind about im- portant issues. In fact, Michael Slater says, gripping narratives may of- ten supersede any logic or more direct tactic: in some cases, it can be the only strategy for getting someone to agree with you or behave in a cer- tain way, where any direct appeals would be met with resistance. The con artist, after all, often gets what he wants without ever having to ask. You yourself kindly offer it up. The more absorbing the story, the stron- ger the effect. And that's what the play is all about—finding the best approach to get the strongest effect. As they say, you only have one chance for a first impression.

The Marc Antony gambit, taken from Shakespeare's *Antony and Cleopatra*, is a particular favorite of con men. "I come to bury Caesar, not to praise him," Marc Antony says in his first speech to the Roman peo- ple. His listeners hated Caesar; that note sets them on the same page and ensures their attention—and their loyalty, since they are primed to think they will agree with what follows, given their wholehearted endorse- ment of the opening line. Of course, Antony then goes on to praise Cae- sar. And he gets away with it. No one quite realizes what's going on.

"I'm not trying to sell you anything!" "You can take it or leave it!" "I'm not looking for charity!" So many prefaces to a story can catch you off guard Marc Antony–style. No self-respecting con artist goes straight for the kill. It's a relationship built on trust, and a story that evolves over time. In June 2014, a persistent journalist, Jen Banbury, published an exposé of a legitimate-seeming businessman who had lured a substantial number of investors from the Amish community into a land scheme in Florida that seemed more suspect by the minute. Tim Moffitt had spent five years building trust within the Lancaster County enclave, operating a produce business, hiring some Amish, getting to know others. Now he wanted to start the next big thing: a wonderful opportunity to get in on an RV park in Bushnell, Florida, that would be sure to yield a 9 percent return on investment. It was the perfect Marc Antony gambit: start by saying you aren't selling anything at all, building the trust of the audience, and only then change course for the true kill. Hundreds of thousands of dollars poured in—and not a one has come back.

In other words, even if you don't really trust the story of the con artist (or Roman conqueror) in theory, in practice a good story can change your actions. You might be skittish of or on guard against scam artists—especially if you're a police officer. But how can you turn down a lost child who has clearly gone through major trauma? She isn't asking for anything, is she? Merely the barest of human kindness.

Paul Zak, a neuroeconomist at Claremont Graduate University and director of its Center for Neuroeconomics Studies, looks at the power of the story in our daily interactions, be it with friends, strangers, or even objects (books, television, and the like). What he has found repeatedly is that nothing compels us to receptivity, emotional and behavioral, quite like the neat, relatable narrative flow.

In one study, Zak and his colleagues had people watch a father talk about his child. "Ben's dying," the father tells the camera as it pans to a carefree two-year-old boy in the background. He goes on to say that Ben has a brain tumor that, in a matter of months, will end his life. He has resolved, however, to stay strong for the sake of his family, as painful as the coming weeks will be. The camera fades to black.

Watching the film made about half the people donate money to a cancer charity. Why? And what was going on with those who didn't?

Zak didn't just ask people to watch "Ben's Story," as he calls it. Instead, he had them watch it together—all the while monitoring their neural activity, specifically the levels of certain hormones released from the brain into the blood. For the most part, the people who watched the video released oxytocin, a hormone that has been associated with empathy, bonding, and sensitivity to social cues. Those who released the hormone also reliably donated to charity, even though there was no pressure to do so.

Then Zak switched the story around. Now Ben and his dad were at the zoo. Ben was bald. His dad called him "Miracle Boy." But there was no real story arc, or immediate mention of cancer, or tension about any life outcomes. The people who watched Ben now drifted away from the story. Their arousal signs fell. They donated little or no money.

Those who'd seen the original story and donated more money were also happier and more empathetic after the fact. In a further study testing the effects of different ads on donations, Zak and his colleagues sprayed oxytocin into the nose of some subjects. Their donations increased substantially: they gave to 57 percent more causes, and when they gave, their donations were more than 50 percent greater.

Zak's work explains how someone like Neil Stokes was able to raise a substantial sum to pay off a heroin debt by pretending instead to be soliciting donations for the family of his nephew, Ashley Talbot. He'd gone door-to-door, recounting the (true) tale of how the teen had been run over by a school minibus, and asking each time for a small amount to either offset funeral costs or help with the family's Christmas celebration. He would take out his phone and show a picture of the smiling Ashley. People gave willingly—and would have given even more had Stokes's mother not accidentally reported him to police. She'd heard a man was raising money for the family, and to her it sounded dodgy. Stokes was promptly apprehended.

Keith Quesenberry, a marketing professor at Johns Hopkins University, found much the same thing in his two-year systematic study of the most scientific of topics: Super Bowl ads. He wasn't coming in cold. For seventeen years, before turning to teaching and research, Quesenberry had worked in the advertising industry as a copywriter and creative director—he'd been the one creating the content from the ground up. Now, however, he took a more systematic approach. He looked at each ad, analyzed the content, and tried to determine what, if anything, predicted how successful it would be. In total, he looked at over one hundred spots.

One thing, he found, was central in a commercial's success: whether or not it had a dramatic plotline. "People think it's all about sex or humor or animals," he told the *Johns Hopkins Magazine*. "But what we've found is that the underbelly of a great commercial is whether it tells a story or not." The more complete the story, the better. When the interviewer asked him to predict, based on his findings, which ad in the 2013 Super Bowl would take the prize, he offered up the Budweiser spot about the friendship of a puppy with a horse. "Budweiser loves to tell stories," he said. "Whole movies, really, crunched into thirty seconds. And people love them." He was right. The ad was the highest scorer on both *USA Today*'s Ad Meter and Hulu's Ad Zone.

Think about how similar "Ben's Story"—and even Budweiser's winning spot—is to so many successful cons. The grandparent scam: your grandchild has been in a horrible accident and you need to send him money right away. And no, he can't talk to you. He's in surgery. The sweetheart scam: the lovebirds of social media who want nothing more than to be with you, but have sudden unforeseeable difficulties and need money, and quickly. Not to mention the impostors who pull at the heartstrings—not just Azzopardi, but Demara playing the "little lost lamb" each time he joined a new monastery, pretending to be a new religious convert who just wanted some solace. That's one con Demara pulled not once, but over and over again. He would come to a religious order pretending to be a sophisticated secular figure who'd found himself emotionally adrift and was looking for meaning. He'd be taken in. And he would, in turn, do the taking in. Or recall the many Countesses Anastasia who litter history, playing on the global love of and fascination with the young Russian princess whose body was never discovered when the rest of the Romanov family perished. The good story that raises your emotion: it's what the successful play is all about.

In the TV show *It's Always Sunny in Philadelphia*, one episode centers on Charlie's mom succumbing to cancer. Except she doesn't really. She just manipulates everyone to think she has. It's a far more common ploy than we'd like to believe—and one that seems every bit as real as its sincere equivalent. A recent real-life Charlie's mom was a patient who had been doing her one better: Alan Knight, a forty-seven-year-old in South Wales, faked being a quadriplegic in a coma for almost three years. He not only got benefits for his paralysis but avoided going to court to pay his neighbor back for a £40,000 prior scam.

All of these cons work because they appeal to your emotions by drawing you into a story that can't help but move you. From that point on, you are governed by something other than reason. Emotion is the key to empathy. Arouse us emotionally and we will identify with you and your plight all the more. Keep us cold, and your goal is far away.

"Our results," Zak told psychologist Jeremy Dean, "show why puppies and babies are in toilet paper commercials. This research suggests that advertisers use images that cause our brains to release oxytocin to build trust in a product or brand, and hence increase sales." Increased oxytocin makes us more generous—with our money, our time, our trust, ourselves. The better the story, the more successful the play, and the more we give. And the better the con man, the better the story.

A successful story does two things well. It relies on the narrative itself rather than any overt arguments or logical appeals to make the case on its own, and it makes us identify with its characters. We're not expecting to be persuaded or asked to do something. We're expecting to experience something inherently pleasant, that is, an interesting tale. And even if we're not relating to the story as such, the mere process of absorbing it can create a bond between us and the teller—a bond the teller can then exploit.

It's always harder to argue with a story, be it sad or joyful. I can dismiss your hard logic, but not how you feel. Give me a list of reasons, and I can argue with it. Give me a good story, and I can no longer quite put my finger on what, if anything, should raise my alarm bells. After all, nothing alarming is ever said explicitly, only implied.

When psychologists Melanie Green and Timothy Brock decided to test the persuasive power of narrative, they found that the more a story transported us into its world, the more we were likely to believe it. All of it—even if some details didn't quite mesh. The personal narrative yardstick is much more permissive than any other form of appeal. And if it's especially emotionally jarring—How amazing/awful! I can't believe that happened to her!—that somehow seems to ratchet the perceived truthfulness up a notch. The more extreme the play, in other words, the more successful it could ultimately be.

Mamoru Samuragochi was a musical phenomenon. Not only was he one of Japan's most prolific and popular composers—his music graced concert halls and video game scores alike, and his composition "Hiroshima," inspired by his parents' survival of the bombing, had sold an astounding 180,000 copies—but he had a remarkable, and remarkably emotional, story that made his accomplishments all the more impressive. He was deaf. When he turned thirty-five, a degenerative disease caused the loss of his hearing—and despite it all, he'd gone on to compose beautiful pieces of art. The "modern Beethoven," the media dubbed him in the 1990s, when he first emerged as a composer to be reckoned with. The resemblance was more than passing. He, too, had long, flowing hair and a penchant for stylish suits. A pair of sunglasses was never far from his face. In 2001, Samuragochi told *Time* that his deafness was "a gift from God."

He remembered well the moment he'd lost his hearing: he had had a dream, he wrote in his autobiography, *Symphony No. 1*, in which he was pulled slowly underwater, losing the ability to hear as the water hit his ears. When he woke up, he went immediately to the keyboard. He couldn't hear a thing. He was distraught. Composing was his life. It was then that he decided to try a small experiment: could he hear Beethoven's Moonlight Sonata—the symbolism wasn't lost on him—in his head and re-create the notes from memory? He could. His resulting score perfectly matched the original.

It was only after he'd lost his hearing that Samuragochi's career took off in earnest. In 2001, the year of his deafness, he wrote his first symphony. Hiroshima, his birthplace, chose his composition to commemorate the bombing in a ceremony in 2008. In 2011, he became the only living composer to be included in a list of favorite classical CDs in *Recording Arts* magazine.

On February 5, 2014, Samuragochi made a stunning confession. Since 1996, he had employed a ghostwriter. Takashi Niigaki was a forty-three-year-old lecturer at a Tokyo music college, and for almost twenty years, he had written over twenty songs on Samuragochi's behalf. He'd been paid approximately $70,000 for his efforts. He'd wanted to stop, he told the press, but Samuragochi wouldn't have it: he threatened to commit suicide if the deception were to come to light. For Niigaki, the breaking point was an unprecedented piece of publicity: one of his ghostwritten compositions would be used in the Olympics by a Japanese skater. "I could not bear the thought of skater Takahashi being seen by the world as coconspirator in our crime."

But there was more, Niigaki said. The songs weren't simply ghostwritten. Samuragochi wasn't even deaf. The illness had been largely faked for the benefit of the story. Alone, the music might have been good, but not remarkable. Together, the story became irresistibly incredible—so much so that a number of red flags in the lead-up to the February confession were ignored. In one interview, a reporter noticed that Samuragochi was responding to some questions before the sign interpreter was done making his interpretations; another time, he'd reacted to a doorbell ringing. Samuragochi was a con artist of the highest caliber, the media concurred. But part of the blame, wrote *Asahi Shimbun*, one of Japan's most widely read newspapers, was with the press. "The media must also consider our own tendency to fall for tearjerking stories." The story had made the composer.

Samuragochi's tale seems crazy. But when we become swept up in powerful narrative, our reason often falls by the wayside. That's the whole point of the play: get us off balance by hitting us hard with a rousing yarn. In one study, readers were given a short story to read, to see how engrossed they would become in different types of narratives. One of the stories, "Murder at the Mall," based on a true account of a Connecticut murder from Sherwin Nuland's *How We Die*, followed a little girl, Katie, as she was brutally murdered in the middle of a mall under the shocked gaze of her family and shoppers. Her assailant, as it later turned out, was a psychiatric patient who had been let out on a day pass.

After reading the story, participants answered a series of questions about the events, the characters, policies about psychiatric care, and the like. Then came the key question: were there any false notes in the narrative, statements that either contradicted something or simply didn't make sense? Green and Brock, the study's authors, called this "Pinocchio circling": did any elements of the story signal falsehood akin to Pinocchio's nose? The more engrossed a reader was in the story, the fewer false notes she noticed. The sweep of the narrative trumped the facts of logic.

What's more, the most engaged readers were also more likely to agree with the beliefs the story implied (namely, the types of policies that should go into effect for mentally ill individuals). It didn't matter what they believed before the story; the tale itself created a new, strong set of views. A well-executed play doesn't just capture your emotion in the moment; it makes you more susceptible to the precise version of reality a confidence artist wants to create to further his scheme.

According to a theory of persuasion known as the elaboration likelihood model, we process a message differently depending on our motivation level. If we're highly motivated, we will focus on and be persuaded by the arguments in the message itself. If we're not motivated, we're more likely to be influenced by external cues, like a person's appearance, what she's wearing, how she's talking, and the like. Visceral cues, like the basic emotion brought forth by a powerful story, however, can override even motivation. Instead of processing a message logically, we act like the unmotivated person and take in all the wrong things. That's the power of the play. Even if we're trying hard not to get conned, if the play unrolls in the right way, it eventually won't matter; the narrative sweep will take over.

The con artist has several possible ways to hook us into the narrative stream. There's the Katie case—something so awful that we can't help but empathize. It's the choice the Sammy Azzopardis of the world make all the time. But there's also a less directly emotional possibility. The con artist can employ something called "wishful identification." We don't feel sorry for the character; we want to be him. He has attained precisely what we want. And don't we deserve that, too? Now it's our turn. The more similar the characters in the story are to us, whether because of appearance or social position, the more likely we are to relate to them. The more we like the confidence man, the more we relate to him.

Richard Harley was making $500 a month on social security benefits when he swindled investors out of $323,000 for an "oil development" in Texas. His approach was quite straightforward: he simply pretended to be wealthy to the tune of hundreds of millions in bank instruments. He was, he told potential clients, the owner of a fine art collection, and had a billion-dollar oil reserve in Texas. It was wishful identification at its finest: invest with me, and you, too, will have all this and more. Don't you want others to see your exquisite taste? According to his indictment, Harley had been at it since 1999—the con that keeps on giving.

Harley's 2014 indictment wasn't his first encounter with the law. Ends up, he was an expert in all elements of the play, in all its guises. Starting in January 1989, he and his wife, Jacqueline Kube, had the story to beat all stories: a cure for AIDS. For years, they said, they had been searching for something that could overcome the horrible disease. And recently, they'd had a breakthrough. Their medical company, Lazare Industries, had pioneered a treatment that seemed truly "groundbreaking." What was more, it was completely natural—not the toxic filth that drug cocktails introduced into the body. It was based on ozone and oxygen, two harmless substances that we are all naturally exposed to. A series of enemas, delivered by an "ozone generator" pump, at bursts of thirty to forty-five seconds a day, could cure the disease. The treatment, Harley and Kube went on, had been tested in extensive clinical trials at a major New Jersey hospital. It was one of the only patented approaches for treating the virus. Each treatment cost $250—or $7,500 for an entire month—a small price to pay for a deadly disease.

Over six years, the couple told their tale in colorful prose, through targeted mailings and ads; they looked at lists of subscribers to popular gay magazines, and tailored their message accordingly. By the time they were charged, in 1996, they had raised over $1.4 million in subscriptions. The treatment, of course, didn't exist. But the story had been so powerful—and the will to believe so strong—that dozens of people fell victim to false hope. Eventually, Harley served a five-year sentence—and it wasn't long after his release that he refashioned himself as the oil tycoon of the day.

Serial con artists like Harley are better at the play than almost anyone else. Yaling Yang came to a temp agency looking for subjects for a study. Yang was a psychologist researching pathological lying. She wanted to see whether, out of the habitually, or at least temporarily, unemployed, she could spot anyone who was also an inveterate fib teller. A possible reason for the unemployment of at least some of the temp workers, she reasoned, was a history of deceitful action at work.

As Yang walked through the temp agencies of Los Angeles, she asked over one hundred people questions about their past employment, families, and general history. She then checked their responses against court records and accounts from family and friends. Were some consistently inconsistent? Indeed, twelve people stood out. They lied often, and they lied without much incentive. Next, Yang asked everyone, liars and not, to come into the lab for a brain scan. What she found was that the habitual liars had 25 percent more white matter than anyone else.

Those extra connections also play a crucial role in in-the-moment storytelling, or the ability to spontaneously weave a compelling narrative. In fact, for the normal developing brain, white matter experiences a large jump in volume between the ages of six and ten. That is also the time frame in which most children learn to intentionally lie. What Yang had found, in other words, was that practiced deceivers were better at one of the basic skills of the con: the ability to tell a good story.

As Epstein puts it, "It is no accident that the Bible, probably the most influential Western book of all time, teaches through parables and stories and not through philosophical discourse." Narratives, he argues, are "intrinsically appealing" in a way nothing else quite is.

Sometimes a story is so powerful that it fools even the teller, creating unintentional con artists in the process. Consider the debacle, in the winter of 2014, that surrounded the publication of a major *Rolling Stone* feature on campus rape at the University of Virginia. It was perfect. A gripping story that couldn't help but tear at the heartstrings: a young, innocent freshman, Jackie, who doesn't drink, doesn't dress provocatively, doesn't do drugs, and is brutally gang-raped by seven men at one of her first frat parties as part of some perverse initiation. Sabrina Rubin Erdely had done a masterful job, finding a compelling spokesperson for an important social issue. She was interviewed by most every outlet and hailed as a brilliant journalist who had created just about the perfect vehicle to make people sit up and take notice.

Until those who took notice also noticed some alarming gaps in the story. Where were the attempts to reach the alleged perpetrators? Where were the corroborations from Jackie's friends? Over the coming weeks, journalists at the *Washington Post* meticulously re-reported the article, contacting Jackie's friends, the fraternity, even tracking down two of the alleged perpetrators. The more they learned, the more holes they found, from the relatively mundane (the fraternity in question didn't have a party the night Jackie had said she'd been to one, and initiations are in spring, not fall) to the more overtly disturbing (Jackie's friends hadn't callously stood by; they'd urged her to seek help when she appeared to be in emotional distress). That night, she had said nothing of gang rape, only that she'd had to perform oral sex on several men. And the man who she said she'd gone on a date with: it looked like she had made up texts, photographs, and an entire backstory where none existed. In March, a police investigation concluded that there was "no substantive basis" to say that Jackie had been attacked by any man, let alone a gang. Of course, the police chief couldn't say that nothing had happened, he hastened to add—there was no way to prove that definitively—but from the perspective of the law, the evidence didn't pass muster. The investigation was suspended.

Let's be clear: the *Rolling Stone* fiasco was not in any way Jackie's fault. Memories of traumatic events are notoriously unreliable; details blur and fade; accounts fail to coincide. But it did show what looked like a blatant disregard for a basic journalistic practice: believe, but question. Don't let your story get away from you. Never turn off your skepticism, no matter how gripping the tale may be. Instead, it was left to the *Post* to question, where *Rolling Stone* had just believed.

And let's be clear about something else: Erdely wasn't consciously setting out to con anyone, that we know. She wasn't, as far as we can tell, a fabricator, a plagiarist, or a malicious bender of the truth. And yet, think about the ones we do now see as fitting that bill—Stephen Glass (the *New Republic* journalist who fabricated multiple stories over three years at the magazine) or Janet Cooke (the *Washington Post* journalist who won a Pulitzer for what turned out to be an entirely fictional story; the prize was subsequently revoked) or Jayson Blair (the *New York Times* writer who fabricated and plagiarized a number of stories) or Jonah Lehrer (the short-lived *New Yorker* staff writer who plagiarized and fabricated parts of multiple stories and had two of three books pulled by publishers as a result) or even Ruth Shalit (another plagiarizing writer at the *New Republic* who, like Erdely, had multiple lapses in fact-checking). Perhaps they started out innocently enough, too, getting swept up by the beauty of their narratives. Their stories worked for the very same underlying reason as hers. Perhaps Erdely, like others before her, was just carried away by the arc she'd created. She ended up being conned by the lure of the tale itself, letting down normal journalistic checks in the process; it was the perfect play almost in spite of itself. And *Rolling Stone* reacted apace. It, too, was enamored of the story. Erdely had sold it so well. They didn't even need a con artist. They conned themselves.

We believe because we want to. Con artists are just there to spin the yarn. And even when we think they've told their last, they have the uncanny ability to resurface.

* * *

In 2010, Dakota Johnson appeared in Brisbane. She was fourteen and had gotten away from a sexually abusive relative, she told the police, and she desperately needed help. She had been traveling to Australia with her European uncle and, along the way, on Lord Howe Island, they'd parted ways—whether because he'd abandoned her or she'd escaped was unclear. Whatever had happened had been traumatic. The Brisbane support system gave her shelter and food. She wanted, she told her support group, nothing more than to go back to school and finish her education, just like any normal teen.

Johnson had very little with her—she'd left in a hurry and taken what she could. Just a few possessions. Some clothes. A laptop. There was a letter of introduction from Le Rosey, a ritzy private school in Switzerland, on a sprawling campus by Lake Geneva. There was a receipt from a Lord Howe Island bank. And there was the diary, pink. In its pages, a vivid, violent account of sexual abuse by a close relative.

It wasn't much to go on. But the authorities wanted to give her a good chance at a normal life—and Le Rosey, well, that was some reference. A local high school accepted her for the following term.

The police, however, didn't feel that enough was being done. Schooling was well and good—admirable, in fact. But a child who had been so abused needed, they felt, more assistance. Concerned for her welfare, they searched her computer while she was out.

There was the smiling girl with her family, standing atop the Sydney Harbour Bridge. The photo had a date, and that date was a clue. The local police contacted the tour company in charge of bridge tours and asked to see records of the participants. It wasn't long before they found a match: the twenty-two-year-old Samantha Azzopardi. She wasn't fourteen at all. And Dakota Johnson? An alias based on the actress who stars in the movie of *Fifty Shades of Grey.* The Le Rosey letter: a fabrication crafted on her laptop. The bank receipt: another fudged fake. When the police dug deeper, they discovered that Dakota was far from her first foray into conning. At the time she appeared on the Brisbane streets, she was already wanted for fraud in Queensland. It appeared our old friend Samantha Azzopardi had attempted to use a fake Medicare card to procure services in Rockhampton, a small coastal town in the area.

On September 14, the Brisbane Magistrates Court charged Azzopardi with two counts of false representation, one count of intention to forge documents, and one of contravening directions. She was convicted. The sentence, however, would be lenient; Azzopardi was to pay a $500 fine. The next month, Sammy was again convicted of four counts of false representation: yet another identity, yet another attempt at fraud through sympathy. Again, the charge was $500. And then, for a few months, she dropped off the legal radar.

But only a few. In 2011, Sammy transformed into Emily Azzopardi, a gymnast, the role borrowed from a past identity as Emily Sciberas. She was a top athlete, she told a new friend in Perth, where she was now living. When she stayed over at her friend's house—an increasingly common occurrence—she repeated the story to her parents. She'd lived in Russia, she said, to train. And she had been the top under-sixteen gymnast in the country.

One month later, a disturbing notice appeared on Emily's Facebook page. Her entire family had died tragically in France. Alongside the announcement, she posted a newspaper article: a murder-suicide. A man had killed his wife and fifteen-year-old daughter before shooting himself. There was, the article said, a twin who had survived. Emily was that twin. Her friend's family, moved by her plight, asked to adopt her. She would love that, she replied; she was just then in the United States, she told the family, with an adoptions specialist. He would smooth everything over.

Azzopardi proceeded to steal the identity of a Floridian judge, indeed an adoptions expert, to e-mail the family and receive the requisite adoption paperwork. To finalize everything, she met them in Sydney, claiming she had been raped in Perth and couldn't go back.

But when the family enrolled her in school, everything fell apart. Her birth certificate as Emily was, predictably, a fake.

In 2012, Azzopardi was again sentenced, this time to six months in prison for attempting to illegally collect social welfare benefits. The sentence, however, was suspended for a year—as all her charges had been, every time. She was a lovely girl. In June of that same year, she stood in Perth Magistrates Court to plead guilty to three counts of opening up accounts under a false name, one of inducing someone else to commit fraud, and one of intent to defraud by deceit. On October 2, she was sentenced to six months in prison, again suspended for twelve months.

Some might call Sammy a pathological liar: someone who is mentally incapable of telling the truth, in the throes of an illness rather than a malicious malingerer. And, in one sense, it's true. There's no denying her proclivity for telling a truth that's as far from reality as they come. Except, for con artists like Sammy, it's not a pathology; Sammy, you may recall, received a clear mental bill of health. It's a deliberate choice: it's the essence of the play. Pathological liars lie for no reason at all. For them, lying is a form of obsessive-compulsive disorder, or may point to a deeper psychopathy. (Indeed, pathological lying is listed as a symptom on the Psychopathy Checklist.) Con artists lie for a very specific reason: personal gain, whether it be financial or other. They lie to set the play in motion, so that they can gain your confidence and then lead you down a reality of their making. And their lies are believable whereas a pathological liar's are often too big and elaborate to be taken seriously.

Azzopardi lied in a very deliberate fashion: she crossed a social taboo. An area so rife with emotion that to lie about it would be to betray our trust in humanity. Unfortunately, because of the power of emotion, such taboo ruses are far from unique in the confidence game; many a play revolves around the topics that no one would dare question. In fact, the same exact ruse was used by Somaly Mam, the prominent head of a global charity who, as it turned out, had fabricated her own history of sexual abuse. What's more, she coached the girls her organization was supposed to be helping on the most harrowing—and often untrue—narratives to relay to potential donors. Each girl would "audition" as a face of the charity. As *Newsweek* reported in an exposé, one girl "confessed that her story was fabricated and carefully rehearsed for the cameras under Mam's instruction, and only after she was chosen from a group of girls who had been put through an audition." She was told it was the only way to help other women who really were sex trafficking victims.

It's a quintessential Machiavellian dilemma. Do the ends justify the means? Even after it was revealed that Somaly Mam's foundation was based on a lie (her own story) and had perpetuated further lies to increase funding (coaching girls on the ideal victim story designed to tug at the maximum number of heartstrings as hard as possible), many supporters didn't abandon her. After all, she had raised money for and awareness of an important cause, and many of the funds had gone to real victims and women in need. Was she a con artist or someone who'd just gone too far?

It's no coincidence that cons tend to thrive in the wake of disaster: natural disaster, illness, economic disaster, national disaster, personal disaster. The play is almost built into disaster zones from the start. Emotions are already high. There's already a compelling story line. We are, in a sense, primed for the grifter to plunge into his game; he doesn't even have to try all that much to up the emotional ante or think of a dashing good yarn. It's all there for the taking. In the wake of the Ebola crisis in the fall of 2014, an investigation from a team of reporters at *BuzzFeed* found that the man who'd been put in charge of the cleanup effort in New York, Sal Pane, was, in fact, a confidence artist and convicted felon, with no proper qualifications in biohazard work. The play, for him, was a matter of child's play: we are already desperate for someone to step in—and who in his mind would lie about something like that? In the wake of the Iraq War, two enterprising British businessmen, Jim McCormick and Gary Bolton, decided to capitalize on the fear of explosives by marketing a fail-safe bomb detector. They faked a few tests, and soon their first-class machinery—little more than glorified golf ball finders at £1.82 a pop to make—was being sold for as much as £15,000 apiece. Again, a child's version of the play: a ready-made story, desperate, emotionally vulnerable clients—and once more, who would ever play with people's lives so callously? Customers flocked, not only from postwar Iraq but from Thailand, Mexico, China, Niger, Saudi Arabia, Singapore, Pakistan, India, the Philippines, Egypt, and Tunisia. Each year, the duo would make millions. And people, confident an area had been swept for bombs, would lose lives. "The culpability and harm of what you were doing is at the highest level," Justice Hone told Bolton at his sentencing, "because when used for the detection of explosives, in my judgment the use of the GT200 . . . did materially increase the risk of personal injury and death."

Their sentencing didn't stop others from trying to find the next best use for the fraudulent devices. In October 2014, Samuel and Joan Tree were arrested for, among other things, claiming that a similar detector could find Madeleine McCann, a young girl who had been missing. If you just placed a photo of the missing child into the machine, it would home in on her location. The emotion and story were built in; all that was needed was the right con artist to set the play in motion.

* * *

Why is the emotional approach so successful when it comes to the play? Simply put, because emotions cause us to act in a way that nothing else quite does—and action is just what the confidence artist wants. That is the con's entire endpoint. When our emotions are awakened, we tend to rely on them more than on anything else. In the 1970s and 1980s, psychologists Norbert Schwarz and Gerald Clore ran a series of studies that looked at whether people's emotions colored how they processed information and made subsequent decisions. What they found, time and time again, was that when we're asked to make a judgment, we usually ask ourselves, "How do I feel about it?" When the answer is negative, we see it as evidence of something being wrong. This room just gives me a bad feeling, you'll tell yourself. When it's positive, however, we think we're satisfied. This phone has amazing features, we'll say—even if we haven't actually evaluated any of them. When we're angry, we think future events that are bad are the result of human error; when we're sad, that they're situationally determined. They called the phenomenon "mood as information." How I happen to be feeling is giving me concrete evidence of how I should act—even if, in fact, my decision is totally distinct. The way I process the information will be colored by my emotion all the same.

Another name for it is the affect heuristic: we make decisions based on whether we feel that something is "good" or "bad," without much conscious analysis. Each person we meet, each thing we hear, each event or sensation we experience is immediately marked by an emotional tinge, a tinge acquired over years of similar experiences and memories. When we hear an emotional story or experience an emotional event, our mind tends to go back immediately to anything like it that we've felt in the past. Paul Slovic, a psychologist at the University of Oregon, calls this the affect pool. We then act not just based on the current moment but based on the associations with all the prior moments like it, be they good or bad.

In one sense, it matters little what we're actually feeling: any emotional arousal will cloud our judgment to some extent. It makes us unthinking and it makes us malleable. It's perfectly understandable why it's the favored approach of many a police interrogator and lawyer, not just con artists. Arousal can compel us to act against our long-term interest—because, in the immediate term, we suddenly can't quite tell the difference. The most primitive parts of our brain take over the rational. In one study, arousal alone was enough to get someone to agree with a request for help; it little mattered what the content of the request might happen to be.

What visceral states do is create an intense attentional focus. We tune out everything else and tune in to the in-the-moment emotional cues. It's similar to the feeling of overwhelming hunger or thirst—or the need to go to the bathroom—when you suddenly find yourself unable to think about anything else. In those moments, you're less likely to deliberate, more likely to just say yes to something without fully internalizing it, and generally more prone to lapses that are outside the focus of your immediate attention. (In fact, one study showed that having to pee made people more impulsive: they were so focused on exercising control in one area that their ability to do so elsewhere faded.)

Cons, long and short both, thrive on in-the-moment arousal: we have no time to repent. The best play makes use of that tendency. Con artists heat us up. That is their living. As one put it, "It is imperative that you work as quickly as possible. Never give a hot mooch time to cool off. You want to close him while he is still slobbering with greed."

Emotion in the moment matters. But we find it almost impossible to anticipate future emotion—like the regret that might come from being too hasty now. "Today's pain, hunger, anger, etc. are palpable, but the same sensations anticipated in the future receive little weight," George Loewenstein writes.

In 2001, Jeff Langenderfer, a behavioral economist at Meredith College, and Terence Shimp, professor emeritus at the University of South Carolina, decided to test directly what factors could make someone more susceptible to the influence of a con artist. That year alone, scams had cost the United States over $100 billion, some $40 billion of that from phone scams. The numbers were rising quickly, but, Langenderfer felt, little was being done to get at the root causes: an understanding of who was most likely to fall victim, and how and why they would do so.

Some people don't see the signs of fraud, true, but, he felt, this couldn't be the fundamental reason. If it were, there wouldn't be nearly as much diversity in the victim pool. It was, he concluded, a question of visceral influence: greed, hunger, lust, and the like. "They are so eager to get their hands on the proffered scam payoff that they fail to pay even rudimentary attention to the details of the proposed transaction and ignore scam cues that may be obvious to others not so overwhelmed by desire," he wrote. The emotional outcome becomes the center of focus, and logic falls away. And that is precisely what the play is all about.

But although most any emotion can make us act, emotion isn't a homogeneous mass. Specific emotions can make us act in specific ways and process things in specific patterns—patterns that the savvy artist can readily exploit. We don't make decisions the same way when we're upset or anxious, for instance, as we do when we're happy. The play must be directed at the precise sort of con the grifter is planning to perpetrate. It's not always enough to make us emotional; you have to think ahead and tailor the approach with the eventual touch (the actual moment of fleecing the mark) in mind.

Sometimes the process in play is mood congruity: we process information in a way that corresponds best to our emotional state. When we're upset, for example, we tend to focus on the negative inputs that come our way; the result is a different sort of action than we'd undertake in, say, a happy moment. In one study, people who were sad wanted to partner with someone who had better interpersonal skills, like a "friendly" person, rather than someone good at the task they had before them—for instance, someone who "usually does well on his exams."

Sadness likewise makes us more prone to risk taking and impulsivity—the perfect play for a certain type of con. If you want someone to take a risky financial gamble? Say, invest in your perfect scheme or chance it on a game of three-card monte? Sadness is your best friend. Target the person in the midst of a life crisis, not the one who happily has everything.

Indeed, the play often works best when we're at emotional low points already. Con artists love funerals and obituaries, divorces and scandals, company layoffs and general loneliness. Sometimes they actually read about personal news—local papers are treasure mines for what is happening to whom, and Facebook's ubiquity makes even those look obsolete. A friend of mine—call her Alexis—found herself the victim of an attempted scam after a series of Facebook posts made it clear that she was going through a breakup. (She had inadvertently befriended the con artist, an all too common occurrence.) Other times, they simply read people. A dejected walk is easy to spot if you're looking for it.

But the play need not rely on sadness. Certain types of cons thrive on positive moods, and the expert con man knows precisely which is which and runs the play accordingly. When we're happy, we don't analyze data nearly as systematically as we otherwise would, and thus, become far more open to persuasion. In one study, happy people were equally persuaded by a strong and a weak argument, whereas sad ones were only swayed by the strong. A separate study found that happy individuals were more reliant on heuristics, things like the status of the person doing the persuasion or perceived expertise, whereas sad ones relied more on content—what the person was actually saying.

Some emotion also makes us more irrational than others. It's good to make someone happy or sad if you're trying to con them, but what if you can also make them fearful—like the natural play during the Ebola crisis or a war? If the emotion is strong enough, we don't see anything else. We'll drive hundreds of miles to avoid flying, even though our risk of dying on that trip is much higher than in a plane crash. We'll avoid vaccinating our child for fear of autism when the risk of measles is actually quite real, and that of a developmental disorder caused by a vaccine, nonexistent. In the fall of 1991, a plane made an emergency landing midflight. The reason: there was a mouse on board. People ran screaming into the aisles, thereby putting the aircraft in danger. Irrational fears trump rational reasoning.

When executing the play, fear is one of the con artist's great friends. In one study, a team of psychologists decided to test the effects of different types of fear on people's willingness to comply with a request. First they located cars that had been parked illegally on the streets of Opole, Poland. Then they employed some deft perceptual trickery: on the windshields of some cars, they placed fake parking tickets; on the windshields of others, they placed advertisements that were designed to look ticket-like. As a control condition, they placed advertisements on car doors, a place where no self-respecting cop would ever put a ticket. After the drivers returned and had a chance to inspect the researchers' handiwork, each driver was approached for a favor. The measure of interest: would she comply?

The premise of the setup was relatively straightforward. Drivers who received fake tickets would feel nothing but anxiety. Until they were told otherwise, they thought they'd been caught red-handed (redwheeled?). Drivers who received the ads that looked like tickets would feel anxious first, but then immensely relieved that they had, in fact, escaped. And those who'd gotten the ads on the door wouldn't feel much of anything, other than perhaps annoyance at the intrusion. What the researchers wanted to know was whether these different emotional setups would result in different susceptibility to requests. And, indeed, they did. The single most persuadable type of driver: the one who had just experienced a wave of relief following anxiety. The second: the one who'd experienced only anxiety. The least: the one who'd felt nothing. The authors concluded that the emotional drain of anxiety followed by the wave of emotional relief created a state of relative mindlessness. It's the classic good cop–bad cop, or, rather, bad cop–good cop approach.

In a follow-up, the researchers discovered something else: people were more likely to give money to a stranger asking for a donation after they'd heard a police whistle when they'd been jaywalking. As they reached the other side of the street, a student would approach them and ask for money. She'd either give no justification ("Excuse me, would you please give us some money?"), a bogus justification ("Excuse me, we are collecting money. Would you please give us some, because we have to collect as much money as possible?"), or a real justification ("Excuse me, we are from the Students for the Handicapped organization. Would you please join our charity action, because we have to collect as much money as possible to cover the cost of a holiday camp for mentally handicapped children?"). If no police whistle had blown at all, people were likely to give money only in the last condition—a real donation for a real cause. If the fake police whistle sounded, followed by the relief of knowing no actual fine was coming, however, their mindlessness increased apace. Now they'd reach for their wallets in any situation, whether justified or not. Imagine the implications for the play: create a sense of fear, and then the feeling of relief (not to worry! there's a solution!), and your mark is all but guaranteed to fall.

From the first snake oil sale, cons that play on our anxieties about our health have been among the leading scams of the world. They have everything needed for the fear-based play built into them: a health concern, real or not, followed by the relief of knowing there's a remedy. There's the late-nineteenth-century salesman of actual snake oil, Clark Stanley, prone to dramatic demonstrations with rattlers, who promised an end to everything from rheumatism to headaches to paralysis. (His concoction was 99 percent mineral oil.) There's John Brinkley, who, in the nineteen-teens, preyed on the male fear of impotence to peddle the perfect solution: a transplant of goat testicles. There's William Bailey, who, at the turn of the twentieth century, convinced hapless marks that radium would reinvigorate the lowest of energy levels (it glowed, after all; it would make you glow, too!) and cure coughs, flus, and other woes. And today, of course, there are the detox diets, pills, and supplements that promise everything from curing cancer to letting you lose weight with no effort, the countless unregulated companies and spokespeople who hold the perfect cure for whatever ails you. Fearmongering knows no expiration date. It is a venerable course for the play to take—one of many, but one that is endlessly powerful.

* * *

On September 16, 2014, Aurora Hepburn walked into a Calgary clinic. She was fourteen, she said, and had been abducted, sexually assaulted, and tortured. "There was considerable impact to a lot of the professionals that were working on this investigation," Kelly Campbell, a sergeant with Calgary Police Service's Child Abuse Unit, told media. "Our concern was that there were actual victims out there, more victims."

If this scenario sounds oddly familiar, it's because it is: even after her Irish escapade and deportation, Samantha Azzopardi was back. And she was just as talented at weaving her deceptions as she'd ever been. Canadian authorities spent $157,000 on identifying her before her identity became clear—yet another foreign government expending resources to track perpetrators that had never existed.

How had Sammy managed it, after the deportation, the travel bans, the familial monitoring? Like so many impostors before her, she seemed to have a rubber knack for resuming her chosen lifestyle moments after each unmasking. Azzopardi hadn't been back in Australia for six months after her Irish caper when she again managed to secure a passport. She made her way back to Ireland—she'd been booted too quickly. She wasn't done. She'd spent months preparing her return, corresponding with a Midlands family with two children, this time to work as a potential au pair.

Alan and Eilis Fitzgerald needed someone to help care for their small sons, four-year-old Jack and two-year-old Harry. And so, they began to look at au pair sites for a possible match. One young woman stood out immediately. Her name was Indie O'Shea. She was eighteen, had Irish roots herself, and was eager to come to Dromod. They took up a correspondence. "We were in contact with her for ages online," Eilis later said. "And she seemed a perfect fit and really lovely. We were friends before she even arrived."

She got on famously with Harry and Jack. Eilis and Alan quickly came to see her as part of the family. "She was great with the boys and around the house," Eilis said. But the family didn't know much about her. She would drop hints here and there—private jets, powerful relations, false names out of necessity—but nothing definitive. "It was like Hansel and Gretel," Alan recalled. "She was leaving crumbs for us to find so we could discover who she was." Soon the crumbs started adding up. Indie O'Shea wasn't really Indie O'Shea. Instead, she was the illegitimate daughter of Princess Madeleine of Sweden. She had been raised by one of Madeleine's cousins and her biological father.

The next day, O'Shea tried to open a bank account. It was denied: her papers didn't add up. The family found her sobbing on the floor. Her mother, she said, had died in Miami.

A few days later, her passport, she said, had run out. But no fear. She'd previously been an au pair for Jens Christiansen, a Danish politician. He would sort it out. Eventually, she returned with a British passport. It had a fake name and a different photograph. It's okay, she assured them. She was allowed to do this. "The 'family' had organized it," Eilis said.

Six weeks later, O'Shea left, unexpectedly. Searching through her belongings, the Fitzgeralds found multiple papers with a name they had never seen: Samantha Azzopardi. They were confused to no end. "We got on brilliant and she was really such a nice person," Eilis recalls. How could she not be who she said?

It was then that Sammy made her way to Canada, where she turned up as Aurora Hepburn.

As 2014 drew to a close, she was charged with public mischief, pled guilty, and was sentenced to the two months she'd already served in custody. She was deemed such a high flight risk that she was locked up until her extradition flight—and guarded on the flight itself. "Ms. Azzopardi has a long history of impersonating others, lying, and committing fraud," said Rhonda Macklin during Azzopardi's immigration hearing. No resource would be spared to make sure she was returned to Australia. And, preferably, kept there.

CHAPTER 4
THE ROPE

Ultimately, anyone can be conned, if you have the balls to do it.

—SIMON LOVELL

Mervyn Barrett had been working for Nacro, a British charity dedicated to crime reduction, going on thirty years. In 1999, he was made an Officer of the Most Excellent Order of the British Empire (OBE) and by 2012 he had decided that perhaps it was time for bigger things: his time at the charity, as head of resettlement, was slated to end in June, and he needed to think ahead. What about running for police commissioner of his old home county, Lincolnshire, as an independent candidate? one of his young employees suggested. Matthew de Unger Brown told him that his mother was a member of the German aristocracy. Her views were in line with Barrett's, and she would be happy to finance the campaign. All Barrett had to do was say yes. And why not? He'd been thinking about crime reduction for decades. Perhaps now it was time to act.

Matthew had joined Nacro as a volunteer in the early days of 2012; he had a legal background, he said, and independent wealth. It was an important cause and he would be more than happy to dedicate his energy toward its advancement. The young man quickly charmed his officemates, impressing them, Barrett later said, "with his skills and intelligence." He was "undoubtedly a brilliant and charismatic character." Initially shy about his past, Matthew had, over time, opened up to the older man, perhaps seeing in him a sort of mentor and role model. His father, he told him, was Lord Malcolm Brown. He had served as a senior envoy to Hong Kong. His mother, the Baroness Renate Margaret de Unger, was a Prussian royal. But not all was rosy for little Matthew. He had, he confessed, a dark secret in his past. Maybe it was because his parents had left him so much to his own devices. Maybe it was all the travel. But whatever the root cause, he had, a few years earlier, been in prison. The charge: corporate tax evasion.

Matthew's revelation only led to a deepening of his and Barrett's growing trust. And to Barrett, he seemed like a perfect fit for the organization. After all, it was part of the organization's mission to rehabilitate criminals. And Matthew had told him, in confidence, of course, that in prison "he'd developed a social conscience and wanted to help others while working out what to do with his life." "It seemed right to give him a chance," Barrett said.

And so, when his young protégé suggested an election campaign, he listened. What convinced him above all, though, wasn't the young man's enthusiasm—he was impressionable, and Barrett was his boss—but a letter Matthew received from his mother, the Prussian royal. In the letter, he later told the *Sunday Times*, she affirmed her faith in his abilities, and even asked him to join the board of the family charity, established to honor Matthew's twin brother, Sebastian, who had, alas, died unseasonably young in a drunk-driving accident. It was called, simply, the Sebastian Foundation. Barrett was touched, not only by the offer but by the show of trust from a woman so cultured and experienced. "Up until that point I hadn't been convinced by Matthew's arguments," Barrett recalled. "But when I saw the faith she had in me it was the turning point."

Matthew was thrilled at Barrett's change in heart. And his entreaties went a step further. He not only thought a bid for commissioner was a brilliant idea, but he persuaded Barrett that he himself would be the perfect man to run the whole thing for him. He'd had substantial election experience, he said, both as a member of the Young Conservatives movement and during his time on American campaign trails. That, coupled with his "towering personality" and "considerable talent for everything he undertook," persuaded Barrett that he'd found just the man for the job. Yes, he told Matthew. He would run, and Matthew would be his right-hand man.

The campaign got under way. Matthew was living up to his promise. Polls, pamphlets, even a television spot: he was pulling no punches in his bid to get Barrett into the commissioner's seat. His intelligent, canny handling of the run convinced the would-be commissioner to give him access to his private bank account. Matthew would need a few last-minute funds, understandably, in those instances his mother wasn't immediately available. They agreed to a spending limit: £10,000 of Barrett's own money, and a total campaign budget of £25,000, the balance supplied by the wealthy aristocratic family who was placing such trust in him.

Whatever Matthew was doing, it seemed to be bearing fruit. Proudly, he showed Barrett the numbers from the independent poll he'd commissioned with his mother's money. Barrett's popularity was on the rise. Matthew set the older man up with a respectable social media presence: a spiffy new Web site, a Twitter account that soon began accruing followers at a steady pace.

On the evening of Wednesday, October 24, 2012, Mervyn Barrett issued a surprising official statement. The whole campaign, he told the press, had been an elaborate ruse on the part of his ill-intentioned campaign manager. He was resigning "after discovering that I have been the victim of a bizarre and hugely embarrassing deception by the person who was acting—and I use the word 'acting' quite deliberately—as my principal adviser and campaign manager."

Barrett had learned the truth. The Fund for the New American Century, the think tank where de Unger Brown had said he had connections, didn't actually exist, according to Andrew Gilligan's subsequent exposé for the *Telegraph*. Nor did MatthewPAC, its associated political action committee—a committee whose name was linked to Barrett's campaign Web site. That healthy Twitter following? Sixteen thousand fake followers, an investigation by the *Times* of London found. The tracking polls de Unger Brown had presented for Barrett's inspection, the pamphlets he'd handed out to secure more votes: all "purely figments of his imagination." They had never existed.

Barrett was now poorer to the tune of tens of thousands of pounds—according to him (the case is still pending), Brown drained his account of £84,000 and left £16,000 in bills—his reputation in tatters. He had only £4,000 of his life savings left. When he opened his bank statement to see what could have possibly happened, he saw campaign charges, yes, but also "rent," donations to charities, direct debits to the Treasury, drinks at a bar in the West End. None of them had been authorized by Barrett. "To my knowledge," he later said, "there has been no funding for my campaign, other than from my own bank account, to which Matthew had access."

"I realize I was completely unsuitable for this position," Barrett admitted to the *Sunday Times* after his resignation from the race. "In fact, after what I've let Matthew get away with, I'm not sure I'm suitable for any position of responsibility.

"He has deceived me on a shocking scale," Barrett went on.

How had it happened? Barrett wasn't quite sure. What he did know was that he was "swept away by it all"—the references, the charisma, the talent. It was the full package. Whenever Barrett asked for clarification on something that seemed off, he would immediately receive a plausible explanation. Over five months, the two men had built a bond of friendship and trust, Barrett felt. "I feel totally betrayed and very hurt that he used me to perpetuate some kind of Walter Mitty fantasy," he concluded. "I also feel very foolish that I fell for his fabrications, when I have a track record of sound professional judgment, but I have to accept the reality."

* * *

In 2003, Eric Knowles, a social psychologist at the University of Arkansas who has been researching persuasion since the 1970s, and Jay Linn, an organizational and social psychologist at Widener University, posited that all persuasive strategies could be categorized into two types. The first, alpha, was far more frequent: increasing the appeal of something. The second, omega, decreased resistance surrounding something. In the one, you do what you can to make your proposition, whatever it may be, more attractive. You rev up the backstory—why this is such a wonderful opportunity, why you are the perfect person to do it, how much everyone will gain, and the like. In the other, you make a request or offer seem so easy as to be a no-brainer—why *wouldn't* I do this? What do I have to lose? They called the juxtaposition the approach-avoidance model of persuasion: you can convince me of something by making me want to approach it and decreasing any reasons I might have to avoid it.

The rope, then, is the alpha and omega of the confidence game: after finding a victim and lowering his defenses through a bit of fancy emotional footwork, it's time for the actual persuasive pitch. It's Matthew roping Barrett in by convincing him that he's the perfect person for the job (alpha) and that there's no good reason why he *shouldn't* do it (omega). What's the worst that could happen? The put-up identified the mark and mapped out his idiosyncrasies, hopes, and fears. The play caught the mark's attention and baited the hook. The rope makes sure he bites and the hook sinks deep—else, with a bit of wiggling, the almost-sure-deal prey swim hastily away.

The psychologist Robert Cialdini, one of the leading experts on persuasion, argues that six principles govern most persuasive relationships: reciprocity (I rub your back, you rub mine), consistency (I believe the same thing today as I did yesterday), social validation (doing this will make me belong), friendship or liking (exactly what it sounds like), scarcity (quick! there isn't much to go around), and authority (you seem like you know what you're talking about). These are all alpha principles, used to increase persuasive appeal—and while Cialdini's own motives in setting them out are laudable ones (improve leadership, persuade people about important issues), they can, as so often happens, be used in most any direction. Get some combination of his principles, add some resistance-overcoming omega tactics, and your chances of roping your targeted mark are good—especially if you've done your legwork in the put-up and laid the right groundwork in the play. The result is a number of persuasive techniques that have been in the repertoire of the confidence artist centuries before they were articulated by Cialdini.

On a strip of land along Honduras's Black River, spreading over some eight million acres—about the size of Maryland and Delaware combined, or a bit larger than Wales—lies a small nation whose modest size belies its promise. The land is so fertile it yields three maize harvests a year. The water, so pure and refreshing it could quench any thirst—and as if that weren't enough, chunks of gold line the riverbeds. The trees overflow with fruit, and the forest teems with game. The weather is lovely—warm, welcoming, sunny. Quite the contrast with the rainy darkness and rocky soils of Scotland. The natives are friendly and solicitous, and just happen to have a soft spot for British settlers. It is, in other words, something of a paradise. And it is called Poyais.

In October 1822, Gregor MacGregor, a native of Glengyle, Scotland, made a striking announcement. He was, he said, not only a local banker's son, but the Cazique, or prince, of the land of Poyais, on the shores of South America. The country was rich beyond compare, but what it lacked was willing investors and settlers to develop and leverage its resources to the fullest. At the time, investments in Central and South America were gaining in popularity. From Mexico to Brazil, the financial opportunities seemed endless. And Poyais appeared to be a particularly appealing proposition. It was unclaimed—and Scotland didn't have any colonies of her own. Could this not be a corner of the new world for her own use?

MacGregor was a master salesman. The opportunity he presented seemed too good to pass up—and the cost of missing out, perilously high. MacGregor published interviews in national papers touting the perks that would come from investing or settling in Poyais. He highlighted the bravery and fortitude that such a gesture would demonstrate: you wouldn't just be smart; you would be a *real* man. The Scottish Highlanders were known for their hardiness and adventurous spirit, he wrote; Poyais would be the ultimate testing ground, a challenge and gift, all in one. He pointed those who needed more convincing to a book on the virtues of the small island nation, by the elusive Thomas Strangeways (actually MacGregor himself). His prospectuses enticed the public with their masterful promises, their lure of opportunity, their appeal to scarcity, their admonitions not to let this perfect moment pass by.

And they were beyond successful. Not only did MacGregor raise £200,000 directly—the bond market value over his life ran to £1.3 million, or about £3.6 billion today—but he convinced seven ships' worth of eager settlers to make their way across the Atlantic. In September 1822 and January 1823, the first two, the *Honduras Packet* and the *Kennersley Castle*, left for the mythical land, carrying some 250 passengers. The mood was high; MacGregor's salesmanship had been unparalleled. But when the settlers arrived just under two months later, they found the reality to be a stark departure from the allure of MacGregor's brochures. No ports, no developments, no nothing. It was a wasteland.

For Poyais had never existed. It was a figment of MacGregor's fertile mind. He had drawn his investors and colonizers to a desolate part of Honduras—and soon, the hardy Scotsmen began dying. The remaining settlers—only one third would survive—were rescued by a passing ship and taken to Belize. The British Navy recalled the remaining five ships before they reached their destination. MacGregor escaped to France.

If he was at all remorseful, he had a strange way of showing it: not long after his arrival he started the Poyais pitch all over again. His initial investment may have evaporated, but his mastery of the art of persuasion was undiminished. In a matter of months, he had a new group of settlers and investors ready to go. France, though, was a bit more stringent than England in its passport requirements: when the government saw a flood of applications to a country no one had heard of, a commission was set to investigate the matter. MacGregor was thrown in jail. After a brief return to Edinburgh, he was forced to flee once more, pursued by the wrath of the original Poyais bondholders. He died in 1845, in Caracas. To this day, the land that was Poyais remains a desolate and undeveloped wilderness—a testament to the power of the rope in able hands.

In 1966, Stanford University psychologists Jonathan Freeman and Scott Fraser observed an interesting phenomenon in their experiments: someone who has already agreed to a small request—like opening the door for you—would become more, not less, likely to agree to a larger request later on. In one study, they asked 150 housewives in Palo Alto, California, if they would sacrifice two hours of their time: a research team of five or six people would come to their homes to classify the household products they used. It was, as anyone would agree, a fairly big ask—invasive and time-consuming both. It didn't seem likely that many people would be willing to comply. Some of the women, however, had already been contacted once before. That time, in a phone call, they'd been asked to spare a few minutes to answer some brief questions about their preferred brands of soap.

When Freeman and Fraser looked at the results, they found a striking difference between the willingness of that one group and the rest of the women in the study. Over half of them agreed to the second request—as compared with one fifth of those who had not had to respond earlier. In other words, once someone does you anything that can be perceived as a favor—picking up a dropped glove (how many con artists love the dropped clothing article!), lending you a quarter for the phone (only a quarter! it's an important call), spending a few minutes on that phone with you in conversation—that person becomes more likely to keep doing even more on your behalf. Freeman and Fraser called it the foot-in-the-door technique. The funny thing is, they later found, the approach worked even if the person doing the requesting the second time around was someone else: doing a small favor seemed to open the door to being nice, generally speaking. It's one of the reasons that con artists often work in groups. There's the roper, the one who makes the first request, engaging his chosen persuasive strategies of choice, and then there's the inside man, a second member of the group who sweeps in for the kill, with the *real* request (the con that will be played out). You are already in a giving mood, and you become far more likely to succumb than you would've been without the initial prime.

It makes sense. We often make judgments about ourselves based on our actions, something psychologist Daryl Bem calls self-perception theory. If we yell at someone, we're rude, but if we open the door for them, we're nice. As nice people, well, we do nice things. That's just who we are. And there are few things we like more than thinking ourselves good: we like proof that we are decent, giving, generous human beings. As Cialdini points out, one of the elements that make us more vulnerable to persuasion is our desire to maintain a good image of ourselves. If something is framed so as to make us feel like worthy people, we are much more likely to comply with it. We want to be behave in a way that's consistent with the image we've created.

Consistency here plays a crucial role in the other direction, too—not just in our evaluation of ourselves but in our evaluation of the person we're helping: if I've helped you before, you must be worth it. Therefore, I'll help you again. If I've given you a job in my company, I will keep helping you with your "redemption" and will keep trusting you, and may even give you my campaign to run. You are worthy. Otherwise, I wouldn't have invested my time and resources in you. If I've given you an investment for your new colonizing mission, I will keep providing you with capital and eager settlers, maybe even some ships. You must be worth it: otherwise, I wouldn't have given you any money to begin with. It's the logic behind many a successful rope, and the logic that has propped up one of the longest-running cons of them all: the Nigerian prince.

In the early years of the twentieth century, newspapers abounded with ads for almost all manner of things—medicines, miracle workers, business deals, lucrative investment opportunities, land and gold investments, riches galore. One day, however, a new sort of ad appeared in the pages of several dailies: an appeal from a certain Prince Bil Morrison. The prince was of noble birth and hailed from the far reaches of Nigeria. All he wanted was some American pen pals. So moving was the wording of the ad that the papers had published his mailing address free of charge. Should not the poor prince find some good old American correspondents?

He did find them, and aplenty. After a few letters were sent back and forth to his new friends, Prince Morrison made a simple request: would his American acquaintances send him a mere four dollars, and an old pair of pants they no longer needed? In exchange for such a small thing, he would send them vast quantities of ivory, diamonds, and emeralds. To him, they were but worthless baubles. Friendship, however, was priceless. The money and pants poured in. But where were the promised jewels?

Complaints flooded the post office. Where was the wealth Prince Bil Morrison had promised to send? Suspecting fraud, the authorities ferreted out the wealthy Nigerian. As they soon discovered, his wealth had been a creation of his fertile mind, as was his nobility. He was American. He was anything but wealthy. And he was fourteen years old.

Though Bil Morrison's age stopped further legal action in its tracks, the undeniable success of his letters had proven the worth of the successfully thrown rope. Americans had just been taken in with the first Nigerian mail order con—the old-fashioned predecessor of the e-mail phishing scam that is probably sitting in your spam folder this very minute. (A quick check of mine reveals a note from Elena. "Hello!!!" it begins in great excitement. "My name is Elena. I looked yours profil and have become interested in you." She's from Russia, too, she tells me. Cheboksary. "Write to me at once on mine e-mail," the lovely young lady concludes.)

The Nigerian fraud is a classic foot-in-the-door approach. Prince Bil made his way up to his requests for money. First it was just a pen pal— something so small and touching even money-conscious newspapers ran his ad for free. Then it was a few letters. Only then was it cash. And pants. The pants, I am at a loss to explain. And look at nice little Elena. She didn't ask me for a single cent. All she wants is for me to reply to her touching note.

The foot-in-the-door is also the exact approach Matthew de Unger Brown used with Mervyn Barrett. From the smallest of favors (let me volunteer in your organization) to the largest ask of all (give me access to your bank account). But all accomplished slowly, incrementally, with great patience and finesse. (Not unlike the psychics like Sylvia Mitchell who rope you in with a low-fee reading and proceed to ask for increasingly ludicrous amounts of cash.)

But niceness isn't the only way to go. Another effective technique that Cialdini first identified in 1975 is the door-in-the-face, a near opposite of the foot-in-the-door. When someone we don't really know asks us for a large favor—or even someone we do know catches us on an off day—and we (understandably) refuse, we *do* indeed feel rude, just as Bem would have predicted. But we don't like feeling rude. And so we also feel something else we don't like: guilty. So what happens when the person we turned down asks us for something else, something smaller, something that seems far more reasonable in comparison? We say yes. Guilt assuaged—and con artist's mission accomplished.

In fact, Cialdini found, more people agreed to a relatively small request—volunteering to chaperone at the zoo for a few hours (if you think about it, not a small request at all)—*after* they'd rejected a much larger one—volunteering two hours a week at a juvenile detention facility over a minimum of two years—than if they'd only gotten the smaller request in isolation. Half agreed to it if it came second, while only 16.7 percent agreed to it on its own. Here, though, a confidence man must operate alone. The technique only worked, Cialdini found, if the same person did the asking both times. If you're nice, you're nice to everyone. If you're guilty, only one person can assuage that guilt: the one who caused it in the first place.

The evening had gotten off to a promising start. Tracy Ward, Marchioness of Worcester, surveyed the room. Slight and elegant, the former actress—she had starred in *C.A.T.S. Eyes*, a detective series from the eighties, and in *Cluedo*, as Miss Scarlet, before retiring from the screen—smiled with approval. They were at London's No. 41, an exclusive Mayfair club that has made its home in the Westbury Hotel, and the room had filled up nicely. The chilly weather hadn't prevented a brilliant turnout. All for the best, since it wasn't just any party. Tonight would be the charity auction for the Marchioness's foundation, Farms Not Factories. The group, dedicated to ethical pig farming, had already drummed up support from an exclusive list. RFK Junior. Sir Paul McCartney. Tom Parker Bowles. And its film series, *The Pig Business*, was off to a good start. But this evening was important. It would mean fresh funds and fresh endeavors to better the lives of porcines everywhere.

The Marchioness, Lady Worcester, remembers well the moment when the mysterious young man made his appearance, gliding down the stairs in full evening regalia. Tall, with wavy blond hair, piercing blue eyes, just a hint of a five-o'clock shadow, a touch of foundation framing a perpetual tan. A whiff of expensive aftershave. He didn't hesitate to seek out the hostess.

His name, he told her, was Sebastian Von Anhalt, a millionaire from Monaco who just so happened, he said, to be dating one of her acquaintances. He took her arm. Wouldn't she like to join him at the family compound in Monte Carlo? He laughed often and contagiously. On the spot, he pledged to raise £100,000 for her charity. Tracy Ward wasn't particularly charmed. "He came across as a drunken upper-class twit," the Marchioness later recalled. But the offer of money was welcome all the same. Donations were donations, whomever they came from.

The evening wore on. Von Anhalt worked the room, throwing a smile here, a compliment there. Soon it was time for the auction. Up next: *Dittisham Lady*. She stood proud, at nine inches of solid bronze. And she stood long, too, measuring twelve inches from nose to tail. She was, after all, a pig. A statue of a black Berkshire sow, by the sculptor Nick Bibby. Von Anhalt signaled his interest. For £4,000, *Dittisham Lady* was his.

At this point, Lady Worcester recalls, Von Anhalt took a folded check from a Canadian bank from his pocket. It was for $18,000 Canadian, about $10,000 more than the cost of the statue. Take the proceeds from that amount, he told her. Equal parts baffled and embarrassed, Lady Worcester accepted the paper. Normally, a buyer would not be entitled to his winnings until a check clears. In this case, though, Von Anhalt proved too quick: before anyone could rightly disentangle what was going on, he was out the door and into a cab, the *Dittisham Lady* tucked snuggly under his arm.

When the check failed to clear, Ward wasn't particularly worried. Von Anhalt had seemed rather a twit, true, but a wealthy twit. And his boyfriend was someone she rather liked. She was sorry for the mix-up, she told Von Anhalt. Would he transfer the money directly to the Farms Not Factories account? Certainly he would.

When the cash failed to appear, Lady Worcester found herself stymied: none of her calls or texts were returned. Whatever she tried, there was silence. Von Anhalt seemed to have evaporated, and the bronze statue along with him.

She turned to their mutual friend. How could she not have thought of it sooner? It was that connection that had acted as an instant guarantee on their first meeting—the ever-friendly glow of the familiar. Sebastian Von who? Her friend was baffled. Yes, he'd met the young man a few times, but he'd broken off contact after he found he wasn't "who he claims to be," he told her. The more Lady Worcester inquired, the stranger the situation became. This, it seemed, was not Von Anhalt's first offense. "I spoke to more people and found he's actually this Talented Mr. Ripley type who just goes round wrecking lives," she told the *Sunday Times*. The £4,000 was lost, she was afraid, and she felt "blindingly gullible." "He was completely plausible, and utterly brazen," she later said.

And it didn't end there. After his failure to pay, the Marchioness involved the police. Every accusation, said Von Anhalt's lawyer, was a brazen lie. He didn't even *have* the pig. "He even told me to check the club's CCTV," she says. They promptly did just that. "It clearly shows him going off with the pig. The maître d' saw him go off with it. Someone else saw him in the taxi with it." The lawyers changed their tune. He had the statue, they now said, but he'd come across it lawfully. Everyone had been paid in full. As of this writing, pig and check both remain at large.

Von Anhalt was in fact the same young gentleman we met earlier in the guise of Matthew de Unger Brown. Only now, instead of the foot-in-the-door as his rope of choice, he came with a full-on door-in-the-face. His first approach to Lady Worcester: an unsuccessful attempt at charm that left her thinking him as something other than charming—her polite demurral of his offer of a visit to Monaco was the cultured way of saying "never" (who would want to spend more than a minute in the "twit's" company?)—followed by a second favor, far more reasonable-seeming, of honoring a Canadian check. The request, in the moment, seemed a small one. And, as the Marchioness herself admitted, she was feeling embarrassed. It wasn't usual policy, but, well, maybe this once . . .

In 1986, Santa Clara University psychologist Jerry Burger proposed a persuasion—or roping, if you will—tactic that relied not on a comparison between two separate favors but on a comparison within the favor itself: the that's-not-all technique. An effective approach, Burger found, is to start with a false baseline (that is, not at all what you're planning to eventually propose) and then, in quick succession, make changes and additions to that starting point that make it seem increasingly attractive. You make an initial bid—how would you like to get in on this land deal in Florida?—and before your mark can respond, you turn it into something else. "That's not all. You also get a guaranteed return on your initial investment." People who were approached with a that's-not-all story, Burger found, were more likely to buy into it than those who heard the great offer right away. (The that's-not-all-ing, incidentally, can continue for a while. You need not stop at one.)

That's-not-all is actually a member of a broader set of persuasive tactics, known as disrupt-then-reframe techniques. First you disrupt someone's understanding of an attempt to influence her, and then you reframe the attempt in a way that makes her more vulnerable to it. Here's how it works. Harvard psychologist Daniel Gilbert proposes that we understand the world in two stages. First we take it at face value, in order to decipher the sense of what someone is telling us. And then we evaluate it, in order to judge the soundness of what we've just deciphered. Disrupt-then-reframe attacks the evaluative part of the process: we don't have a chance to give a proper assessment because each time we try to do so, the situation changes.

Consider this illustration. In 1999, Barbara Davis and Eric Knowles, psychologists at the University of Arkansas, went door-to-door selling holiday or note cards—three-dollar holiday or note cards, that is. Not a bargain fifteen years ago, and pricy even today. When the door opened, they greeted the would-be proud owner of a set of cards with one of several pitches. "They are three dollars," was the simplest. "They are three hundred pennies" was the disruptive approach—it takes a second to evaluate and recalculate. Each of those could, in turn, be followed by either "It's a bargain"—a way of reframing the offer as positive—or "They're three hundred pennies . . . that's three dollars. It's a bargain," the disrupt-and-reframe. The only time that people bought more cards than in the control condition—the simple three-dollar request—was when their three hundred pennies were immediately made into three dollars and then immediately remade again into a bargain. Between 65 and 70 percent of people then went on to buy the cards—as compared . with a quarter when the price was named alone.

Disrupt-then-reframe techniques are legitimate sales tactics, but in the hands of con artists, those cards can easily turn into something else—like the perennial favorite of selling bogus health products that are immediately presented at a multi-month discount, and alongside another product that does something equally wonderful and is being thrown in *for free*. It's a limited-time offer, of course. Better get ordering.

In 1984, psychologist Joel Brockner pioneered a new approach, one of the street hustler's favorites: the even-a-penny-would-help. Similar to the foot-in-the-door, here, asking for a little helps you get a lot. But it's not quite the same thing. You're not looking to make two different-size requests. Instead, you're looking to exploit something known as the "legitimization effect." A request for a tiny amount of money legitimizes you in the eyes of others. If you were a swindler, you'd ask for a lot, wouldn't you? If you'd be happy with only a penny, what kind of a thief are you? It works the same way for organizations. If you're looking for a tiny donation—a dollar or another inconsequential-seeming amount— you look like you're working hard for very little. You're not the type of person to go all tricksy on me.

Glafira Rosales perpetrated one of the largest art frauds of the twentieth century, selling dozens of fake Abstract Expressionist paintings to unsuspecting buyers over the course of twenty years. Her success lay in targeting the Knoedler Gallery, formerly the oldest art gallery in Manhattan, as her seller. And why did the Knoedler trust her? For many reasons (we'll come to that in a later chapter). But a strong indicator of Rosales's personal integrity in the eyes of Ann Freedman, the gallery's then-director, was the fact that Glafira wasn't focused on money. "She didn't care how much it sold for," Freedman told me. "She was quiet, not at all pushy. She deferred to my judgment." She would be happy, she told Freedman, as long as the art sold "fairly"—and for that fairness, she trusted Freedman implicitly. The prices, of course, did just what you would expect in the even-a-penny scenario: they increased. By a hell of a lot. The more paintings were sold, the more legitimate the collection and provenance appeared, the more money they brought in, and the more Rosales and the Bergantiños brothers (Rosales's accomplices) were paid. It worked like a textbook charm. But it never would have been possible if the initial starting point hadn't been a humble one. It was a truly expert rope.

A closely related approach is Cialdini's lowball technique. This time, you tell your intended victim that what you want is actually quite small—and once he commits to doing it, raise the stakes. A car salesman can give a ballpark (lowball) estimate on a car. Once the buyer is enamored with the actual car he already thinks he's buying—a different model altogether from the one initially quoted—he can raise the price: "Actually, sir, this particular model comes with . . ." and so forth. Many a person will say yes where they would have originally said no. It only works, however, if you made your initial decision with a good amount of freedom. If you felt at all compelled or pushed, it can backfire. It's the con artist's bait and switch. Bait with one, switch with another. In some ways, one of the oldest cons of all time—the biblical replacement of Rachel with Leah. You have your eye on one model, but . . .

Most persuasive strategies—the con artist's rope—work by promising more. But there are, as well, those that operate on Cialdini's principle of scarcity. The scarce is inherently valuable by very virtue of its scarcity: there isn't much to go around, so only the very lucky few can have it. The limited edition. The forbidden fruit. The offer only good till midnight. The members-only sale. The collector's item. Pose something as unique or rare, and takers will line up where there used to be none. It works for goods. It works for information. It works for most anything.

Bernie Madoff didn't take investment from just any old sucker. You had to work your way in. You had to earn his trust. Some people tried for months, even years, to get him to accept their investment. It only increased the allure. And insider trading, of course, is built entirely on scarcity—scarcity of information.

Rudy Kurniawan, perpetrator of one of the master wine frauds of the century, didn't let just anyone buy his wines—and never right away. Wilf Jaeger, a wine collector who has known Kurniawan since the start of his foray into the world of fine wines, told me—over a glass of wine, of course—that he'd worked for months to get the charismatic young collector to sell him some of his elusive bottles.

Kurniawan had come seemingly out of nowhere. A wealthy young financial type, he'd made quite a splash at wine auction after wine auction, buying up expensive lots, throwing millions after the choicest of bottles. Then the dinners started. Not just any wine dinners. The wines served here were as exclusive as they come—some bottles not available for sale anywhere, at any price. The company, too, was a rarefied one. A true sampling of the best in the wine world: the finest tasters, the best-reputed collectors, the cream of the luxury world and high society. People skirmished and angled for an invitation. A Kurniawan dinner was an affair to remember. It certainly didn't hurt that Rudy himself was an extraordinary taster. Going blind, he could guess most any wine down to the proper vineyard.

Old-time collectors were, frankly, stunned. Here was a relative upstart, and somehow he was able to get his hands on bottles they'd been tracking for years. How was it possible? Rudy had a secret, he let it be known. He'd unearthed a new private cellar in France, and the owner was shipping him the bottles directly. They had never left the basement, and had been waiting for years for just such a discovery.

It wasn't an unprecedented story. New cellars did come to light all the time, Michael Egan, a former wine director for Sotheby's who specializes in tracking and authenticating private collections, told me. He's examined quite a few newcomers himself. Who was to say Rudy hadn't lucked out?

Soon Rudy began to share his wealth. Not just at small dinners. Now he would sell you cases of some of his wines at the right price. He had many, and he wanted others to have the same tasting opportunity.

Yet try as he may, Wilf couldn't seem to get his hands on even a single case. "I asked for months, practically begged," he recalls. Finally, Rudy relented. Wilf could be one of his exclusive buyers.

A few days later, the cases arrived in Wilf's cellar. Wilf buys vast quantities of wine. He can't taste everything, but he makes it a practice to spot-test his new acquisitions, to make sure the bottles are in proper condition. He cracked open a crate and took out a Lafite. It tasted . . . off. "I didn't think it was fake," he says. "Just bad. Maybe it wasn't stored properly. I don't know. It just tasted wrong." He returned the entire purchase to Rudy, who, without argument, offered him a full refund.

In retrospect, Wilf was remarkably prescient: the wines had been fake, and for several years investigators had been looking into Kurniawan's sources. There had been one event that tipped the scales: an auction in New York, run by Acker Merrall and Condit, an old and renowned wine store and auction house. The auction was scheduled to include a case of particularly rare bottles from Kurniawan's cellars, including several magnums. The only problem, according to the owner of the château in question: that particular vintage never came in magnums. They had never bottled any in that size.

Against protests, Acker went forward with the sale all the same. Who knows; records at the time were patchy. Who's to say the magnums weren't bottled elsewhere?

Of course, just like Jaeger's wines, these were not miraculous exceptions. And soon the evidence reached a tipping point. Police raided Kurniawan's house. In the basement, they found old labels, fake labels, "recipes" for various wines and vintages, the whole panoply of paraphernalia needed to manufacture old and rare bottles.

It was indeed an exclusive club, fueled by true scarcity. Too bad it was also fake. Kurniawan is now serving his sentence in Southern California.

* * *

Matthew de Unger Brown, or Sebastian Von Anhalt, if you will, was born Matthew Edward Brown in 1984, in Doncaster, South Yorkshire, the son of a Hong Kong–based telecom's director of legal affairs. When his father died suddenly of a heart attack at forty-two, Matthew, then thirteen, moved in with his mother, Jane, a social worker. They lived in a house not far from his school, by all accounts a middle-class life. (In 2007, Brown's mother died of a sudden heart attack as well.)

As a teen, Matthew attended the Oakham School, an expensive second-tier private school in Rutland, where he was both prefect and, at one time, librarian. School, however, didn't particularly suit him. As former classmate Andrew Cummine later recalled, "He wasn't very popular. He was strange, always putting on an act. A complex character. He never revealed himself or his feelings but he loved public speaking."

What Cummine recalled most, however, was Matthew's manner. He had his own stationery, his name emblazoned on top, "a bit strange for someone of thirteen." He was, he'd said, the leader of the Young Conservatives. And he always carried around a thick novel. Ask him anything, and he would quickly formulate an articulate response. And yet he "was in the bottom sets for most subjects." Somehow, the veneer covered nothing of substance.

In 2005, Brown—by that point openly gay—married up in the world. Four months after meeting Renate de Unger-Bloeck, an art restorer thirty years his senior with a sizable personal fortune derived in part from her own first marriage, he proposed. He moved into her £2 million London town house, close to Buckingham Palace. His legitimacy was increasing by the second. In short order, his new wife appointed her dashing young husband to the helm of Icehome, her art restoration company. He soon proved, however, to once again be more charm than chops. The company's finances unraveled, partly due to incompetence, partly, one suspects, to more willful misdeeds, until by 2008, what had once been multiple millions dissolved into bankruptcy. Brown and de Unger-Bloeck soon parted ways. The separation, suffice it to say, was not a particularly pleasant one.

His parents dead, his wife estranged, Brown took refuge with his aunt, his mother's sister. He proved, however, a bitter disappointment. "He is 100 percent trouble," his stepfather, Robert Gant, later said.

In 2010, Renate de Unger-Bloeck died unexpectedly, apparently of alcohol poisoning. Her name, however, lived on. Matthew Brown re-christened himself Matthew de Unger Brown, and transformed Renate into, by turns, his mother and his secretary.

He'd already been Lord Brown of Ardbreckin as a teen, and a vaunted City worker. But his horizons were about to expand. German prince. English QC. Monaco almost-royalty. The boyfriend of CNN anchor Richard Quest. The Honourable Sir Matthew de Unger Brown. The world was his oyster—and he would soon prove himself to be master at all matters of the rope.

* * *

In their influential 1959 work "The Bases of Social Power," John French and Bertram Raven posited that there were five major bases from which power derives: reward power, or the belief that someone is able to re-ward you; coercive power, or the belief that someone is able to punish you somehow; legitimate power, or an actual basis of authority; referent power, or power derived from your affiliation with someone (or desire to be affiliated with them); and expert power, from someone's expertise on a topic.

Con artists are after power: power over you and your future actions. So how do they derive it? From which base does it stem in order for the rope to work its persuasive magic? The grifter will avoid coercion at all costs. That would be unaristocratic. Not to mention unartistic. Con art-ists don't demand, they don't threaten, they don't intimidate. Instead, they use the softer touch: some reward power with a little authority and affiliation mixed in.

In one review of the literature on fraud victims, marks said they often thought that not only was the person doing the conning legitimate, but the reward he was offering was the real deal as well. That is a fairly typical perception in many a confidence game: you're dealing with someone to be reckoned with (legitimate power), and that someone is in a position to reward you, be it financially or otherwise (reward power). Indeed, in establishing their legitimacy, the victims said, their scammers appealed often and early to trust and authority. The logic is clear. If you know someone is asking for something, you need to know early on who that someone is and why, exactly, you should listen.

We get authority in two ways: by virtue of what we know (authority based on expertise) or by virtue of who we are (authority based on position). The confidence artist will exploit both. But the second is much easier to fake than the first; indeed, the first, or at least the perception of it, often follows in its wake.

When Dr. Clifford Berry, a professor of physics at New York State Maritime College, first read the *Time* account of Ferdinand Waldo Demara's escapades, he—like many others—felt his curiosity piqued. "I thought about Demara's case for a long time," he would in turn tell *Life* some two years later. For one simple reason: his name wasn't Clifford Berry at all. In Demara's forays into the professoriate, he glimpsed his own theretofore-successful escapades with academic impostoring.

The oldest of three children, Marvin Harold Hewitt was born in Philadelphia in 1920. His father, Samuel, was a police sergeant. Marvin dropped out of high school just shy of graduation—he claimed he was bored. Manual labor followed—freight yards, factories, anywhere that could use a powerful seventeen-year-old. Rejected from the army, he joined the Signal Corps (also boring, he declared).

Then he saw something that caught his eye: teaching. Now *that*, he mused, wouldn't be boring. In short order, he replied to an ad for an eighth-grade teacher opening at a new military school, Camp Hill

Military Academy. His résumé conveniently forgot to mention his own lack of diploma. Instead, a degree from Temple University had magically appeared in its place. Soon Marvin Hewitt was standing in front of a class of eager thirteen-year-olds, teaching math, geography, and history. That spring, the school closed (perhaps, one thinks, due to its hiring practices). Hewitt's tenure, however, had been a success. Instructor Hewitt he began, and Instructor Hewitt—this time with actual teaching experience—he remained.

It had gone off seamlessly. Why stop at junior high school? Hewitt began to telephone local colleges. Might they be seeking a physics instructor? He soon learned that the Philadelphia College of Pharmacy and Science was indeed in the market for a new faculty member. When department head Robert Jones asked Hewitt for his name, Hewitt promptly provided it: Julius Ashkin. The actual Ashkin was beyond qualified; he had worked at Columbia, Los Alamos, and the Argonne National Laboratory. All Hewitt had to do was borrow the identity. Jones was impressed. Ashkin-né-Hewitt was hired to teach approximately three hundred students calculus, trigonometry, and algebra. Among his other responsibilities: supervising physics laboratory work. There was only one minor hitch. Ashkin-né-Ashkin had also gone on the job market. That fall, he, too, was slated to begin teaching, at the University of Rochester.

For a time, the two Ashkins coexisted in peace. Hewitt had written to Columbia and, for a dollar, obtained an academic transcript. He'd followed his textbooks closely, and the students were scoring on par with other professors' on their departmental exams. One close call: Hewitt's real father was shot and killed by a car thief. Reporters gathered around his home. Afraid of being caught on camera and exposed, he hid inside and, for several days, played hooky from his classes. The danger passed.

The year concluded successfully. But Hewitt felt too close to home. At any moment exposure could strike him unawares. And so he began to write to colleges farther afield. In due course, he received a reply: Bemidji State Teachers College in Minnesota was hiring. Hewitt promptly sent over Ashkin's transcript. This time he added a personal flourish: he had also worked for a year as physics consultant to a certain "Christie Engineering Company." No such company actually existed, but Hewitt was resourceful. Stationery and a secretarial service (the latter legitimate) quickly followed. By the time the college president, Charles Sattgast, inquired as to a reference, Robert Christie, the company head, was ready with a glowing letter.

Hewitt packed up his new wife—he'd recently gotten married to a local girl proud of being the wife of a professor—and moved to Minnesota. He soon had a sixteen-hour-a-week course load. Analytical and solid geometry, college algebra, physics. He covered them all. But somehow it didn't seem enough. Bemidji was *small*. It was, well, boring. He wanted a *real* university, where people of his own intellectual caliber, such as he perceived it to be, would more readily congregate. Once more, Hewitt sent out applications.

He soon received an offer from Saint Louis University. Finally, he thought. A school worthy of his name. He would make appropriate demands. His teaching load had been too high, leaving him little time for contemplation and discovery. Here, he would teach ten hours a week. His students had been of too low a caliber. Here, he would teach mostly to graduates. And college algebra? An insult to his intellect. At Saint Louis, he would lecture on nuclear physics, statistical mechanics, and tensor analysis. Julius Ashkin had finally found an intellectual home. There were some close calls—he was, after all, using the real name of a real physicist—but Hewitt was resourceful. His Professor Ashkin flourished.

Meanwhile, the real Ashkin was successfully publishing from his tenure-track job at the University of Rochester. Hewitt followed his progress carefully, and after each publication he fearfully checked to see whether it would be the key to his undoing. Would anyone notice the disparity in schools and connect the dots?

No, this life of stress was too much. Hewitt needed another change. Again, he began the application process. He would stay Ashkin, but he would lower the caliber of his school. Lesser schools, he reasoned, wouldn't follow the literature as closely.

The University of Utah was thrilled. For references, they received brilliant recommendations from Columbia, Argonne, and Los Alamos—the real Ashkin was a brilliant man making a brilliant career; it was easy to find people willing to vouch for him. His recommendations were far from bogus. They were simply for the wrong man. Hewitt's luck held out. The hiring committee never called Rochester. And one school, Columbia, even offered a convenient excuse for any potential red flags: there had actually been two Ashkins enrolled at the university. While Ashkin-the-first toiled away at the lowly rank of assistant professor, Utah made Ashkin-the-second an unprecedented offer: full professorship, straight off.

And then came the letter. It was addressed to Julius Ashkin—but with a question mark appended to the end. The postmark: Rochester. The sender: Julius Ashkin. Ashkin-the-first was understanding, saying he assumed that Ashkin the impostor was "fundamentally a decent man." He was, he wrote, giving him an opportunity to stop the charade of his own accord, without official action. Someone else at Rochester, though, wasn't so gentle. The president of the University of Utah, too, had received a letter, from a tipster who was a little less willing than Ashkin to let the impostor off lightly.

Hewitt was let go. Quietly. The administration even offered him the option of completing his studies at the university. To Hewitt, that was too low to fall. He wouldn't stoop from full professorship to student status. He ran back to Philadelphia—even spurning another legitimate offer from a friend who had contacted Princeton on his behalf. His Ashkin had simply died. But the great professor lived on—and would go on to teach at the University of Arkansas College of Engineering (electrical engineering) and, of course, at New York State Maritime College (physics and calculus).

When he was unmasked for a second and final time, Hewitt dodged all responsibility for the fraud. It wasn't at all his fault. It was the system itself. The system had flaws. *He* wasn't to blame if they hired him. And, in a sense, he was absolutely right. The process was designed by humans. The same humans who are built to trust. We don't always have nets to catch fraud because we never expect to need them, especially not when we're dealing with a successful—brilliant, even—mind. We trust that mind implicitly. The man who holds power, however illusory it may be, is a man in the perfect position to rope.

We often obey power reflexively, without ever quite stopping to reflect on why we're doing what we are and whether it is, in fact, something we should be doing. While the most famous—or, rather, infamous—study on the phenomenon is Stanley Milgram's obedience study,* in which people thought they were giving dangerous electric shocks to a man with a heart condition but did it anyway because they were told to continue, the phenomenon has been broadly replicated in multiple settings. In one study, personnel managers discriminated against applicants by race when their superiors instructed them to do so. In another, employees engaged in routinely corrupt practices, like stealing or price-fixing, when their higher-ups so directed them. When someone in power tells us to do something, we tend to do it. The rope is often at its most effective when we trust the power of its source, the con man.

A position can be powerful, as French and Raven pointed out, not simply through actual authority. It can also draw us in by its referent nature: the person in power is someone we are affiliated with already or want to be affiliated with in the future.

One of the first things a con artist does is establish trust—often by being the exact type of person he thinks you aspire to be, or at least, want to be associated with. Someone like you. Someone you would like

---

* The study has been criticized in recent years as not showing what it purports, but Milgram's original work—and series of studies, not just the one most frequently reported—do show that many (not all) people will indeed follow orders to a surprising degree. The effect has been widely replicated.

to become. Someone you'd like others to know you're friends with. That way, you are much more likely to bite when he throws the rope your way. One broker who fell for Bernie Madoff's spell remarked that there was "something about this person, pedigree, and reputation that inspired trust."

And there was something else crucial about Madoff: he was part of the Jewish community. A community he leveraged to its full extent. As Michael Shermer put it, "It was an affinity scheme, it was insidery. We have to take care of each other; he's one of us." Madoff is far from alone. Con artists often use communities to quickly gauge character and belief and acquire a veneer of the same. Religious communities are frequent targets—another con man you'll meet later in this book used his Episcopalian ties to their best effect. But so, too, are connoisseurs, members of certain clubs, whatever it takes. The authority we grant someone comes often as more of an afterthought than anything else, by virtue of their belonging to the exact right group, one that we're particularly eager to either join or be liked by. There's a reason Matthew Brown didn't pose as just anyone. He was aristocracy. And aristocracy is something you want to affiliate with.

Brown knew it, too, and took every opportunity—and every new identity—to bolster his credentials, with fake Wikipedia entries (that were, for the most part, quickly removed, but stayed up long enough for victims to chance upon them), and social media accounts, from Facebook to Twitter to more niche markets, depending on his quarry. Some, like Badoo and Google Plus profiles for Matthew de Unger Brown, are still active. The Internet has, in many ways, made establishing a trustworthy identity far simpler than it ever has been. All you need to do is create a firm social media presence—the more accounts, the better—and voilà, you're a real person with whatever pedigree you've chosen to fashion for yourself. Create a few feeder accounts under other names that seem to support your exclusive affiliations ("Great party on your yacht last night!!"), and your value rises even further. People are lazy. Few will bother to check Burke's Peerage when everything else is so readily available. It's why an entirely new set of legal considerations, many of them to do with the implications of bogus reviews, has suddenly emerged with the advent of online ratings and postings, on sites from Yelp to Amazon to eHarmony. The more digital we become, the more difficult it can be to separate reality from fiction—and the easier it is to establish a firm basis for the rope to work its magic.

In some cases, in fact, Matthew Brown's supposed affiliation was the only thing he had going for him—and it worked like a charm, even when it came to things like opening a bank account. An early escapade: On October 14, 2004, the *London Evening Standard* published an account of a recent teen—Brown, as it later turned out—who had done more than his share of teen-gone-wild antics. The young man, then eighteen, had made a habit of convincing credit card companies that he was a member of the aristocracy. He'd posed as a lord and City worker, no less—a salary of £86,000 per year, he said—and, in November 2002, received his first American Express card. The card company failed to conduct the most basic checks because it implicitly trusted the authority lent by the aristocratic connection, not wanting, it seems, to run the risk of questioning the story: it would be unseemly to undermine a gentleman's word.

The month after he'd received his new card, Brown took a Christmas holiday to the Lake District. Five-star accommodations and £500 limousines peppered his five-day trip. But the area seemed a bit too provincial for such a discerning young nobleman. And so, as January turned to February, Lord Brown of Ardbreckin began to travel first class across England and Scotland. He had excellent taste, in food, champagne, and cognac alike. His multicourse meals and profligate wine habit—with generous tips often larger than the bills they tipped on—soon became famous. The debts piled up, but still no one questioned—or questioned hard enough—the notion that the young lord was good for them. He was an aristocrat, a member of the most exclusive club there is. And with affiliation comes power. You want the powerful to like you, not to think you petty for deigning to question their integrity, and so you keep any doubts to yourself—much as the Marchioness would later do when it came time to part with her prize pig statue.

Lord Brown's exploits continued unabated. He would, on occasion, foray into the capital itself. Claridge's was his hotel of choice. Propped now by a Barclaycard alongside his AmEx—one seal of seeming approval feeds into the next—he ran up multi-hundred-pound wine and spirits bills at Oddbins and hefty sums at surrounding tanning salons. He couldn't, of course, be caught on camera with a pallor.

Meanwhile, the bills kept coming. The payments, not so much. The situation reached a tipping point: aristocracy was no longer enough. This was a business, and any business needs to be paid. Authority only goes so far. Soon, American Express issued a "wanted" poster for the errant cardholder who'd run up charges of some £18,000. On August 15, 2003, as Brown boarded yet another train at Plymouth Station, a look of recognition passed over the ticket officer's face. By the time the lord disembarked in London, a police escort was waiting.

Plain old Matthew Brown soon found himself in the halls of Middlesex Guildhall Crown Court. Criminal charges didn't deter him from his usual flamboyance, though. A pink carnation boutonniere, a neckerchief, a trilby, a cane with a silver tip: he greeted the courtroom in style. In 2004, he pled guilty to 9 charges of deception—with an additional 224 taken into consideration—and was given a three-year rehabilitation order, admitted for treatment for alcohol and cocaine abuse at a £12,000-a-month clinic in Surrey. He'd been in jail, just as he would later admit to Mervyn Barrett. Just not quite for the offense he'd let on.

That was Brown's first (that we know of) escapade. And all it took was some credible and choice-sounding affiliations to get off the ground. Position, even if not real, is a powerful thing. Consider how often famous families find their names co-opted for more nefarious uses. Clark Rockefeller successfully convinced dozens of people that he was legitimately part of the Rockefeller clan, until it emerged that he was actually Christian Gerhartsreiter—and a murderer to boot. But for over two decades, he posed not only as Rockefeller (his longest disguise), but variously as a member of British royalty and a Hollywood producer. The guise could change, but the exclusivity remained: he knew well what other people wanted to hear. Who doesn't want to befriend a Rockefeller?

Long before the Rockefeller family grew a new member, there was Cassie Chadwick, who for many years passed herself off as the illegitimate daughter of Andrew Carnegie. Her plan was deceptively simple. She hired a prominent Cleveland lawyer and had him drive her to the scion's mansion. There, she pretended to go inside and visit with the man himself; in reality, she only spoke with the housekeeper. On her way back, she accidentally-on-purpose dropped a (forged) promissory note for $2 million, from Carnegie to her. The lawyer was convinced. He spread the word—hush-hush, of course—and soon Cassie was living a life of luxury on the loans that were pouring in: everyone believed that, on Carnegie's death, the return would be immense. And everyone wanted to be on the good side of the soon-to-be heiress. Chadwick would have gone on indefinitely had she not overreached, drawing the attention of Carnegie himself, who promptly disavowed all knowledge of her identity. In 1904, she was finally arrested.

Fred Demara, too, chose his affiliations with care. He never stole credentials willy-nilly. They were always stolen with an eye to what they represented—and whether they represented a type of power that his target would respond to. Was a given disguise a good basis for this particular rope, or no? In religious orders, he was unfailingly a former academic superstar. The monks felt honored that someone so learned and decorated wanted to put everything aside and join them. They wanted him to like them and accept them as intellectual equals. When he became warden of a Texas prison, on the other hand, he went for a tougher image: a Southern gentleman with a hard streak, who had a fascination with the law and wanted to enter the penal system. He was someone who was just like the prisoners might one day be—a reformed alcoholic, no less—so that they liked him. But he also had what it takes to be the kind-but-firm enforcer—so that the higher-ups liked him. The rope works best when the persuasive base is tailored to the task.

Our desire to be accepted as a member of groups that appeal to us is, according to Cialdini, one of the strongest motivators in our being persuaded by something: it is an important reason that the rope often works effectively. We are more likely to go along with something if it has the stamp of approval of a group we trust or promises us entry in a group we'd like to belong to.

Even when we're anonymous and the group not particularly desirable, we'd still like to be included more than not—and it hurts when we are excluded. Kipling Williams, a Purdue University social psychologist whose work centers on ostracism, found that, in a virtual ball toss game, people who were passed over by the other group members felt worse about themselves and had a greater need for belonging—a psychological concept that measures the general extent to which we want to be part of a larger group. In an unrelated task, those same people were much more likely to conform to their peers' behavior. Now imagine the group had been a well-known one. Imagine you're trying to get on Madoff's or Kurniawan's good side, and he simply won't see you. The effect can be much more pronounced. You'll want to belong all the more. And the rope will find its intended mark all the more easily.

You may be the best roper there is, and have every persuasive strategy playbook down, but the truth is, who you are—or seem to be—will affect how it's perceived. As will precisely how you present it—and what you do if you encounter resistance. The rope depends on multiple elements: not just the persuasive strategy you use and your identity, but how, exactly, you frame the proposition. Power, in other words, can come from the construction of the argument rather than its substance: power through how you phrase something rather than what you're actually saying. A good confidence artist uses the structure of his pitch to manipulate the way we perceive or think about something. He may not be powerful as such—perhaps he's just a nice guy you met in the lobby—but he has power to influence your reality, the way you understand and parse an argument or proposition. If he's a good roper, you will soon be seeing the world as he sees it, and not as you did moments before falling under his sway.

Take this example: by the order in which someone presents us with options, she can reliably make those options look better or worse—even if we wouldn't naturally think so. In 2006, J. Edward Russo, a psychologist specializing in decision making at Cornell's Johnson Graduate School of Management, ran a series of experiments to illustrate just how easy it would be to get us to go against our own best interest with just a bit of clever framing. First, he and his colleagues asked a group of students about their restaurant preferences for two pairs of fictional restaurants that were described according to ten different attributes (atmosphere, daily specials, driving distance, speed of service, and the like). Two weeks later, they asked everyone to come in for a follow-up. This time, the list of attributes was modified and ordered in a very specific way. The information was identical, but now the characteristic that most favored the inferior restaurant was placed first—and the less favorable last. Everyone was next asked to rate the restaurants a second time, and then to say how confident they were of their choices on a scale of zero (uncertain) to one hundred (completely certain), where fifty represents a toss-up.

This time around, a majority of people—62 percent—favored the previously inferior choice. The fact that the first attribute supported it skewed all subsequent information. In fact, after the first attribute alone, a full 76 percent said the inferior choice was the leader. What's more, they had no idea they were doing it. People were choosing a restaurant they would not have naturally liked nearly as much as other options, but they remained equally confident in their choice no matter what option they'd picked.

In the choice of food, effects like these may seem minor. But the order effect—what Russo was demonstrating—is but one of the many elements of decision architecture—how information is presented to us— that can get us to make decisions in a very precise way, and not necessarily in a way that corresponds to our stated preferences.

There's the positive side of decision architecture, the nudge, popu-
larized by behavioral economist Richard Thaler and legal scholar Cass
Sunstein in their 2008 book by the same name. The idea behind the
nudge, in its positive guise, is a simple one. In many cases, our choices
aren't based on some innate preference. Instead, they are constructed at
any given moment by a combination of situational factors. I may not
have thought about drinking wine with dinner, for instance, but if the
wine list is right in front of me, I may find myself ordering a glass all
the same.

The psychology of why nudges work forms the entire basis of a
confidence artist's soft power. Just as a grifter never coerces in any
observable way, a nudge never actually forces one behavior or forbids
another—a smoking ban is not a nudge but a policy regulation—but
rather changes the nature of the choice itself. That is, you influence a
decision by changing how, precisely, that decision is presented. Thaler
and Sunstein explain their reasoning in terms of a seeming oxymoron:
libertarian paternalism. The environment affects our choices no matter
what, the argument goes, so why not make sure it's doing so for the better? Or, in the case of the con artist, for the worse?

The order effect is the tip of a very large iceberg that includes things
like position effects—where something is located physically. Con artists
manipulate this all the time by placing objects or people they want you
to gravitate toward in more privileged positions. There are default
effects—or what your choice is by default. Cons like the infamous Publishers Clearing House sweepstakes use default effects to get you into
more subscriptions you never asked for than you can ever unsubscribe
yourself from—a subversive take on the old marketing ploy of automat-
ically receiving e-mails from a retailer you've placed an order from, even
though you don't recall ever signing up for a list. There are anchor
effects—the initial cues you see that then influence your subsequent decision, like the price that first catches your eye on a menu, that then
makes other prices seem more or less fair, or a monthly payment plan
that forms a reasonable-seeming anchor for a sum you might otherwise

question as too high. And the list goes on. The final message, though, is simple. Precisely how something is presented to you matters a great deal. And you can be certain that the confidence man knows exactly how to engineer any game so that the odds are stacked against you. That is the art of the rope.

One evening over a dinner of pasta, Apollo Robbins, gentleman thief extraordinaire, had me convinced for a good ten minutes that he could read my mind. He'd grabbed three objects from the table, lining them up side by side behind a screen, and asked me to choose the one I wanted. And then, over and over, he would be able to tell me what I had chosen and what hand it was in. I was mystified—until he explained that he was forcing my choice with clever wording. Each time, he would word his instructions slightly differently to make it seem as if he could predict my every move: I had perfect freedom, yet he could tell the future. I can't give away the trick, alas, but it was all about game engineering: how to frame choices, in what order, and using what precise words to make it seem he was always a step ahead. It's the rope on a miniature scale—a demonstration of the power of minute presentation in influencing things as weighty as your perception of the future.

Con artists can even influence choice by limiting it—a take on the default effect. When Ohio State's Curtis Haugtvedt surveyed the literature on persuasion—specifically how we're influenced by conversations and interactions, the Internet, radio, television, and books—he found certain characteristics that make a message more likely to hit home. One of them is the element of choice itself. We often like to have our choices constricted. Too much choice, and we just shake our heads and walk away—a phenomenon known as choice fatigue. But if a persuasive statement engenders a strong negative reaction—"There is no choice"— it will draw more attention to itself, and as a result, be more likely to be remembered. If the statement seems persuasive—your granddaughter is in trouble and you have no choice but to send money immediately to help her—we'll be all the more likely to concede the point rather than stop and think about alternatives. When a con artist appears to make a decision for us, making it seem as if we've already decided when we actually haven't, it can actually work to his advantage. The magazines or products that already arrive at your door. The wallet that has already been found—and the plan to return it that you didn't even have to think through.

Another effective tactic, Haugtvedt found, is to prime as much information as possible: order effects where you make sure to seed the first impression ahead of time. That is, throw in just enough early, hard-to-pin-down references that set the mark's mind thinking in a certain direction. Then, when the grifter makes a suggestion or actually raises the point explicitly, the victim has already been considering it, however subconsciously. It's almost like a meeting of the minds: you were just thinking that yourself.

Information priming works so well because it exploits an effect we've already seen several times: the ease that comes from familiarity. Mention something in passing, and then when you elaborate on it later—especially if it's a few days later—it seems that much more convincing. It's a phenomenon known as the illusion of truth: we are more likely to think something is true if it feels familiar.

Consider a turn of phrase the con artist often uses: "Picture this," "Imagine that . . ." Imagine you've actually gone to claim the lottery winnings that you already have, if you just make the effort. What will you do with the money? How will you spend it? Where will you go? Suddenly you're on a warm beach or strolling the streets of Paris. One of Cialdini's many studies of persuasion had people watch an ad about cable television. Those who were told to "imagine the benefits" were much more likely to actually subscribe to it a month later than those who were simply told about "the benefits of cable TV." The call to "imagine the benefits" can come even before any concrete proposal. Just a seemingly throwaway remark, a casting of the rope, so to speak, before you even realize that anything is on offer. You've planted the suggestion and, when the time for the real proposal comes along, the mark is more likely to see it as coming from her own initiative. (Apart from being a favorite gambit of the con, it's a famous marital trick.)

And a final construction that can win an argument: it doesn't actually matter what you say, in what order, or how. All that matters is that you say a lot, quickly, and that it sounds convoluted and has many moving parts. Simply put, we tend to make worse decisions when we have a lot on our minds—even after that "lot" is removed. Con artists exploit this by making us have to keep track of multiple things at once: multiple acquaintances, multiple moving pieces, multiple histories. At the most basic level, consider sleight-of-hand cons, like three-card monte, where we're asked to "follow the lady" as she moves from hand to hand. Or the "pig in a poke," where a wallet we thought full of money ends up being full of paper scraps—a dexterous last-minute switch that succeeds because our minds are busy following the rest of our deceiver's story. In all cases, there are too many things for our minds to take in, and so we miss the crucial detail. We're simply too busy trying to register it all.

Tyler Alterman, a psychologist turned Bay Area entrepreneur, was eager to be allowed into local Chicago bars when he wasn't yet of legal drinking age. He didn't use a fake ID. Instead, his strategy was wholly derived from his psychology training—the so-called pique technique, in reverse. The premise was simple. Bombard the bouncer with so much information that he didn't actually process the dates on the ID. "How's it going, man?" he'd open his conversation. Before the bouncer could answer, he would launch into an unrelated demand. "Do you know where I can find a place to get cinnamon pita chips around here?" while handing the bouncer his real, under-twenty-one ID. "My girlfriend loves cinnamon pita chips for whatever reason, and I promised her I'd get some." The bouncer would hand back the ID. "Is there a store or bodega where I can get some?" Finally the bouncer had an opening. "Cinnamon pita chips? Nah, I can't help you." By that point, Tyler was inside: his ploy to increase the bouncer's cognitive load had succeeded. And it succeeded, in various guises, all the way through his college career. A rope that derives entirely from the argument's presentation can still be amazingly effective.

Derren Brown, one of Britain's most famous magicians, had a field day with the same approach on a 2007 visit to New York. Except in his case it was to make the point that, with the right cognitive load, people won't notice if you're paying with paper. Stop one: a fishmonger's. The goal: three filets of sole. "It's a fantastic place. Are you a local? How long have you lived in this area?" Brown warbles off as he selects his fish. Twenty years, the shopkeeper responds. "So how much was that—$18.55?" Brown repeats, before launching into a riff on the subways. "I was a bit intimidated by the subway system. I didn't want to go on it and then someone said, 'It's okay—take it, it's fine.'" Money exchanges hands. "Where'd you live before this? Staten Island? That's just over the water, isn't it? Well, thank you." Out he walks, fish in hand, leaving behind a stack of blank pieces of paper. The same gambit works like a charm in a jewelry store. One platinum ring for $4,500: out the door with blank notes in its wake. The only one who doesn't fall for Brown's wiles: a hot dog street cart vendor. He calls him out the moment that blank bill hits his hand. "Asshole," comes his parting comment as a sheepish Brown walks away.

Something else happens, too, when our minds feel bombarded from all sides. In situations where we're overtaxed, psychologist Katherine Milkman has found, we are more likely to make decisions that fit with what we *want* to do rather than what we *should* do. The two are often in conflict, and even without outside help, it can be difficult to choose the path of the "should." "Shoulds" like saving money. Exercising. Always reading the fine print. Controlling our temper. In the moment, the rational "should" recedes and the emotional "want" tends to dominate. "Want" to spend, not save; to eat, not deprive myself; to just get this thing, not worry about how it will turn out; to just let my anger out, not rein it in.

When psychologist Baba Shiv asked people to keep in mind a seven-digit number—a common way to mimic mental overload—and at the same time choose between eating a chocolate cake and a fruit salad, two thirds chose the cake. Less than half—41 percent—did so when recalling a two-digit number. The difference was especially marked for people who were impulsive to begin with. The con artist knows how to create the equivalent of seven digits from two, in effect making us less likely to choose the "right" thing and more likely to "indulge"—in this case, in the con. The rope is all about the presentation.

That approach, in fact, is precisely what Anthony Pratkanis, a social psychologist at the University of California at Santa Cruz, found when he looked at actual cons as they unfolded. Beginning in 1998, Pratkanis took charge of a team of researchers and experts devoted to understanding and fighting fraud—the Consumer Fraud Research Group. In 2004, he and his colleagues received some of the first direct evidence of the con process, told not from hearsay or memory but as it was happening: over six hundred tapes that had been collected undercover by twelve law enforcement agencies. They covered seven types of con: investment schemes, like the Ponzi; coin scams, where real money is exchanged for coins that aren't quite as they seem; recovery room scams, so called because they target existing victims with the promise of "recovering" their lost funds, for a fee, of course; credit card or identity theft; sweepstakes scams, based on false promises of assured winnings; lottery scams; and travel scams, where a great deal on an exotic vacation never materializes. Here was the con artist mid-sell, while his every word was taken down.

When Pratkanis analyzed the tapes, he found, as expected, that the first part of each con was taken up by the put-up: the first hallmark of the successful scammer, he found, was the extent to which the perpetrator customized his scripts to would-be marks. A con artist would begin a call with a gambit to establish a victim's psychological profile—the types of needs, wants, and pressure points detailed in the put-up. A lonely widow, say, would receive a very different approach from a devout housewife. Then came the play, perfectly tailored to establish the trust of the intended mark. One con artist professed to spend fifteen minutes of every call with a particularly religious victim in joint prayer. She wanted God's help in making her decisions. The grifter was only too happy to comply.

Only then did the con men begin to persuade, or rope, the mark—and when they did, they for the most part favored the "overwhelm them" strategy, hitting the victim as quickly, with as many approaches, as possible. Every persuasive tactic was there, but not in isolation. It was a kitchen-sink-like approach, and it was remarkably effective. As one con man put it, "My pitch put the victim in a haze of ether . . . I wanted to sell them as soon and as often as I could before the ether wore off."

As for the tactics that were used: there were all the expected culprits, neat as you'd like. Scarcity (get it while you can!). Credibility appeals (I'm from a legitimate institution). Phantom fixation (the promise of future wealth—that is, a fixation on a future phantom). And social consensus (everyone else is doing it!). Real scammers, it turns out, operate just as we would theoretically expect them to.

* * *

What was Matthew Brown after in his escapades? Despite the fact that Brown had ruined him financially and destroyed his reputation, Mervyn Barrett retains a philosophical view. "He clearly feels inadequate, and you have to question whether his father's absence from his life and his premature death have something to do with that," he said. "He simply does not feel able to be himself. He clearly believes that no one will like or love him for himself alone. It's tragic when you think about it." A bit later, he added, "I think he wanted to be loved. I thought he was absolutely adorable. He was charming and fun and flirtatious, but it was all an act." As it always is.

CHAPTER 5
THE TALE

The whole secret to our success is being able to con ourselves into believing that we're going to change the world—because statistically, we are unlikely to do it.

—Tom Peters, businessman

In late April 2014, the University of North Carolina at Chapel Hill did something almost unprecedented: it fired a tenured professor. He'd wanted to retire. No, the university told him. A peaceful resignation? No. He was, Chancellor Carol Folt reiterated, fired. "You committed misconduct of such a nature as to render you unfit to serve as a member of the faculty of this University," she wrote in her letter to the professor, informing him of the Faculty Hearing Committee's decision. The professor in question had held the Louis D. Rubin Jr. Distinguished Professor of Physics and Astronomy chair at the university. He had published 271 papers and racked up more than 7,000 citations, and had the support of nearly one hundred tenured faculty from across the country behind him. So what had happened to render such an absolute judgment?

Paul Frampton had first met Denise Milani online, on a popular dating site, Mate1.com. He was sixty-eight, divorced, and lonely, a theoretical particle physicist whose work had devoured much of his personal life. But he wanted more: children. A rewarding home life. Love. And there she was, his perfect mate.

Denise Milani was gorgeous. A Czech model who, at thirty-two, was forty years his junior, she had been crowned Miss Bikini World several years before. Why would someone like her fall for someone like him? In his mind, it made perfect sense. She liked older men, she told him, and photo shoots had grown draining over time. People always ogling her, seeing her as nothing more than a body; it could all be a bit much. She was ready for a change.

For eleven weeks, Frampton and Milani corresponded. Their messages, the *New York Times* reported in a lengthy profile, were frequent, intimate, and passionate. Often, she told him that she loved him. They'd never met, but sometimes love just happens. You have to embrace it when it comes, whatever guise it might take. He asked to speak on the phone. She put him off. Why not just go all the way and meet in person? She was going on a photo shoot to Bolivia, she told him. He could meet her there. At long last, they would be united.

Frampton was born in Kidderminster, Worcestershire. He came from a lower-middle-class family that doted on his academic accomplishments, heralding them throughout the neighborhood and encouraging him to do much the same. He graduated with a double first from Oxford's Brasenose College, received his DPhil in 1968, and from there made his way to Chicago for a postdoc with Yoichiro Nambu, a Japanese physicist who was a leader in his field. In 1985, he became a professor at UNC Chapel Hill, a post he would occupy for close to three decades.

It wasn't the first time Frampton had been lured to a foreign country by the prospect of new wedded bliss. After his divorce from his first wife, Anne-Marie, he'd flown to China to meet a twenty-something woman he'd met online. She had said she would marry him. But after their initial meeting, the marriage was called off; she allegedly backed out. It just wasn't meant to be, Frampton reasoned. Denise, though—now she just might be his soul mate.

On January 13, 2012, Frampton arrived in Bolivia. He checked into the Eva Palace Hotel and awaited word from his love. Alas, she had been called off to Brussels on another shoot. But in her haste, she'd forgotten a bag—these whirlwind engagements, they really mess with your head; one of the reasons she couldn't wait to leave it all behind and start a new life in Raleigh. Could he bring the bag with him on his way to see her? Frampton was only too happy to oblige. That evening, in the darkened streets outside the Eva Palace, a man approached him with a nondescript black cloth suitcase. Frampton took it inside, found it empty, promptly stuffed it full of dirty laundry, and went to bed.

The next day, he flew to Buenos Aires. From there, Denise promised, she'd send a ticket to Brussels. For the next thirty-six hours, Frampton sat in the airport, Ezeiza International, awaiting instructions for the next leg of his trip from his future wife. (He'd calculated the chance of their getting married, and found it to be a near certainty.) The promised airfare never came. Instead, a friend bought him a ticket home. Disappointed but sure that he and Denise would soon reunite in North Carolina, Frampton checked his bags for his new flight and sat down to await boarding. It was now January 23, ten days after he had arrived in Bolivia.

His name was called over the loudspeaker. He later told the *New York Times* that he was expecting it to be about an upgrade to first class. Who else, if not him? Distinguished scholars deserve distinguished treatment. Instead, it was a police summons. That nondescript suitcase was descriptive enough. Inside the lining: two kilograms of cocaine. After a brief questioning, Frampton was promptly arrested and taken to prison. How could Denise have betrayed him so? Maybe the man in the street had betrayed her, too, jealously stuffing the drugs inside to keep them from their perfect happiness. At this stage, anything was possible.

Frampton was placed in the Villa Devoto jail.

It took some time for the severity of the situation to dawn on him.

He and Denise were still practically engaged, as far as he was concerned. "Paul is a charming man, but he has the emotional maturity of a child," his ex-wife, who had always remained a close friend, remarked. He even laughed as footage of the model appeared on the television, alongside news of his current predicament. "The other prisoners burst into cheers and shouted 'bravo' and treated Paul like a hero when they saw her," Anne-Marie said. He also continued to think of himself as the true standout of the prison's inmates. Everyone else who was there with him, he said, was guilty. He, however, was the exception. "Some people will say they're innocent, but when I talk to them further, it becomes clear that they were somehow involved," he said. "I think people like me are less than one percent."

* * *

At this stage in the confidence game, the mark has been chosen, the play has begun, and the rope has been cast in a very specific way. We're no longer deciding between abstract, cold courses of action that we don't much care about. We're emotionally involved. We've already had the case persuasively laid out for us, in a way that makes it seem like a version of what we ourselves would most want, in the way we most want it. And so when the tale is told—that is, we're told how we, personally, will benefit—it's no longer really being told *to* us. We are the ones who are now doing the telling. The good confidence man has been working his way up to this very moment, the moment when "Too good to be true" turns into "Actually, this makes perfect sense": I am exceptional, and I deserve it. It's *not* too good to be true; it is exactly what I had coming to me. The chances may be less than 1 percent, but then again, I'm a less than 1 percent kind of guy.

One of our fundamental drives is the need for self-affirmation: we need to feel worthy, to feel needed, to feel like we matter. But how do we attain that reality? Throughout the first part of the twentieth century, psychologists saw the self as a realistic entity. They felt that it was somehow crucially important for us to have an accurate representation of our selves and our place in the world. In his seminal 1950 paper "Self-Actualizing People: A Study of Psychological Health," Abraham Maslow, a founder of the humanist school of psychology and famous for his eponymous hierarchy of needs, argued that the fully realized, or "self-actualized," human being must perceive reality "efficiently" and accept herself, with all her quirks and ways, no matter how much that reality might deviate from her ideal vision of herself. Only then will she reach her fullest potential as a person.

Eight years later, Marie Jahoda, one of the earliest pioneers of positive psychology and empirical research into the foundations of mental health—she was a founding director of NYU's Research Center for Human Relations—defined the healthy psyche as one that could perceive the self as it is in reality, without skewing it to fit a particular image or desire. Accurate perception of reality was one of the six criteria she put forward for full mental health. And in 1967, Harold Kelley, a psychologist who was one of the originators of attribution theory, or the theory of how we ascribe causes to different events, agued that humans were like naïve scientists, striving for truth through unbiased, systematic research. Accurate perceptions, he wrote, made us function at our most effective.

Starting in the 1970s, though, that emphasis on accuracy started to shift. As it turns out, not only are we not particularly accurate at how we see ourselves, but that accuracy would be self-defeating: brutal honesty likely wouldn't allow us to reach our goals. The self we most want to affirm isn't the self a stranger would describe if he were to simply observe us for an hour, or even a minute. Instead, we want to affirm our best, most deserving self: the skewed ideal, not the unvarnished original. And so we systematically represent ourselves and our reality in a way that favors our preferred version. In the things that truly matter to us, the core characteristics that we view as central to our identity, we exhibit the greatest bias of all. We all become, in a sense, Frampton's "less than one percent." Each one of us is exceptional in our own minds.

And exceptional individuals are not chumps. Exceptional individuals are in charge. They don't get conned. Which is precisely why the tale works as well as it does. We are ready—eager, even—to believe we will personally benefit, no matter what. Exceptional people, after all, have good things coming to them.

When Ghislaine de Védrines, a member of the old French aristocracy and the director of a successful Paris school, first met Thierry Tilly, a man who had almost, but not quite, completed a law degree and had few professional qualifications, she could hardly have known that within a few years he would come to dominate not only her life but that of her entire family, in an intricate plot that would rival any of Dan Brown's fictional creations. By the time Tilly and an accomplice were sentenced to prison for "despoiling" the de Védrines family and "depriving them of ten years of their lives," in November 2012, eleven family members, spanning three generations, had handed over $6 million in assets, the three-hundred-year-old family estate, and countless personal items to the conning duo. Tilly had managed to convince them all that they were protectors of an ancient secret—and that they were being hunted by Freemasons, Jews, and multiple other "sinister" forces. And so, little by little, they entrusted their entire lives to his keeping. At the end of it all, they would be living in England, working at menial jobs and subsisting on little more than biscuits and water, their wealth, education, and aristocratic pedigree a thing of the distant past.

When the story came to light, the public was shocked. How could an intelligent, educated, successful family fall, one after the other, for a story that more resembled fiction than fact? How could they, day by day and year by year, impoverish themselves for a vision with no proof, a fantastical creation that looked like it wouldn't pass muster in even the most accommodating of circumstances? Therein lies the power of the tale: it is a story of your exceptionalism.

Tilly was savvy. He didn't just create a fantastical story. He created a fantastical story in which the aristocratic family became guardians of a precious part of history. He knew they were proud of their heritage—the family's friends often said as much—and so used that heritage as an entry point into their trust. He, too, was noble, he told them, a descendant of the Habsburg line. And as such, he was privy to some inner workings of the nobility that might have passed them by. Their family name was the key to an ancient treasure—and the target of an elaborate Masonic plot. They weren't simply an aristocratic family. They were an exceptional aristocratic family with a legacy no one else could ever dream of, and that legacy was under threat of extinction. It was their duty—no, their calling—to protect it. To prove themselves exceptional and worthy of the trust history had placed in them.

It seems impossible to believe, but Tilly was persuasive to no end. A master brainwasher, a master manipulator with a master intuition of the way to weave the most convincing tale. "I heard someone on the radio talking about us and saying we were cultured, educated, intelligent and this should have armed us against Tilly," Christine de Védrines told the *Observer* in one of her first interviews after Tilly's sentence. "But it didn't. We were simply not armed to deal with someone who lied on such an extraordinary scale."

In June 2013, Tilly's appeal of his sentence came before the court. He had wanted clemency. It was too much to believe he had had the power over such discerning people. Surely they were to blame. The judge listened closely. And he did award him a new sentence: ten years, instead of the original eight.

It goes by many names. The Lake Wobegon effect. The better-than-average effect. Illusory superiority. Superiority bias. Whatever you call it, it means the same thing: we believe we are singular, whatever the circumstances. It could be that we're especially attractive and brilliant, in the case of Frampton, or that our family legacy is unique in history. Regardless of the specifics, we hold an unwavering commitment to the notion that we are special—and not just special, but more special than most anyone else.

Of one million students who took the SATs in 1976, 70 percent thought they were above average in leadership ability and 60 percent in athletic ability. Eighty-five percent of students put themselves above the average in their ability to get along with others—a full quarter going so far as to place themselves in the top 1 percent. In 1977, a full 95 percent of the faculty of the University of Nebraska thought they were better than average at teaching; over two thirds placed themselves in the top quarter. In a survey that behavioral economist Richard Thaler performed on his own students, he found that less than 5 percent of the class expected to do below average, and over half thought they would be among the top fifth of performers. And, of course, almost all of us are better-than-average drivers, far more skillful and less risky than the next guy. In one study, researchers asked drivers who had been hospitalized after a car accident—which over two thirds of them had caused—to rate their driving skills. They said they were better than average—and the ratings were identical to those of similar drivers who had no accident history.

Professionally, we are also all better than our colleagues at our jobs, despite any potential protests to the contrary. (We're not egotistical braggarts like Bill in the next cubicle over.) Would-be managers and actual executives think their future or current firms will overtake competitors quickly. In self-evaluative performance reports, we tend to rate ourselves above average on the skills that matter for our job. And where we are asked to list areas for improvement, we tend to focus on areas that matter only peripherally, if at all, to our main job. (As a writer, I might tell my editor that I need to improve on, say, my public speaking abilities—hence shielding my writing talents from self-critique. That's a hypothetical example, though. I'm an exceptional public speaker. One of the best, really.)

Consider it honestly. What do you say when an interviewer asks you to share your greatest weakness? Chances are, you have to think long and hard to prepare the answer in advance. That's not because you don't have weaknesses, but rather that you still think you're better than others, kinks and all. You're far more likely to say something like the dreaded "I'm a perfectionist"—a strength that cleverly (or so you think) masquerades as a weakness—than to admit an actual professional failing. And when something goes wrong at work? It's the boss. You're on a bad team. The markets went haywire. It's not your fault.

It's the exact reason the Gondorf brothers, Fred and Charles, originators of the original wire fraud and big store game, were able to tell the tale to so many victims for so long: each mark wanted to believe himself the lucky beneficiary of an exceptional tip; no one wanted to see himself as a dupe. Over fifteen years, the brothers would bring marks to what looked like a respectable bookmaking parlor, telling them that they had an in at the telegraph: a disgruntled employee who could tap the lines and get the race results seconds before they became public. (No such in actually existed.) So proficient were the Gondorfs at their craft that, for a time, the big store game was known as the "Gondorf game," with sucker after sucker remaining perfectly convinced that the brothers had given him access to an inner line, and that it was the savvy investment decision to go along—or risk regretting it forever. One victim, William O'Reilly, didn't even want to believe a police inspector who'd told him he'd been conned: "He had been loath to believe them other than the honest tipsters they seemed," the *New York Times* reported on June 5, 1915, when Fred Gondorf was finally apprehended. By that point, the duo had made off with approximately $15 million.

We are, as well, much better citizens than everyone else. Over the course of twenty studies, Jean-Paul Codol, a social and cognitive psychologist who studied the effects of superiority on behavior, found that people think they behave in ways that are more in line with good social norms than others. We recycle our trash more than the average person. We help others more than our fair share of the time. We turn off unused electrical devices and walk instead of drive more than the average guy. We donate more to charity than usual—sure, I might have given only ten dollars this year, but I bet the average person gave nothing at all.

Oh, and, frankly, we're just far better people than most. We're nicer.

We're more liked. In fact, on almost all desirable categories, we rate ourselves better than the majority of those around us. On almost all undesirable ones, we rate ourselves below average. In six studies, Cornell University psychologist David Dunning and his colleagues demonstrated that people overestimated how they fared on socially desirable characteristics, like accepting social norms, liking knowledge for its own sake, reading widely, being imaginative, and being willing to take a stand on important issues. At the same time, they dismissed any potentially negative tendencies, like aloofness and submissiveness. What's more, even among positive attributes, they rated traits that they had earlier described themselves as possessing as more desirable than those they hadn't considered.

When we're asked to select which words better match our personalities and key characteristics out of a list of possible contenders, we overwhelmingly select more positive than negative options. We are better at remembering the good things we've done than the bad, and the positive attributes we possess rather than the negative. Our memories for events, too, are skewed: we are worse at recalling the details of failures than successes. That's why the good con artist is able to plant false memories so easily: it was my idea all along. I was the one who thought to make the investment or place the bet. I was the one who decided to go to South America to meet my future wife. No one forced me to. It was all my idea. Of course it was. The tale almost tells itself: we *know* we'll personally profit. We are savvy like that.

As for when the events are actually happening, we tend to attribute the good aspects to our own prowess and dismiss the bad as environmental consequences—something known as the locus of control, or where we see control residing. In one study, people who worked in pairs were told that they'd collectively done below, at, or better than average. When the score was good, both members of the team individually accepted the credit. If the score was below average, each team member blamed the other. And when the score was average, the above-average performance was, without fail, assigned to oneself. We also tend to dismiss the skills we're not that good at as not particularly important in the first place—a tendency con artists love, as most people are not particularly skilled at things like financial management, nuanced statistical analysis, or whatever the con of the day happens to be.

When we compare ourselves to others, we tend to emerge ahead for a simple reason: we focus on our own most positive traits. And, no, we aren't just all wonderful people. In one experiment, a group of outside observers watched as students took part in a group interaction activity. They then rated each student on a number of dimensions, like warmth, assertiveness, and friendliness. Meanwhile, the students rated themselves on the same scales. Inevitably, the external judgment was significantly more negative than the students' own.

Most people are average by definition, although nobody wants to think themselves so. In Lake Wobegon, all the children have above-average IQ and above-average looks. They are all above-average athletes. In artistic pursuits, they excel—not that they're any slackers on mathematics. They're above average there, too. And while they may not be Mozarts—well, a few of them might; *I have a sneaking suspicion my child is one of those*—they're certainly still above average in their musicality. And as they grow up and disperse around the world, leaving Lake Wobegon behind, they remain persistently, universally the best.

The confidence artist will do everything in his power to bring our better-than-averageness front and center. Grifters appeal to our vanity, not about just anything, but about the things that are most central for us—after all, they've spent the entire put-up casing our psychology. How intelligent you are, Professor Frampton. Just what I want in a man. So intellectually stellar that my looks are a perfect complement. What a savvy investor you are, Mr. Koufax. What a great judge of character, Mr. Barrett. The tale centers on our singular talents.

And we believe it. Not because it's plausible—a supermodel is on a dating site and she targets *me*?—but because we want it to be. The more exceptional we see ourselves, the easier we may be to con. As one grifter—a player of the short con known as the *tat*, played with a crooked die that has fives on four sides and sixes on two and is subbed in at the last moment for an identical but fair one—told David Maurer, "A New Yorker is the best sucker that ever was born. He is made to order for anything. You can't knock him. He loves to be taken because he's wise." Because New Yorkers fancy themselves so cosmopolitan and sophisticated, they are the easiest fish to catch.

The tale tells itself: it's how so many con artists justify their actions to themselves, getting swept up in their own stories so strongly that they forget, at least for a moment, that they are lying. The belief in exceptionalism, after all, applies just as much to the con artist as to the mark: I am allowed to act like this because I am an exception to society's rules. In one of his escapades, our old friend Demara took on the role of Ben W. Jones, a proper Southern gentleman who had decided to turn his eye to crime, in the guise of a prison warden in Texas. The Texas penal system has never been known for its leniency, and its potential guards are no exception. Prior to being hired, Demara was asked to provide references from his three last employers, as well as personal references from eight different acquaintances. You'd think that such a burden of proof would scare him off. But no: Demara inhabited his role so completely that he sincerely believed it was rightfully his and everything would work out. And after it did work out (Demara himself helpfully supplied the majority of the references), his belief in his exceptionality— that even here, he would not be caught—is what led to his downfall. So invulnerable did he think himself that he handed one of the inmates the very *Time* magazine where he'd first been profiled, picture and all. The prisoner promptly reported the rise of the impostor, and B. W. Jones was quietly dismissed.

The same I'm-the-exception reasoning applies across all types of schemes. It's true of people from Jonah Lehrer to Lance Armstrong, Michael Shermer points out. "Lehrer's mea culpa was a bit like Lance's Oprah moment—not much of a moment at all." There is no sense of guilt, but rather a sense of entitlement followed by regret at getting caught. "People like Stephen Glass and Jonah Lehrer are just smaller, less harmful versions of Madoff, but still in the same category. Like Lance said—all cyclists dope in that circuit. I got caught, whatever—that's the only thing he's sorry about."

* * *

Prison did not agree with Frampton. He had a lung condition that left him coughing amidst the smoke-filled air, and an elevated blood pressure that the stress of cell life did little to alleviate. But, he said, although it was a "very dehumanizing experience to be in prison," adding that he and his fellow inmates were "treated like cattle," he was staying creative, using the computer at Villa Devoto to continue with his research and follow field developments, like the Higgs boson discovery.

He continued to post works in progress on ArXiv, an Internet repository of preprints in mathematical and scientific fields. Over the phone, he persisted in supervising two graduate students. He even found time to referee some journal articles.

In October 2012, Frampton was allowed to leave the prison and instead spend his days under house arrest at an old friend's home. His lawyers had convinced the judge that his lung condition was too dire, and ever-worsening, in the Villa Devoto cells.

UNC, meanwhile, suspended his $106,835 annual salary. Frampton appealed. Over eighty professors signed a letter in support of his case, calling it a threat to the tenure system everywhere. The suspension remained in place.

The trial lasted for three days. Piece by piece, the prosecution laid out the evidence against Frampton. And his situation began to seem ever more dire. There were the texts with "Denise." He worried about "sniffer dogs." He was taking care of the "special little suitcase." "In Bolivia this is worth nothing, in Europe it's worth millions," one text to his beloved read. Another: "Monday arrival changed. You must not tell the coca-goons." Another: "Need to know if your loyalty is with the bad guy-agent & bolivian friends—or good guy, your husband?" Frampton explained them away as jokes—in retrospect, jokes in poor taste, but in the moment, fairly hilarious, he said. Besides, he had been severely sleep deprived. Then there was the back-of-the-napkin calculation about the drugs' street value. But he'd only written it out *after* he'd been detained, he argued. He was prone to calculating everything in his line of sight.

On November 21, 2012, nearly a year after he was first arrested, Frampton was found guilty of drug smuggling and sentenced to fifty-six months in prison. "I am in a state of shock and disbelief," he told the *Raleigh News and Observer* a day after the sentence. "This is a gross miscarriage of justice. If this had happened in the U.S., a jury would have obviously acquitted me."

Soon after the sentence, he received further bad news: the provost of UNC at the time, Bruce Carney, told him that he was going to be fired. Frampton requested a hearing from the Faculty Hearing Committee.

* * *

Why did Frampton persist in believing that he deserved an exception? Why did he appear to be so seemingly oblivious to things that, to an outside observer, seem nothing short of overtly incriminating? Could he truly believe his actions would be taken for a practical joke—and then expect the university to bend its rules and let him keep his position? What seems like sheer stupidity at best, and more likely willful igno-rance, is actually quite understandable in the moment. The power of the tale isn't the strength of its logic; it's that at the point it's told, we're past being reasonable. The superiority bias doesn't just make us more vul-nerable to tales that seem rather tall to an objective eye. It colors how we then evaluate evidence and make decisions.

In one early study, Ziva Kunda, a psychologist who devoted her ca-reer to motivated cognition—the process by which our views of the world are motivated by our own self-serving, better-than-average bi-ases in perception—found that, when personal outcomes were at stake, people's ability to reason logically went out the window. When she had students read descriptions of individuals who were either like them or not, their predictions of their likelihood of personal and professional success vacillated strongly. The more similar the person, the less objectively the students weighed the evidence, skewing in favor of a positive outcome—a successful marriage, a stellar academic career—even when it didn't seem warranted. The students, concluded Kunda, were interpreting the world with what she termed the self-serving bias.

That bias, moreover, didn't just manifest itself in hypothetical predictions. In another study, Kunda gave students an article about the risks caffeine consumption posed for the development of fibrocystic disease in women. (She told them it was from the *New York Times* Science section but had really taken it from a medical journal, where its findings had later been disputed by other researchers.) She then asked them to rate their own risk for developing the disease within fifteen years and to evaluate how convincing they found the article itself. A curious pattern soon emerged. Women who were heavy or moderate caffeine drinkers themselves acknowledged that they might be at higher risk, but were also far more skeptical of the article. They wanted, they said, to see some additional evidence; to them, the study seemed shaky at best. Everyone else, however—men and women who drank little or no caffeine—found the work convincing.

So what does this suggest? Simply put, when it comes to ourselves—our traits, our lives, our decisions—our personal attachment overshadows our objective knowledge. We systematically misevaluate evidence based on our own characteristics, and if we're given evidence that something about us poses a threat, instead of thinking about how to change our own behavior, we call the evidence itself into question. To put this in conning terms, if I paint a picture of a perfect mark for you, and you recognize yourself in it, you are more likely to think I'm a poor researcher than yourself a good target. Nah, you'll say. Those aren't *actually* the things that get someone conned. I bet this girl didn't do any research and is just constructing this out of thin air.

Frampton's texts look beyond incriminating in retrospect. But at the time? "I am not generally the suspicious type," he told the *Telegraph*. "So although it seems very odd in retrospect, even to me, it all seemed perfectly plausible to me at the time. I really did not suspect anything was wrong until I was arrested." This is less far-fetched than it may at first appear. We don't see objectively. We see the version that best suits our own desires. And because the tale is all about telling us how we'll personally benefit, it is in many ways the easiest part of the confidence game to stomach. We're on the exact same page as the grifter: we deserve this.

When Frampton evaluated his chances of success with Milani, he looked past the fact that he had never met her, that she seemed to vanish every time he got close, that he was dealing with an unsavory character instead of his sweet bride-to-be. Instead, he focused on the texts of love and adoration, the photographs, the vision of the future. In that haze, any signs of drug-related banter were simply that: banter.

Because of our self-serving bias, we tend to rationalize after the fact, focusing on reasons that justify our choice rather than those that went against it. It's a kind of confirmation in reverse: we want to decide to do one thing over another—take the suitcase for Denise—and we want to think our decision good—this is what a good husband does—so we marshal evidence that makes our decision seem well reasoned even when we didn't actually use any of that evidence in reaching our choice to begin with. There's nothing wrong with this suitcase. It's perfectly normal to carry an empty bag for a girl you've never met, that was given to you by a man in a dark Bolivian street. She has always joked with me, so the cocaine texts are jokes—and I want her to like me and think that I'm "cool" and "with-it" and able to play along. The woman of my dreams would never actually hurt me. Oh, and if she *were* out to get me: I'm a brilliant man. I would know. And I know real love when I see it. Real love would not *actually* give me cocaine. So I'll text away. After all, there's no actual danger. And she will be even more fond of me when she sees how playful I can be. I may be older than she, but I can be hip and lighthearted with the best of them. I will pass her every test.

Paul Slovic's work centers on how we make decisions, especially under conditions of risk—that is, when we're taking some sort of gamble, be it financial or personal. He proposes that when we want to go for something, for whatever reason, the reasons in support of the choice will loom much heavier than those against it. If, however, we want to reject it, the negatives will suddenly seem much meatier. We focus on the rationale that retroactively justifies our choice rather than actually base our choice in the moment on the most pertinent rationale. If Frampton had found Denise unattractive, he would have likely evaluated her identical dating profile much more negatively. He might have even called it a scam, one of many so-called sweetheart cons that line the pages of dating services. He would have said he was basing his conclusion on the evidence, when he was doing no such thing. He would have already decided he didn't like her, and so would be looking for reasons to justify that conclusion.

Even after he'd been imprisoned, Frampton remained unconvinced of Denise's duplicity. For months, the *New York Times* reported, he held that they had both been set up. "When he first called me, he thought he'd be home in a couple of days," Anne-Marie Frampton told the *Telegraph*. It would all turn out to be a big misunderstanding, he assumed. She, however, was more alarmed. Not mincing words, she summed up the situation this way: "I realize that for anybody who doesn't know Paul, it must seem crazy that someone could both be so intelligent and so devoid of common sense . . . Even his friends would tell you that he's completely daft. He's a naïve fool—he is, really, an idiot savant." She concluded, "His stupidity could cost him his life."

One of the reasons that the tale is so powerful is that, despite the motivated reasoning that we engage in, we never realize we're doing it. We think we are being rational, even if we have no idea why we're really deciding to act that way. In "Telling More Than We Can Know," a seminal paper in the history of social and cognitive psychology, Richard Nisbett and Timothy Wilson showed that people's decisions are often influenced by minute factors outside their awareness—but tell them as much, and they rebel. Instead, they will give you a list of well-reasoned justifications for why they acted as they did. The real reasons, however, remain outside their knowledge. In fact, even when Nisbett and Wilson pinpointed the precise inspiration for a choice—in one case, someone casually walking by a curtain to make it swing back and forth in a manner that suggested the swing of a pendulum, prompting the subject herself to swing a rope as a pendulum to solve a puzzle—the vast majority of people persisted in a faulty interpretation. It *wasn't* the power of suggestion, they insisted. It was an insight they had reached after meticulous thought and evaluation of alternatives.

In the 1970s, a new kind of art started to gain traction in the New York art market: nineteenth-century American painting. The paintings had existed for over a century, to be sure, but they had never been particularly popular. Suddenly, they were all the rage. By the end of the decade, they were commanding prices in the hundreds of thousands, selling at auctions at the best houses and gracing the walls of the chicest art collectors. The art world is notoriously fickle. Trends come and go. Artists who sold for nothing become popular. Artists who were popular sell for nothing. But in this particular case, part of the market wasn't altogether accidental; it was, rather, the doing of an incredibly successful confidence man, and one who was master of the tale if ever there were.

Ken Perenyi feels no guilt about his past as a fine art forger who duped galleries, collectors, and auction houses alike into buying his faux-nineteenth-century creations. He's downright gleeful. "I loved what I did," he tells me one winter afternoon, sitting in his Florida living room. "It was a contest of wits. I regret nothing—well, the only regret I have in my life is that the FBI walked in on me." One of the things he's most proud of is his ability, with a few accomplices, to convince people that a Butterworth is exactly what they'd been wanting for their collection all along. "It was the ground floor of a rapidly developing new market," Perenyi recalls. No one knew quite what to expect, or quite what they wanted—so Perenyi was all too happy to plant the seeds of suggestion, and then create the perfect painting to make that suggestion a reality, all the while letting the gallery owner or collector think he was the one calling the shots, asking for the precise painting he wanted, playing Perenyi for the fool by extracting a good deal on the price. By 1978, the Sotheby's catalogue contained two full-page prints of Butterworth paintings that would be up for sale. Both were hot commodities—the nineteenth-century sweet spot. And both had been painted in the last few years by Perenyi.

Perenyi was never formally charged. After the FBI caught up with him, he was eventually let off with a warning not to do it again. (He now paints "legitimate forgeries," that is, the same fakes but without passing them off as such.) He doesn't know why, but he suspects it would be too embarrassing for the major auction houses: "The nineteenth-century American painting department is the jewel in the crown of Sotheby's. They started it. They developed it. It had never been tainted by any scandal," he speculates. "If my story came out, they would have to say, 'Oh, my god. How deep does this go? How many did we sell?'" Perenyi didn't just enter the market. He helped create it, convincing marks of what they'd always wanted, and then nicely filling that request—because don't they deserve the best?

Not only does our conviction of our own exceptionalism and superiority make us misinterpret events and mischaracterize decisions; it also hits us a second time long after the event in question. Because of this, we rewrite the past in a way that makes us less likely to learn from it, selectively recalling everything good and conveniently forgetting the bad. We rewrite positive events to make us more central in their unfolding. As for negative events, sometimes we don't even remember they occurred. In other words, someone like Frampton, after being released, will likely fail to learn something about the future from his behavior in the past.

Memory is a tricky thing, and once we've been taken once, it becomes all the more likely that we will fall for a con again. There is no better mark, many a con artist will tell you, than one who has already been duped. When Bluma Zeigarnik, a psychologist from the Gestalt school, discovered her eponymous effect—we remember interrupted tasks better than completed ones; our minds haven't quite given up working on them, and we feel a strong need to attain some sort of closure—she also noted a far less frequently cited exception. As it turns out, we don't remember all uninterrupted tasks equally. Zeigarnik found that for some people the effect was reversed. If a person felt she had performed poorly, the task was promptly dismissed from the mind. The privileged position reserved for unfinished business was no longer so privileged if the business in question wasn't a particularly good one. For a con artist, that tendency is pure gold: you will try your best to dismiss any moments when you acted like a dupe, rationalize them away as flukes. So next time the tale rolls around, you will once more think it's your lucky chance.

In 1943, Saul Rosenzweig, a psychologist at Clark University and Worcester State Hospital, further elaborated on Zeigarnik's exception. What if, he wondered, he took it one step further: an interrupted task that signaled personal failure, whereas simple completion would mean success? Rosenzweig recruited a group of students to complete a series of jigsaw puzzles—pictures of everyday objects like a boat, a house, or a bunch of grapes—each the size of a square foot. Each student would be allowed to complete only half of them; the other half, as in Zeigarnik's prior setups, would be interrupted. Not all the puzzle-completing sessions, however, transpired in quite the same way.

In one case, Rosenzweig had recruited students from the student employment office for a small hourly fee. These students were told that they'd be evaluating puzzles for a future study; what the researchers were interested in was figuring out how well the puzzles worked for the purposes of their research. "This is not in any way a test of your ability or anything else about you," each student was explicitly told. "Don't hurry or feel in any way constrained." And one more thing: "Do not be surprised if I interrupt you before you finish," he said. "I doubtless shall do so if I find out what I want to know about a particular puzzle before you finish."

The other group, however, was set up for an altogether different experience. This time, they weren't recruited by just anyone; they were the freshman advisees of the director of the clinic, and he personally invited each of them to take part. This time around, the puzzles were presented as a test of intelligence, "so that you may be compared with the other persons taking the test." Each puzzle would count the same in the final score, but different puzzles had different levels of difficulty, and so the time allowed to work on each would vary. "If you do not solve any puzzle in the allotted time, I shall naturally be obliged to stop you." And one more thing: "Your work will be interpreted as representing the full extent of your ability, so do your best." As if they weren't going to already.

Immediately after the last puzzle, each student in the study was asked to list as many of the puzzles as he could remember, in any order they occurred to him. When Rosenzweig compared the lists, he found exactly what he had hypothesized. The first group exhibited just the expected Zeigarnik effect: their recall of the interrupted puzzles far exceeded their recall of the completed ones. In the second group, however, the effect was completely reversed; now memory for the completed tasks surpassed recall of the interrupted ones by a long shot. It was, Rosenzweig concluded, a battle of excitement and pride: excitement at working on something in the first case, and pride at finishing in the second. (Despite the shaky ethical standards adhered to in social experimentation in 1943, the poor students in the second group were promptly debriefed to disclose the true nature of the study. They did not leave feeling that their intellect had taken a sudden plunge.)

Cons are often underreported because, to the end, the marks insist they haven't been conned at all. Our memory is selective. When we feel that something was a personal failure, we dismiss it rather than learn from it. And so, many marks decide that they were merely victims of circumstance; they had never been taken for a fool. In June 2014, a so-called suckers list of people who had fallen for multiple scams surfaced in England, It had been passed on from shady group to shady group, sold to willing bidders, until law enforcement had gotten hold of its contents. It was 160,000 names long. When authorities began contacting some of the individuals on the list, they were met with surprising resistance. I've never been scammed, the victims insisted. You must have the wrong information.

Of course, it's not particularly pleasant to dwell on moments that put our skills or personalities in question. We'd much rather pretend they never happened. And even if we do remember, we're much more likely to shift some of the blame in other directions. The test was rigged and unfair. It was her fault. He was being mean. She didn't give me a chance. He asked for it. I was tired/hungry/stressed/overwhelmed/thirsty/bored/worried/preoccupied/unlucky. Unfortunately, by this kind of dismissal, we fail to learn what we could have done differently—and in the case of the con, we fail to properly assess our risk of getting, well, conned. We fall for the tale because we want to believe its promise of personal gain—and don't much feel like recalling any reasons why that promise may be more smoke and mirrors than anything else.

In fact, Baruch Fischhoff, a social psychologist at Carnegie Mellon who studies how we make decisions, even has a name for instances of past misdirection: the knew-it-all-along effect or, as it's more commonly known, hindsight bias. I knew it was a scam the whole time. So the fact that I don't think that *this* scheme is a scam now speaks all the more highly for its integrity. The confidence man need not even convince us by this point. We're quite good at getting over that hurdle ourselves.

We don't see what the evidence says we should see. We see what we expect to see. As Princeton University psychologist Susan Fiske puts it,

"Instead of a naïve scientist entering the environment in search of the truth, we find the rather unflattering picture of a charlatan trying to make the data come out in a manner most advantageous to his or her already-held theories." That charlatan isn't the con artist who's out there. That charlatan is us conning ourselves.

* * *

Alas, our belief in our own superiority persists in the most unfortunate, and ironic, of places: in our assessment of the extent to which we believe in our own superiority. Of course, we realize that some things are simply too good to be true, there's no such thing as a free lunch, and any number of other clichés we bandy about for just this purpose. We understand this in general. And yet. The illusion of unique invulnerability to all those biases is a tough one to break. We simply never think that, in any specific instance, it applies to us. In 1986, Linda Perloff and Barbara Fetzer, psychologists at the University of Illinois at Chicago, published the results of a series of studies aimed at testing how our beliefs in our own personal vulnerability may differ from our beliefs about vulnerability more broadly. Over and over, they found, people tended to underestimate the extent to which they were susceptible to any bad turn in life: their risks were reliably lower than the risk of the "average" person, at least according to their own estimate.

When Perloff and Fetzer tried to get their subjects to adjust their estimates by changing the comparison point from "average" to someone they knew—say, a friend or family member—in the hopes of making the risks seem more concrete, the attempt unexpectedly backfired. It didn't make them feel more vulnerable at all; instead, it made them think that their friends and family were similarly less vulnerable. Sure, it could happen in general, but it won't happen to me or my friends and family. In other words, instead of adjusting their own risk, their overconfidence widened to enfold the others in their lives. Whenever we have an opening to do so, the authors concluded, we will compare downward—that is, we will place ourselves and those closest to us at lower risk than the abstract mass of others, whether that risk is for a heart attack or a crime.

This is true of just about every better-than-average effect. When it comes to our friends, our relatives, our coworkers, even complete strangers, we tend to be fairly good at spotting biases even as we miss them completely in ourselves. In one set of studies, Stanford University students and random travelers at the San Francisco airport were shown to be capable of evaluating the susceptibility of the average American or their fellow students to a range of subjective evaluations—but when it came to themselves, they remained completely blind. Completely and, it seemed, almost willfully—much like Frampton or de Védrines. Even when the experimenters described the bias and pointed out that people tended to weigh themselves more positively on positive attributes and less than average on negative ones, the overwhelming majority insisted their initial rating was accurate—and 13 percent went even further, to say they'd been too modest. Others see the world through a prism of subjectivity; my view, however, is accurate. I'm fairly good at being objective, if I may say so myself.

In the summer of 2014, I had the chance to speak to a rather unusual family: one in which two grown siblings had, completely independently, gotten conned, trapped in schemes that had little to do with each other. Dave was the victim of an unfortunate ticket exchange on Craigslist. Unable to go to a show, he posted an ad looking to exchange his tickets for another evening. A few days later, he received a reply: Ashley was willing to exchange, but she unfortunately had e-tickets. (Trying to protect himself from getting scammed, he had asked for paper tickets only.) Dave was a bit worried, but no one else had offered to trade, and he really wanted to go to the show. And Ashley seemed legitimate. A quick Google search revealed a LinkedIn profile and a valid-seeming, upstanding occupation. They went ahead with the switch. Everything seemed good, up until the moment he and his girlfriend got to the show: their e-tickets had already been scanned, the guard informed them. They had been the victims of a well-known ticket fraud, where one person legitimately buys electronic tickets but then proceeds to sell them to multiple buyers.

Meanwhile, on the other coast, Dave's sister Debbie found herself out some fifty dollars after buying bogus magazine subscriptions from a man who'd come to her door with a tale of trial and redemption: he had been in prison and was now working his way toward a better life. She hadn't wanted to buy a subscription—she didn't need any more magazines—but his story, and his mention of the tax deduction she'd receive, swayed her. She had pledged to be more charitable, and here was a good deed that would make her a kinder person. When she later checked up on the organization, its Web site had disappeared. The magazines, of course, never arrived.

Both fairly innocuous, small-stakes cons. Except for one thing: the siblings could spot the scam and the gullibility a mile away when it came to each other's stories. When it came to themselves, though, they were certain, in the moment, that they were the exception. Sure, Dave knew all about Craigslist scams. But he really wanted to go to the show, and the chances of him, personally, falling for a scam were slim to none; he had been careful. Debbie, however, would never buy e-tickets from a stranger—how silly could you be? Sure, Debbie knew that there were many impostors claiming false hardship for easy cash, but she wanted to donate more to worthy causes, and his story seemed on the level. The chances of her, personally, falling for someone who *wasn't* sincere were slim to none. Dave, however, would have done his due diligence before he parted with any cash—how trusting could you be? When it comes to you, I see clearly. When it comes to myself, I see what I want.

Marie Jahoda—Mitzy, as she was known—had a nose for prejudice. She had to. A Jew born in Vienna in the winter of 1907, she found herself in prison in 1936—not yet for her Jewishness (Austria was yet to be annexed by Hitler) but for her political views as a social democrat. She managed to escape and make her way to London. Her first book, however, which had expounded on her research to date, was rounded up and most of its copies summarily burned. This time, because its author was Jewish.

When she made it to the United States and was teaching at NYU, she focused not only on mental health but also on social prejudice. And there she came to a very different conclusion from her earlier view that an accurate perception of reality was a prerequisite of solid mental health. "People with prejudices seldom like to admit it," she wrote in one study of opinion researchers who had themselves used biased questions to detect bias in others. What she then failed to deduce was that it wasn't just anti-Semitism that they didn't like to admit. If you can't see one shortcoming, chances are you don't accurately see any, or at least many, of them. If you tell someone they are prejudiced, they will laugh in your face and give you all the reasons why they aren't. If you tell people they aren't superior in all the ways they think themselves to be—that they aren't objective, aren't exceptional, and actually do exhibit many biases in their worldview—they will promptly dismiss what you've said.

Or, to put it in other words, after reading this chapter, you will be intrigued by all of these forays with exceptionalism. But you will remain convinced that you, personally, have already properly taken them into consideration. Your present understanding of yourself and of the world around you is now fairly objective. Everyone else, however, is a potential sucker.

Cons work so widely because, in a sense, we *want* them to. We want to believe the tale. And we want to believe things that are too good to be true more than anything. Cons aren't about money or about love. They are about our beliefs. We are savvy investors. We are discerning with our love interests. We have a stellar reputation. We are, fundamentally, people to whom good things happen with good reason. We live in a world full of wonder—not a world of uncertainty and negativity. We live in a world where good things happen to those who wait. The teller of the tale has us hooked.

In August 1835, Sir John Herschel, son of the astronomer Sir William Herschel, made a remarkable discovery. Using the latest in telescoping technology, he had been able to view the moon in unprecedented detail. And what a view it was. Beaches of white sand abutting lakes and oceans of blue. Buffalo-like beasts wandering through lush forests over a rocky marbled path. There was, too, something disturbingly like a unicorn, with a single horn and a goat- or horse-like appearance, but blue in color. And a beaver-like animal that walked as humans did, on two feet. And best of all, there were what seemed to be a species of human: batmen, with semitransparent wings sprouting from their backs. Their lives, it seemed, were much like ours. Herschel had seen some bathing in the waters, shaking out their wings "as ducks do theirs." He'd seen others sharing a meal—fruit from the wondrous trees. They seemed to be altogether happy, prosperous, and peaceful. Or so wrote Richard Adams Locke for the *New York Sun*, as he reported on Herschel's incredible findings.

And incredible they were, in every sense of the word. The whole thing had been an elaborate hoax, planned over multiple installments to goad credulous readers. It worked better than expected. Not only did the news consumers fall for it completely, but so did the rest of the media. According to the *New York Times*, the story was "probable and plausible." At Yale, students and professors alike discussed the news. And when it was revealed for what it was—a hoax—many refused to believe it. It wasn't a hoax. It was a conspiracy and cover-up. The men existed, but when word got out, the government had moved to cover it up. It's an all too familiar course of events: spectacular news, spectacularly covered, spectacularly accepted. At least in this case, it was an in-good-fun con without any real victims or repercussions. But the persistence with which readers clung to it despite its obvious outlandishness underscores the power that the aptly told tale has over our minds. Our world is an incredible place where incredible things happen.

"The secret of rulership," wrote George Orwell, "is to combine a belief in one's own infallibility with the power to learn from past mistakes." The con artist has learned that; the rest of us would do well to catch up.

———

Paul Frampton, in the end, was exceptional. In January 2015, two years and six months before his sentence would have been up, he was allowed to leave Buenos Aires for London—a luxury not afforded to many prisoners. He's currently seeking another academic appointment, if you happen to hear of anything.

CHAPTER 6
THE CONVINCER

I was the realization of their dreams. The idol. The hero. The master and arbiter of their lives.

—CHARLES PONZI

In March 1889, William Franklin Miller asked a group of friends for an investment of ten dollars. Affable and boyish looking, coming in at just under five and a half feet, with a touch of gravitas lent him by a dark mustache that framed a nose broken in some other life, Miller was a prominent member of the community—a congregant of the Tompkins Avenue Congregational Church, a leading church in Brooklyn, and past president of its charitable arm, the Christian Endeavor Society. It was there that he had met the three young men—Hartman, Bergstrom, and Bragge, the youngest just turned seventeen, the oldest twenty—to whom he now posed his plan. If they each gave him a tenner, he told them conspiratorially, he would make them a promise. Each week, they would receive a full 10 percent return on their stake. They huddled closer; 10 percent seemed an awfully large amount.

Miller spoke in low tones. He had, he told the men, an in at the New York Stock Exchange. His "inside information" would allow him to not only guarantee the promised 10 percent return, but also to protect the initial investment through a mysterious "surplus." Later, he would elaborate that his "inside tips" were "from the fountainhead of speculative interests, and never fail us." And any time they wanted to stop, well, all he needed was a week's notice and they would receive all the money they'd placed with him, safe and sound. The men were intrigued. It seemed a bit too good to be true, yes, but then again, Miller was a trusted man—at twenty-two, he had far more worldly experience than they. And he *had* been in the markets before. (What he failed to mention was that it was as an office boy for Jacob A. Cantor, a job that paid him five dollars a week.) He even had that office, on the corner of Marcy and Park, just above the Heber & Brandt store. Clearly, he could afford it. Who knows. Maybe he really did have an edge. They withdrew to think it over.

On March 16, Oscar Bergstrom arrived at 144 Floyd Street, Miller's new headquarters. Up a flight of stairs, into a room furnished sparsely but well. It was a former bedroom, in the front hall. A desk, strewn with important-looking financial papers. A small table, a handful of chairs. And, of course, a large, prominent safe. This was, after all, a place that saw real money. Miller greeted him alone. He was being careful with his funds and wasn't going to throw money away with needless overhead; this was a man to be trusted to be frugal and measured in his approach to your hard-earned currency. He would not frivolously waste it on things like an assistant.

Ten dollars in hand, Bergstrom approached the desk. With great care, Miller took the money. It would be safe with him, he assured the slightly anxious young man. In return, he gave him a small strip of paper. The money was received, it said, for "speculation in stocks. The principal guarantied against loss. Dividends weekly from $1 upwards till principal is withdrawn." Miller had his first client.

And he was true to his word. Each week through early April, Bergstrom made the trip to Floyd Street, and each week, as promised, he received his 10 percent return. Impressed, Bergstrom gave Miller a further ten dollars.

By August, business picking up, Miller hired a few extra hands: John and Louis Miller and Charles Scherer, fourteen-year-old boys. He'd been a clerk himself and now he was training others. By October, he'd taken over the entire house—and the house's owner, Gus Brandt, had become an investor. Twenty dollars in April. One hundred in June. Ten more in August. Another fifty to follow in November.

The clients grew. Now, Miller wasn't handing out just any stray slips. He had letterhead. "An Investment of $10.00 will Net You a Profit of $52.00 a Year," it read. And below, "William F. Miller, Mgr. Franklin Syndicate, Bankers and Brokers. Stock Exchange, daily, from 10 a.m. to 3 p.m." A picture of Ben Franklin adorned the page, with his wisdom imprinted below. "The way to wealth is as plain as the road to market." By the late fall, his certificates were being professionally engraved, and he'd added "Investments, Stocks, Bonds, Wheat, Cotton" to his qualifications.

In October, his investments a runaway success, Miller decided to incorporate. Beginning December 2, he wrote his investors, his company would be officially known as the Franklin Syndicate and would be launched with an initial capital of $1 million. It was as much for their benefit and protection as his, he said. They could turn in their investment slips for stock certificates—and all who helped him would, in turn, be helping themselves. By March 1, 1900, he predicted, shares would be selling for between $400 and $500 each. Together, they would grow rich. Oh, and from now on, fifty dollars was the minimum deposit. "In conclusion I desire to congratulate all those who have been depositors in the Franklin Syndicate on the wonderful success the Franklin has had under my management."

The incorporation was taking a bit longer than expected—unforeseen obstacles, you understand. Some of the investors began to express their impatience, but in short order they were reminded that "My intention is to make the Franklin Syndicate one of the largest and strongest syndicates operating on Wall Street, which will enable us to manipulate stocks, putting them up or down as we desire, and which will make our profits five times more than they are now." And as always, they were completely, utterly, totally guaranteed against any losses. "Our business is honest, safe, legitimate, and profitable." To the doubters, he had only one thing to say: "This may look almost impossible to you, but you know there must be a way where one can double their money in a short time, or else there would be no Jay Gould, Vanderbilt, or Flower Syndicate, and other millionaires and syndicates who made their fortune in Wall Street starting with almost nothing." He was right, of course—what about them?

The impatient investors calmed themselves. Convinced of his sincerity, many handed over more cash.

The Franklin Syndicate kept growing. Fueled by word of mouth, fabulous returns to new investors, and hundreds of ads in papers throughout the country—Miller spent upwards of $32,000 making sure the ads went out regularly, interspersing self-placed media coverage with headlines that wouldn't be out of place in any modern click-bait forum, like "Wall Street Astonished. William F. Miller's Franklin Syndicate a Big Winner . . . Financial Operations Eclipsed by a New Wizard"—the business flourished. By November, Franklin had over twelve thousand subscribers, and each day between $20,000 and $63,000 was deposited into his account by new eagers.

The lines stretched down the stairs, out the door, serpentining around Floyd Street. You could see the lucky ones who'd already gotten their dividends descending down the stairs, satisfied smiles on their faces. And you would jostle just a bit closer for your own chance. One crisp winter morning, the line had grown so thick that the stoop of 144 Floyd collapsed.

The office, too, had turned sleek and professional. Two rolltop desks, a large table with impressive-looking circulars professing the Franklin Syndicate's prowess, a wooden railing down the middle to separate the deposits from the returns. To the right, a small booth with a glass window through which to pay investors their dividends. Piles of bills, gold and silver coin lining the shelves, for all to see. It made a pretty picture.

By November 24, Miller's deposits closed in on $1.2 million.

* * *

In 1988, Shelley Taylor, a psychologist at the University of California at Los Angeles, proposed that humans have a strong bias toward misperceiving the world. We don't just think ourselves exceptional. We predict our lives will always go well—better than before, even. We are programmed, in a sense, to think a bit too positively about how things will turn out—even the things we have no actual control over. It's a tendency known as the positivity bias or optimistic bias, and it is a version of our belief in our own exceptionalism, but one that centers on our life outcomes: how we'll fare, how things will go for us, the extent to which we control our environment and the events that transpire therein. Even pessimists experience it; it's optimism not about the world or people in general, but about yourself. The most sour skeptic still thinks he will come out on top.

One of the key elements of the convincer, the next stage of the confidence game, is that it is, well, convincing: the convincer makes it seem like you're winning and everything is going according to plan. You're getting money on your investment. Your wrinkles are disappearing and your weight dropping. That doctor really seems to know what he's doing. That wine really is exceptional, and that painting exquisite. You sure know how to find the elusive deal. The horse you bet on, both literal and figurative, is coming in a winner.

The tale made us fully aware of our own exceptional nature: we are good, and we deserve great things. And lo and behold, precisely that now seems to transpire; we are indeed justified in putting our initial trust in the game. That 10 percent return is coming in strong, just as promised. No self-respecting con artist is complete fluff. There needs to be something real there to anchor the whole thing. Just for a moment, the grifter needs his mark to feel as if he is holding a winning ticket.

Glafira Rosales, the master art fraud perpetrator, had some legitimate paintings in the midst of the dozens of fakes she dumped on the market. Rudy Kurniawan and Hardy Rodenstock, the wine forgers par excellence (the first convicted, the second still alleged), threw lavish dinners where the fine wines they served were quite real. All Ponzi schemes, of course, work until they don't. And so on.

We are terrible at predicting the future. It's unpredictable by definition, true, but that doesn't keep us from thinking it isn't. When things are going well, we tend to think they will continue doing so—and, quite possibly, even improve. We tend to think, as Taylor puts it, that "the present is better than the past and that the future will be even better." When Americans were surveyed about their thoughts on the future, most expressed confidence in continued improvement. In one study, when college students were asked to list future possibilities for their lives and careers, the positive outcomes outnumbered the negative four to one. "In effect, most people seem to be saying, 'The future will be great, especially for me,'" Taylor explains.

When it comes to our own lives, we tend to be especially certain that good things are coming our way, and bad things will avoid us—especially if an event is hard to forecast with certainty. We become unrealistically optimistic about events that have to do with us—I'll definitely be able to get this book done before the deadline; nothing stands in my way—and we become unrealistically optimistic that we'll avoid any obstacles. Really? *Nothing* will stand in my way?

In 1990, psychologist Robert Vallone and his colleagues asked students to make forty-one predictions about themselves in the coming semester. The list involved things like joining a fraternity or sorority, visiting San Francisco, playing a sport, voting in the November election, dropping courses, studying more than two hours a day, having a higher GPA in certain subjects, having a steady boyfriend or girlfriend, calling their parents at least five times, changing career goals, changing political affiliation, making post-graduation school or job plans, feeling homesick, continuing in a bad relationship, and so on. Some of the predictions were positive; others, slightly more negative. At the end of the semester, the researchers once more caught up with the students to see how it had all played out.

On twenty-nine of the predictions, or 70 percent, the students had been overconfident by at least 10 percent—that is, there was a 10 percent or more difference between what actually happened and what they had predicted would happen. On another eight items, the gap was over 20 percent. And the confidence error was always in the students' favor: they were much more likely to think positive events would take place and that they would manage to avoid negative ones than was actually the case. For instance, they had predicted with almost full confidence—80 to 85 percent—that they would remain with a long-distance love through the end of the semester. Their actual accuracy: a coin toss, or worse.

Ralph Raines, Jr., was the heir to a large tree farm in Gaston, Oregon—a family fortune valued at $15.5 million. In 2004, when he was fifty-seven, the confirmed bachelor decided to visit a fortune-teller in nearby Bend, Rachel Lee of Lee's Psychic Shop. He liked what he heard—so much so that for the next two years, he made regular visits to Lee's storefront for further consultations. He felt he could trust this woman. She had suffered a great deal in her life—she'd lost a husband to cancer—and she seemed honest and earnest. When Raines's father suffered a stroke, in October 2006, he had the perfect idea: he would hire Lee as his full-time health worker. She had, after all, taken care of her husband for years. Lee started work at almost $9,000 a month. Her boyfriend, Blancey, was hired to fix up the property. By the time Raines Senior died, his son had given Lee power of attorney. Lee started buying real estate—psychic shops in several towns, a house. It would be, she told Raines, a perfect way to "realize investment gains." She had previously worked in real estate, she told him. He trusted her advice implicitly.

And then, in 2007, she upped the stakes: she introduced Raines to her teenage daughter, Porsha. Except, to Raines, she was Mary Marks, a complete stranger. For the role, she donned a blond wig—his preferred hair color—affected a British accent, and arranged a chance encounter.

Raines remembers it well. October 21, 2007. He had been at a tree farm convention and had asked Lee to pick him up from the airport. She'd told him to meet her in the smoking area. And there, on one of the chairs, was a striking blond who addressed him by name. She sometimes got vibes from people, she explained, and she was getting a strong psychic reading from him. Personal facts, even his birth date: the information just seemed to flow from her psychic channels. Raines was completely smitten. He asked her name. Mary Marks, she said, a part-time bookkeeper. They made plans to meet for coffee.

Their friendship soon deepened. In time, Marks-née-Lee confided a secret. She was illegal, and would soon be deported. Raines agreed to marry her, and she proceeded to provide him with legal papers to sign—all fake, it would turn out. By November 2010, Raines's house had been transferred into Marks's name.

And then came the kicker. Marks wanted a child. Would Raines agree to in vitro fertilization? He would. He remembers her bringing him a large pot with dried ice inside and instructing him to place his "donation" inside. As far as Raines was concerned, she would give the sperm to a California clinic for the procedure. Marks, in the meantime, had other plans. She really was pregnant—by another man. When the boy was born—she named him Giorgio Armani—she insisted he was Raines's son. Rachel Lee would serve as his nanny.

In 2012, Marks asked for a second donation. Raines happily obliged. He was proud of his growing family and eager to welcome a new arrival. This time, though, Marks faked her pregnancy, wearing padding to simulate the baby bump around the time it was expected to show. And then she called with the devastating news. Gloria Jean—Raines had already picked out a name—was no more. She had had a miscarriage. Raines was devastated.

But why the fake second child? Rachel Lee needed just a bit more time. By the time of the "miscarriage," she had concluded the liquidation of Raines's property, draining the once prosperous farm of all resources.

On February 19, 2015, the sixty-seven-year-old Raines took the stand. He appeared baffled and distraught, not quite comprehending what had happened. "I thought I was married to a person named Mary Marks. I don't know where she's at," he told the court. And he wasn't quite ready to believe what people were telling him. "For reasons of my own, I'm just going to wear the ring." Lee was sentenced to eight years and four months in prison. Her daughter, Porsha, the twenty-five-year-old Raines had known as Mary Marks, pleaded guilty to co-conspiracy. Her sentence: two years and ten months. Blancey Lee would serve two years.

It wasn't at the trial alone that Raines acted as if he were in denial. In the decade that he had become enmeshed with the Lees, he had heard warnings of disaster. At a local event that he attended with Rachel Lee, several friends voiced their skepticism. And when he attended his high school reunion with Mary in 2010, his cousin Karin Fenimore expressed shock. She had no idea he was married. Before, she later told prosecutors, he had been in the habit of stopping by her house every week or two for a friendly chat. But the interactions had gradually decreased. She felt he was being isolated from his support network, and that couldn't have been good. There were, as well, the more concrete signs. His child, for one, looked nothing like him. Raines chose to ignore it all. He could have gotten out, but things seemed to be going so well. And so he did what was easier: kept right on believing. It wasn't until bank officials expressed concern about some of the financial transactions being conducted in his name that the police became involved. Had it been up to Raines, he might have kept believing until the end. It would have been a simpler, happier reality. And that basic desire for a happier, simpler reality is at the center of the convincer's success.

As information from our environment comes in, we home in on the positive and tend to isolate and filter out the negative. That selective perception makes us more empathetic, happier, better able to care for others, more productive, and more creative. When we receive negative feedback, we can (usually) deal with it, because, we rationalize, it's not really our fault. We are good at what we do; it's just that, this time, things went a bit awry. And even if we don't rationalize, it's easier to take the bad when you think yourself capable. Yes, I messed up, but I'll be able to make it work.

But that selective filter also makes us far more likely to attribute Miller's 10 percent returns not to something strange, but rather to our own acumen in choosing investments. Since it is the result of our good judgment, it will continue indefinitely rather than come to an end the moment the environment changes. If we're expecting something to work, we will see evidence for its working even in ambiguous circumstances. Are Miller's returns the result of astonishingly savvy investments—or are they coming from somewhere else? If the money is coming in as promised, we don't dig too deeply into why; we just assume he's a brilliant investor. Isn't that why we invested with him?

Take the stock market. We have reams and reams of data on its performance over time—charts, trends, cycles of boom and bust, expected returns, and the like. But when things are going well, it's tough to convince even the savviest of investors that they may soon enough turn south. When, during the 1998 bull market, investors were asked to predict their annual return for the following year, they guessed an equally bullish 14 percent. Over the next ten years, they grew even more optimistic, estimating 17.4 percent average annual returns—even though the long-term base for U.S. stocks is between 10 and 11 percent, a fact of which, presumably, traders and investment professionals are well aware.

It's one of the reasons that, time and again, bubbles will swell—in the markets on the whole, or in certain sectors—and then, just as fabulously, burst. Everyone realizes, in theory, that the downturn will happen. In practice, though, it never seems to be quite the moment for it. After all, things are going so well. The convincer is precisely that: wholly convincing. Why quit while you're ahead, if you are certain you'll remain ahead in the future?

The ebullient optimism that doesn't see its own demise isn't a function of modern markets, either; it's far older and more pervasive than that. One of the most famous bubbles in history was the great Dutch tulip mania—*tulpenwoede*—of the early seventeenth century. So desired were the flowers, and so high their price, that in the 1630s a sailor was jailed for mistaking one for an onion and eating it. While the story is likely apocryphal, the sentiment is not. At the bubble's peak in 1637, some bulbs had increased in price twentyfold in a three-month period. Semper Augustus, considered particularly desirable, cost about a thousand guilders in the 1620s. In the weeks before the crash, it sold for the cost of a luxury house in Amsterdam: 5,500 guilders. In February, the market crashed. Such is the nature of speculation. And such is the nature of our endless optimism. If we're not expecting it, it won't happen, and if we are, it will. The convincer needs no further evidence than the momentary success it seems to provide.

Though few people would think of bubbles as confidence schemes, the line between bubble and con can be a very fine one: they operate on many of the same principles, occur for many of the same reasons, and are so incredibly persistent, despite past evidence, based on much the same rationale. And sometimes it can be incredibly difficult to tell the one from the other. One man's bubble may well be another man's con.

In 1714, John Law arrived in Paris. Tall and elegant, with a passion reserved in equal parts for women and gambling, Law soon installed himself at Place Louis-le-Grand—a glamorous square in the heart of the 1st arrondissement that boasted the highest echelons of society as residents. Today, it's better known as the Place Vendôme, home of the Ritz-Carlton and the Hotel de Vendôme. Soon after his arrival, Law received an appointment at the Bank of Amsterdam. He had been a noted economist back in Scotland, trained by his banker father, and had a way of making himself liked in the highest of places.

In due course, Law was gambling alongside the likes of the Duke of Orleans, France's future regent. The duke took to the colorful Scotsman. Here was a man, he thought, who knew how to be serious with the best of them, but didn't take himself too seriously. He had hobnobbed with the most learned minds of Europe, from Amsterdam to Venice, but he knew how to be the perfect guest and most charming conversant.

At the time, France was mired in debt. Louis XIV had racked up some two billion livres, in the currency of the time, to pay for his wars and his whims. Precious metal was scarce, and new coins hard to come by. When the king died, leaving a five-year-old heir, the duke assumed the regency. Overwhelmed by the nation's financial quagmire, the duke asked his old financial wizard of a friend for advice.

Law soon assumed control of the Banque Générale, and was shortly thereafter appointed controller-general of the country. He had a plan. For years, he'd been advocating a system of central banking, in which paper currency, backed by a reserve of gold and silver, would serve as the medium of exchange, thus making the financial system more elastic. Today, that seems like business as usual; it's how we operate, at least in theory. Back then, it was quite revolutionary. There was no paper money in circulation. Everything was transacted in precious metal. Paper, though, would increase the monetary supply and, Law hoped, stimulate trade and commerce, getting France out of its slump. Law established a trading company, the Mississippi Company, that would engage in exchange with the colonies. People could buy shares and raise money, the company would trade for important goods and precious metals, and the economy would get a much-needed stimulus.

What happened next has been debated ever since. One thing is certain: the shares in the Mississippi Company collapsed in 1720, after rising to an all-time high the year prior. A few discerning investors saw that more and more shares were being issued, and more and more money printed, with little to show for it: it was a system feeding on itself. And so some—notably two prominent princes—decided to cash out. Others soon followed suit: shares were worth a great deal, so why not collect the hard cash now? Quickly, Law printed some 1.5 million livres to cover the conversions—but soon people wanted coin, not paper bills. The Banque Royale, as it was subsequently called, collapsed under the demand. Law himself was forced to flee the country, dressed as a beggar to avoid capture. He died in Vienna eight years later, of pneumonia, poor and friendless.

Some people see John Law as a master con man, someone who brought France to the verge of financial collapse by selling worthless stock in a sham trading company. As one rhyme of the time goes:

My shares which on Monday I bought
Were worth millions on Tuesday, I thought.
So on Wednesday I chose my abode;
In my carriage on Thursday I rode;
To the ballroom on Friday I went;
To the workhouse next day I was sent.

Or as one nobleman put it, "Thus ends the system of paper money, which has enriched a thousand beggars and impoverished a hundred thousand men." As late as 1976, when Jay Robert Nash published his history of the con, *Hustlers and Con Men*, he listed Law among the game's most polished practitioners. In October 2014, John Steel Gordon, a prominent business and financial historian, called Law's the greatest scam of all time.

But today many would argue that Law was no confidence artist. He had a theoretically sound scheme, but got caught up in the bubble mentality. He thought he could continue to issue and print indefinitely as he consolidated his trading companies and set the whole thing in motion. Confidence would remain high because it was high already, and the share price would continue to rise because, well, it had never fallen in the past.

So was he a hustler, or merely unlucky? Ultimately, we'll never know: it is, for the most part, a question of knowledge and intent. Did you seriously want to help the economy, or did you weasel your way into a position you had no business being in with the knowledge that you could get rich, and flee when the going was good? The jury is out. Before his stint in France, back in his homeland, Scotland, Law had run his father's banking firm into the ground in pursuit of an extravagant gambling habit, and was later sentenced to death for his role in a love duel.

(He escaped to Amsterdam, and later returned to Scotland.) By the time he made his way to the French court, his proposals had already been rejected by Scotland and Amsterdam. France looked an awful lot like the ideal con victim: the nation was mired in debt and close to bankruptcy. It would try anything. And for a while, Law did seem to be making headway. Those who were poor now prospered. Those who had clamored for revolution were now satisfied. Who's to say the good times couldn't keep coming? The convincer is all about getting your mark to dedicate himself to his commitment for the long haul, and, willful con artist or not, Law certainly knew how to play the part well. There is a thin line between a reformer ahead of his time and a savvy con artist who knows how to exploit optimism about the future. Up until the last moment, France and its people kept piling more and more resources into the scheme. How could it burst when it had all gone so smoothly?

It's simply how our minds so often work. We cannot fathom failure in light of success. Well, we can *fathom* it. We just don't really think it's going to happen—not yet, not now, not to us. Our optimism in the future runs ever-strong.

So strong, in fact, that we often create the illusion of successful outcomes ourselves, even without the sorts of cash incentives a Miller or a Law or a Madoff offers. We see a con going well, and read our desires into ambiguous signs, to convince ourselves that we've invested wisely, be it money, time, reputation, or any other precious resources. When we want to, we see signs of good fortune everywhere. It's one of the reasons for the famous hot-hand fallacy that Cornell University psychologist Thomas Gilovich identified in 1985. Gilovich had first observed the phenomenon among basketball aficionados when they pronounced players on a "hot streak" or playing with a "hot hand." The players and coaches, too, seemed to believe it—even going so far as to select certain draft picks because they were perceived to be playing hot at the time.

To Gilovich, the whole thing seemed highly unlikely. He was a cognitive psychologist, studying rationality and its departures, and there was simply no reason to assume that people's talent and skills could show such tremendous, lasting deviations. He'd also been working with Amos Tversky, who, along with Daniel Kahneman, had identified the "belief in the law of small numbers" some ten years prior: that we believe that chance rates seen over the long term should also be reflected in the short term, and if they are not, something else must be going on. For instance, since a coin is supposed to land on heads half the time, we expect it to do so if we toss it, say, ten times. We don't take into consideration the fact that averages are derived over a broader timescale. And so, if we see tails coming up time and time again, we tend to think that we're particularly lucky.

Simon Lovell, con artist turned legitimate magician, wrote a book about exploiting such tendencies when you're out on the grift. One of the simplest short cons revolves around getting people to place bets on outcomes they think either highly unlikely or highly likely because of their recent experience (an experience that, in the convincer, is unerringly positive)—and then to upend those perfectly reasonable-seeming expectations. In what's called a proposition, or prop, bet, you first make a claim, and then ask for any takers to bet against you. One example: betting that you can tie a cigarette into a knot without tearing the paper. Impossible, right? Anyone would bet against you after trying it a few times on their own. But it's not actually impossible if you first wrap the cigarette tightly in the cellophane from the box and then tie the cellophane. Prop bets take advantage of what we expect and then do something completely different. They take the psychology behind the convincer and exploit it to its logical conclusion.

Gilovich and his colleagues decided to test our hot-hand-like perceptions by analyzing the shooting records of the Philadelphia 76ers and the Boston Celtics. They failed to find any relationship suggestive of actual hot hands: a player who made one shot was no more likely to make another soon after. Any deviations from their average level of play were the result not of streaks, but of chance: they were to be expected from the probability distributions and were not the result of some magical power that a player suddenly had.

But even though the hot-hand fallacy has been largely disproven—in 2006, a review of twenty years of data found an overwhelming lack of evidence for the presence of sudden bouts of talent—it continues to govern our thoughts of the future. If a player is on a hot streak, we should give him the proverbial ball because he will make the shot. In hedge funds, Kahneman points out, we see the same thing. When a fund has been tremendously successful for a few years, investors pour in: success now, even in something as volatile and chance-like as markets, means success always. Often, though, those phenomenal returns evaporate or reverse. It is, after all, a game of chance. Sure, a manager could be quite good, but ultimately he also has to be quite lucky—and luck can often masquerade as talent when the latter is absent.

Not only do we get fooled into thinking that just because something is working now, the future will be even better, but we often project our desires onto our estimations of likely success. In other words, we tend to think that what will happen is what we *want* to happen, especially if the outcome is an important one. It's Paul Frampton's near certain calculation that Denise Milani will be his wife, Ralph Raines's certainty in a happily ever after with his "family," or Oscar Bergstrom's calculation that he can steadily give all his money to William Miller and live off the returns that will, of course, never end.

In 1935, Jerome Frank, a psychologist at Harvard University, asked a group of people to perform three separate tasks, each repeated a number of times. The tasks were simple enough. In one, they would have to print a set of words as quickly as possible; in another, pitch rings onto a stick (a game called quoits); and in a third, manipulate a series of shapes in their heads under time pressure. Each time a participant finished a particular task, Frank would let her know how she'd performed—and would ask her how well she wanted to do on the next go-around. The better she wanted to perform, he found, the better she'd estimate she would, in fact, perform in the future, even when that performance was in no way warranted by her past experience. We want our schemes to succeed, our investments to go well, our love life to flourish, our luck to hold, our health and looks to improve. And we will that desire into being. It's perfectly understandable—but it's also how a convincer becomes so convincing, and how a con goes from short to long in a matter of moments. We're working just as hard to convince ourselves as the confidence man is working to convince us.

The optimistic illusion applies not only to the con itself; it applies to the con artist. Just as we think, once we've tasted the convincer, that everything is on the level, so we believe that just because someone has been trustworthy—or so we believe—up until now, he will continue to be so in the future.

Victor Lustig was born in Prague in 1890. Early on it became apparent that the child had tremendous linguistic ability; he wasn't yet out of his teens before he spoke not only Czech but English, German, Italian, and French. It would prove a useful skill: Lustig's silver tongue became his livelihood. The Count, as he later styled himself, went on to become one of the master confidence men of the early twentieth century. It was he who sold the Eiffel Tower to unwitting investors—not once, but twice—convincing them it was to be destroyed for scrap metal. It was also he who created a famed money box that could make perfect copies of twenty-dollar bills on demand—yours for the low cost of $4,000 (more if you could afford it; one banker was purported to have bought one for $100,000). He'd seed the box's false bottom with real bills, and almost never failed to make a sale. And it was he who managed to get a sheriff who'd arrested him for fraud to purchase a money box of his own.

Lustig's reputation preceded him. It was even enough, when he found himself in Chicago, to gain an audience with the man who ran the whole place, Al Capone. Lustig had, he told the bootlegger, a proposition. If Capone gave him $50,000, he would double his investment within two months. Capone was naturally suspicious, but he also had many a hired gun by his side. "Okay, Count," he told him. "Double it in sixty days like you said." *Or else,* came the implicit threat.

Lustig was a smart—and cautious—man. He liked to live the fine life, but more than that, he liked to live a life, period. He wasn't about to invest Capone's money and risk losing even a penny. That had never been the plan. Instead, he made his way to a safety-deposit box, where he left the full amount, and from there traveled to his home base in New York. Over the next few months, Lustig went about his business, and on the promised day he returned to Capone's office.

Eagerly, Capone asked for his doubled return. The Count couldn't have been more humbled or apologetic. "Please accept my profound regrets," he told Capone. "I'm sorry to report to you that the plan failed. I failed." He then reached into his pocket, removed the whole of Capone's money, and returned it to the gangster. He'd wanted to make it work, truly, he continued. He needed the cash himself. But the plan had fallen through.

Capone was, for the moment, speechless. He had known Lustig was a flimflammer, he said. And he'd expected either a cool hundred grand, through some shady scheme or other, or zero. But now the Count had shown him another side to his personality, a side he wouldn't soon forget.

"My god, you're honest!" With that, Capone gave Lustig $5,000, to "help him along" in his financial difficulties. That's all Lustig had ever wanted. Capone was a mighty fine judge of character.

Each year, Roderick Kramer teaches a class on negotiation at Stanford's business school. And each time he teaches it, he poses a question: how good are you at judging someone's trustworthiness? About 95 percent of people, he has repeatedly found, think themselves better than average—and not just any average. The average Stanford business student. *Others* may not be good judges of character. But the students, well, they can rate not just trustworthiness but reliability, honesty, and fairness. Over three quarters of the class rank themselves in the top quarter on their character-reading ability—and a fifth place themselves firmly in the top 10 percent. We are confident that we can judge how sound of character someone is. And the moment they prove us right, it will take a miracle for them to lose that trust.

* * *

The same morning that the Franklin Syndicate hit $1.2 million in investments, November 24, 1889, it hit another landmark: a lead headline in the *New York Times*—that is, a legitimate article, not one of Miller's own paid adverts. It ran at a cool three words, exhorting people to no uncertain action: "Desert Miller's Company."

Leading financiers, the story said, were asking questions about the venture: Who was the backer? Where were the deposits being invested? From whence the consistently dazzling returns? Four days earlier, a Franklin Syndicate did indeed apply for incorporation in New Jersey, investigators had found, but none of those concerned knew anything of Miller. "I know nothing of Mr. Miller, of his business affairs, or of the statements contained in the papers as to what he is doing in Brooklyn," Howard Wood, the secretary of the Corporation Trust of New Jersey, told the press. From there, it only got dicier. "They have no officers; there is no general manager; they could only do business outside New Jersey through a vote of the Board of Directors, which has never met, for the reason that there are no Directors."

Miller's fantastical returns had been catching the eyes of journalists for several months. Even as the syndicate heated up, so, too, did the scrutiny surrounding its investments, its methods, its financial soundness. Repeatedly, reporters had come to Miller's door, poking, probing, demanding answers and financial statements. The headline of November 24 was the culmination of the effort. And so, that Friday night, as markets shut down for the weekend and subscribers retired for a two-day break, Miller fled north, arriving in Canada before the week was out.

As Miller was making his way northward, the police were closing in on his operation. Hours after he'd left, they arrived to find the house on

Floyd Street bereft of its proprietor. Cecil Leslie, Miller's public face and press officer, was also nowhere to be seen. Gone was Schlesinger, his partner. The owners, it seemed, had left in a hurry. There was $4,500 just lying there on the table, next to $400 worth of stamped envelopes. There was a large safe, unopened, in the corner. There were some clerks and secretaries, forty-five or so, wandering around in a bewildered haze. They had stuck around for payday: where were their checks?

That evening, a crowd of thousands—two thousand, according to one account—swarmed the syndicate. They weren't particularly anxious, merely curious. Past six o'clock, they were making their deposits. Fifty dollars here. A hundred dollars there. True, earlier in the day some had demanded refunds, but the tide had turned. A few loudmouthed men had screamed at the clerks to return their money, promptly received the entire sum, and then sheepishly returned a second time to ask if it could be re-deposited; they apologized for being hasty and untrusting. Soon, the demands for returns—about a hundred at last count—began to turn into further deposits. And the tide of trust kept rising. "Why, Mr. Miller has never failed us," said one woman who'd been lingering outside. "He's always paid dividends. I put in $100 six weeks ago and have taken $60 out. It is these newspapers and bankers that are causing this trouble. Nobody believes the papers," she continued. "It's envy. They'd like to make money themselves." Investing with Miller was the best thing "that ever happened," affirmed the local druggist H. M. Uhlig.

A young woman who'd persuaded three of her friends to go in with her on the scheme agreed. She'd come that afternoon with the goal of investing further. She was being a fool, someone warned. She replied confidently, "No, never. Mr. Miller will always do as he says." At the livery stable around the corner, where all the employees had invested with the syndicate, an elderly German reassured onlookers. "Miller's all right," he told the *New York Times*. "He can have anything he wants in this section. We'd send him to the Legislature, if he wanted to go." A local tailor, Adolph Breman, had closed his business on the strength of

Miller's dividends—$75 a week for two weeks. He was confident the sums would continue to arrive.

On Saturday, a crowd of some two to four hundred lingered outside the office. "Closed on Saturday," read the sign, as it always had. The crowd seemed reassured. After all, Mr. Miller never came in on Saturdays. Why today? Mrs. Charlton, a Brooklyn sweatshop worker who toiled twelve hours a day for fifty-six cents, anxiously surveyed the crowd. Just two weeks earlier, she had put $160—her entire life savings—in Mr. Miller's keeping. She'd received $32 back—dividends for two weeks. Would her money be lost? she anxiously asked the gathered onlookers. No, they told her. It was all a plot against "poor Mr. Miller." Reassured, she went on her way.

As the afternoon wore on, more investors arrived. There was Carl Preuss, a cripple, who proudly displayed his receipt for $450 from the day before. He wasn't anxious—no, sir. He was just seeing what all the hubbub was about. And he'd be back early Monday—you could count on it—to receive his first week's dividend. There was an equally confident H. D. Strunk (investment: $500). He was a grocer from down the road, and Mr. Miller had always been as good as his word. There was the confectioner, Frank Weinstein, who'd invested $50 and had, just the day before, convinced his cousin that this was the safest place by far for his $200. There was the delicatessen dealer, August Weber, so confident in Miller's returns that he'd also secured investments from his wife and mother-in-law. So large was his deposit that he refused to divulge it, as those around him had so proudly done. "That's none of your business," he retorted. "But I tell you that if Mr. Miller wants $500 from me on Monday, he can have it."

And there was Miss Wolford, there to deposit another $50, to double her account and returns both. She wasn't much of a reader of papers. Mr. Miller, fled and unable to take her money? Nonsense. She wouldn't hear of it.

It wasn't just the locals, either. Policemen, firemen, detectives, mailmen: all had, up until the last, received dividends from Miller. "If the officers are not afraid," chanced someone in the crowd, "why should we be?"

On Monday morning, when the anxious account holders gathered to receive their funds, they found the house taken over by the police.

And yet, even now they didn't panic. So strong was Miller's pull—and their optimism, born out of experience and necessity—that they maintained a quasi-religious faith in his return. It would all prove to be a misunderstanding. Tradesmen, neighborhood housewives, members of his church: all crowded Floyd Street, but only to be there when he returned. It was the newspapers, they repeated, that were the true culprits. They had cast such deep, unfounded aspersions that *of course* Miller was forced to flee. "It seemed yesterday as if the majority of the crowd gathered in front of 144 Floyd Street were awaiting his return," wrote the *New York Times* on November 27, four days after Miller's flight. "To be followed by the announcement that the syndicate would resume business promptly and that he would confound all his enemies."

Captain Lees, the district captain who had been among the earliest skeptics of Miller's venture, sought in vain for someone to pull the trigger on his illegitimacy. "I have yet to hear any of that man's customers speak against him. They all believe in his honesty, and cannot be convinced that his business methods are crooked," he said. Brooklyn detective James Reynolds added, "The people in the neighborhood all had faith in him, and many of the merchants there honor his checks even now. The principal feeling among these people is one of animosity to the newspapers for destroying what the people thought was a 'good thing.'"

On November 28, five days after Miller's disappearance, press at a high and police search going strong, his investors remained undeterred. Letters filled with cash—hopeful investments for when Miller returned and the syndicate resumed, as it surely would, its daily operations—flooded the Brooklyn Post Office. At Station A, at Broadway and Graham, over twelve hundred letters awaited the return of the greatest stock manipulator of all time. Nearby, at the main post office, there sat over $10,000 in money orders. As more than a dozen detectives spread their net beyond New York, scanning European freighters, New Jersey trains, anything that might give a sign as to Miller's whereabouts, crowds gathered on Floyd Street, awaiting the Franklin Syndicate's grand reopening.

* * *

Unrealistic optimism about the future doesn't just make us think everything will continue to go well if we're seeing returns at this very moment. It also makes us complacent—and complacently overconfident—even when we have the chance to get out. It's like Miller's investors, who came to withdraw and ended up depositing. The logic is actually quite clear. You are wavering—maybe things aren't that great—but then you see just a hint of reassurance: Miller's plants, who asked for refunds and then promptly redeposited the cash. (A vaunted strategy of the con artist: work with a gang, and make sure plenty of those who look just like the marks are actually nicely paid to string those marks along.) And you start the age-old game: What will I regret more? Knowing I'm safe, and having missed out on a potentially great investment, or risking it, and knowing that if the fantastic returns continue, I will grow rich along with them?

Anticipated emotion—that is, the emotion we can anticipate feeling if we take a certain course of action—strongly favors the status quo. Anticipated regret makes us want to keep doing what we're doing; anticipated stress makes us want to cope proactively, by not doing anything that might provoke said stress; and anticipated guilt makes us likewise want to prevent it from ever happening.

In one of their famous thought experiments, Daniel Kahneman and Amos Tversky described two individuals who'd been playing the stock market. Both had just lost $1,200 on a certain stock. The difference between them was in *how* they'd lost it. The first had lost it after initially buying one stock and then, after a bit of thought, switching to another. The second had made the mistake of sticking with a losing stock rather than, after some reflection, switching to a winner. Who would feel worse? Almost without fail, the participants who read the two scenarios thought that the first investor—who'd had a winner and switched to a loser—would feel more regret. The thought that you'd been right all along, if only you'd stuck to your guns, is just too painful for most people to consider.

Over a decade later, Maya Bar-Hillel and Efrat Neter demonstrated that the same behavior would hold when it came to actual money. The researchers asked participants to trade a lottery ticket they already had (they'd been handed it at the start of the experiment) for a new one with an equal chance of winning, alongside a delicious chocolate truffle. Three out of five refused to make the trade. The psychologists then sweetened the deal: not only would they give out new tickets; they'd also give out hard cash to anyone willing to trade theirs in. Even still, fewer than 40 percent of the participants made the trade. The number fell to a low of just over a quarter—27 percent—when the possibility of regret was raised explicitly: there would be a public drawing, and a prior owner would know if her ticket had actually won. Even if the ticket was completely withdrawn from consideration—it couldn't win, no matter what—fewer than half were willing to give it up.

It wasn't just about what is known as the endowment effect—the fact that we value what we already have more than what we don't—Bar-Hillel and Neter concluded. The possibility of regret loomed so strongly on the chance that the player had given up a winner that it overcame all rational considerations. Trading pens instead of lottery tickets, in fact—an object without any uncertainty surrounding its value—yielded a 90 percent compliance rate. It wasn't about letting go of what you had. It was about letting go of the chance of winning and having to live with the regret.

A 2007 follow-up found that not only were people reluctant to exchange tickets; they actually judged an exchanged ticket more likely to be a winner. The truth is, when things are going according to plan, we are that much more likely to believe the plan a solid one. If we startle, if we run now, if we walk away, we may live to regret it. And then who's the sucker? As they say, nothing ventured, nothing gained.

And that is precisely what the confidence artist is depending on in the convincer. That nagging feeling in your gut: what if you scream foul and it ends up that it wasn't a con after all?

* * *

Sightings of Miller started popping up around the continent. In early December, a hotel clerk at the Hillago Hotel in Monterrey, Mexico, swore that Miller had checked in with two large suitcases, only to depart for Tampico, and from there on a boat to Central America. Next, he was arrested and headed back to New York—except it wasn't Miller at all. It was a local reporter.

His investors finally started to turn. Elizabeth Timmons, who'd given a thousand-dollar bond for his bail, asked to be released from it; she wanted no responsibility for his appearance. Bergstrom, his first ever victim, sued him for return of the $150 he'd eventually deposited.

On February 8, Miller, the real one this time, was apprehended in Montreal by Captain James Reynolds. On Tuesday evening, around seven, he had been walking down the street with another man when Reynolds spied him in the crowd. "Hello, Miller. I'm Captain Reynolds of New York," he said as he walked up to the fugitive. Miller doffed his hat. "Why, how are you, Captain?" he replied. They shook hands, Miller smiled, and the captain informed him of his impending travel plans back to the States—preferably with Miller at his side. By eight, the two were speeding on a train back across the border. Just before two in the afternoon the following day, Reynolds and Miller arrived at Grand Central Terminal.

"Well, Miller, we are in New York now," Reynolds told him. "I will have to place you under arrest." Miller smiled. "Certainly. I understand."

Misfortune, it seems, did little to make him less brazen. "Anyone with any common sense would know that I was not [in Canada]," he told a reporter who managed to sneak his way into the jail alongside a lawyer once Miller was safely in custody. "Since I have been connected with this enterprise I have been pounded like a football by the police, the lawyers, and the reporters." He was the real victim. He'd done nothing but make money for thousands of people.

At just past four in the afternoon, William Miller arrived at the Brooklyn Municipal Building. He looked as dapper as ever, complete with his usual derby hat, gray covert coat, and black suit of cheviot wool. There, a crowd awaited. Head hung, Miller made his way up the steps, dwarfed by Reynolds at his side. The crowd closed in behind him, following closely on his heels. The courtroom, meanwhile, had filled well past capacity, each seat taken, the aisles crammed with onlookers. As Miller stood before the court, Judge Hurd read back his indictment: two counts of grand larceny in the first degree, and one in the second.

There was no syndicate. There were no shares. Miller hadn't invested in the stock market. He wasn't even a member of the stock exchange. Actually, that's not entirely true. He did invest once. As the Franklin Syndicate took off, Miller seems to have bought some of his own lies and invested $1,000 on some shares he was certain would go up. Wasn't he the one with the inner edge, after all, the genius of Wall Street? At the end of the week, the investment had indeed changed significantly in value. It was worth $5.36.

Miller's was one of the earliest and most successful of what we now call Ponzi schemes in history—only, back then, Charles Ponzi would have still been a seventeen-year-old kid. Take from Peter to give to Paul. All well and good while you have a steady supply of capital. Not so good if that supply dries up. He'd netted what today would be worth over $25 million. The whole scheme was "fraudulent and felonious," the court documents read; Miller's intent, to "cheat and defraud." He'd committed grand larceny and "crime of false pretense."

"Not guilty," came Miller's plea.

As the courtroom cleared, Miller was brought to a small cage next door. For the next hour, he sat quietly on a chair in the corner, reading the paper, joking with his guards. Just past six, he was returned to jail, Cell 6, Tier B, Raymond Street.

On April 30, Miller was sentenced to ten years in Sing Sing. It was the maximum penalty possible by law. Miller was crushed. His lawyer had begged for clemency. The judge stood firm. "It is a grave question whether an enterprise like the one this man carried on ought to be suppressed by the severest punishment under the law. I am of the opinion that it should."

Yes, Judge Jenks Herschberg said, the victims were "ignorant and unthinking." Who could believe in someone nicknamed "520 percent" for his unparalleled rate of return? It practically screamed fraud. But Miller's sins were vast, and he had to pay.

The man who stood in front of the courtroom in June 1903 was no longer the dapper gentleman who had lured thousands of victims into parting with millions. Bent and broken from long illness, a cough racking his body—just the other week he'd suffered a near fatal hemorrhage in his cell—it was all Miller could do to remain upright during his three days' testimony. He was testifying now against his partner, his lawyer, Colonel Robert Ammon. In exchange, he hoped for an early release.

As he geared up for his final appearance, crossing the so-called Bridge of Sighs, Miller collapsed, the only thing keeping him from the void, the grip of two prison guards on his forearms. "Any bitterness I may have felt against Mr. Ammon has been counteracted by my knowledge of what it means to suffer in prison," he concluded his testimony. "I am here to tell the truth, regardless of whether it convicts or acquits Mr. Ammon."

On Friday, February 10, 1905, Miller was pardoned for his cooperation. Ammon replaced him in the cells of Sing Sing.

For the next decade, Miller lived quietly in Rockville Centre, working as a grocer under the name "Williams Schmidt," the last name borrowed from his brother-in-law. His notoriety remained hidden until he and Schmidt quarreled. Miller had him arrested for assault, and in retaliation, Schmidt outed him to neighbors and press. "I had to have an alias," Miller later said, "or else I never would have been able to earn an honest living. Nobody would have trusted Miller, but as Schmidt I got along fairly well."

Meanwhile, Miller's scheme lived on, albeit in new hands. One, the Washington Syndicate Company, even promised the same weekly 10 percent return. Hadn't investors been deterred by Miller? an inveterate reporter asked the new manager. "Don't you, as a businessman, know that it is impossible for anybody to make 10 percent a week regularly on money in Wall Street or anywhere else?"

"I don't know any such thing," he replied. "I've heard of men making a hundred percent a day in Wall Street, and I've seen it figured out how it can be done, but I couldn't do it myself because I don't know anything about stocks. I guess Mr. Lamont knows what he's doing."

And what of the fact that the enterprise was the exact same scheme as Miller's had been? "Well, it isn't just the same," came the reply. "But what if it was? Nobody knows that Miller won't come back and go on with the business. I've heard today that people are offering fifty cents on the dollar for Miller's certificates of deposit, so I guess some believe in him yet in spite of the newspapers."

***

Optimistic biases are among the strongest we experience. And so, just as the convincer is irresistible to the mark, so, too, can it prove the downfall of the confidence artist. The lure of success is simply that powerful. Many con artists operate for years, decades even. Miller rose and fell quickly, true. But Miller's partner-at-heart Bernie Madoff operated his Peter-to-Paul game for over a decade by the most conservative estimates. And our old friend Fred Demara conned his way through the fifties, sixties, and seventies, until being forced by circumstance to go straight. The longer a grifter operates, in some sense, the more likely he is to overshoot.

By the time we hear of a scheme, it may appear incredible. We find it difficult to believe that someone could honestly hope to get away with it. But the logic of the convincer sweeps up many a grifter. It took a long time to get so brazen. Miller's example makes the case perfectly. "This scheme, in its infancy, was quite moderate in extent, but grew by what it fed upon," wrote Judge Goodrich in a dissenting opinion on Miller's appeal. Ten dollars isn't brazen; $1.2 million is. Jonah Lehrer, the journalist who had two books recalled for containing fabrications and willful factual misrepresentations, was finally brought down by falsifying not just anything but quotes from Bob Dylan. Dylan is still alive, and Dylan fans are a loyal bunch, hanging on the master's every word. When the lies were uncovered, people's reaction was disbelief: how could someone be so brazen? The answer is exactly the same as in Miller's case. Lehrer didn't start by fabricating Dylan. He started with a ten-dollar equivalent. But for years, no one caught on. By the time of the Dylan fiasco, he'd likely fancied himself invincible. The confidence artists can grow as complacent and overconfident as those they deceive: I can keep going forever. I'm good, and things are good, and so it will stay. Catch me if you can. And sometimes this mentality is exactly what does catch them. Had they only stayed more modest, perhaps we'd be none the wiser.

Miller wasn't quite destitute during his Long Island days, but he came fairly close. How? Where had the money gone? Much of it was never recovered, and the investors were never fully paid back. (According to author Mitchell Zuckoff, his investors were able to get back, on average, twenty-eight cents on the dollar.)

Miller had grown so confident that he'd fallen for a little trick of confidence of his own. Before leaving for Canada, he had signed over all of the proceeds of the syndicate to his lawyer, Robert Ammon, including some $200,000 in bonds—a total, as he would later tell the court, of $255,000. Trust me, Ammon had told Miller; because of attorney-client privilege, the money would be safe. He'd take care of everything.

Miller had only ever gotten $5,000 back; $5,000 more had gone, according to Ammon, to "fixing" a few problematic people; and $5,000 had gone toward bribing a jury. And for "guarding" the funds, Ammon also agreed to look after Miller's wife, still in Brooklyn: he gave her a princely allowance of five dollars a week.

It starts with one word. One quote. One scene. One massaged fact. One altered data point. Did anyone notice? No one? Then let's keep going. Soon the ruse takes on a life of its own and you're fabricating whole fictional worlds as you bring ever more dupes into the fray. You're not a psychopath. You're probably not even a pathological liar. You're just a grifter who got a bit too enamored of his own scheme, and too certain of his own success, to believe he can ever fail.

And when you're caught? You still can't quite believe it—just as Miller's victims, to the end, refused to believe they would never see their money again. It's just too, well, unbelievable—the convincer has played its role only too well. There's too much at stake. Things had been going so well. It must be a mistake—not the end. And just as the crowds insisted on Miller's honesty, so the con artist caught in his own web insists on his. You protest your innocence until the point where to keep on protesting would signal a final break with reality.

For profit isn't all about money. It's about gaining an edge. Sometimes a financial edge, yes, but also a cognitive edge, a reputational edge, a personal edge. And when we see that edge in our grasp, we hold on to it, and we don't ever want to let it go.

CHAPTER 7
THE BREAKDOWN

And the burnt Fool's bandaged finger goes
wabbling back to the Fire.

—RUDYARD KIPLING

James Franklin Norfleet—Frank—sank back into the plush chair in the lobby of the Adolphus Hotel. It was early November, and it had been a long few days. He needed the rest. He'd been staying at the St. George, arriving just two days prior in order to sell off one of his farms. Stocky and compact, just five foot five in his bare feet, his blue eyes wide-set on a broad face, a "frosty bark of a voice" punctuated by frequent bursts of laughter that belied his handiness with bulls, horses, and firearms alike—"fast on the draw and a deadly sharpshooter," as one acquaintance put it—Frank was a rancher, Texas born and bred. He owned a big swath of land up near Hale County, just north of Lubbock, and was in Dallas to sell over two thousand acres of his land in exchange for the cash to buy a much larger parcel—ten thousand acres immediately across the way—from its owner, Captain Dick Slaughter.

Norfleet was fifty-four years old, and business was good. On his way to Dallas, he'd sold a load of mules. Here, he hoped to sell the land, too.

That would get him where he wanted. He hated debts, credit, all of it. He was a cash man, and soon he'd have enough to close the deal. It couldn't come soon enough. He was feeling lonely, and home pulled at him. He did hate the big city.

It was at the St. George that, just a few days earlier, Frank had met R. Miller, a mule buyer from Hill County, just outside Dallas (and no relation to the Franklin Syndicate). He'd seen many a mule and grain car from West Texas, Miller told Frank, but had never been there himself. What was it like? Norfleet described the flatlands, the sandy patches and the playas, the loamy soil, the way the ranch rambled on into the distance. He mentioned, too, that he was looking to sell a tract of his land up there.

"Norfleet, I may help you," Miller exclaimed. It was Frank's lucky day. A friend of Miller's, W. B. Spencer, was actually a purchasing agent with the Green Immigration Land Company of Minneapolis. He was just that day closing on a patch of land—also two thousand acres, as luck would have it—in Williamson County. But it looked like the deal could fall through. "It is just possible he might be interested in your place as well," Miller concluded.

After a fortuitous introduction and a few false starts, Miller's intuition panned out: Spencer was eager to buy Norfleet's land. Norfleet was thrilled. He'd liked Spencer from the first—mid-thirties, dressed in a simple business suit, elegant but not too flashy. Just the sort of straight shooter he fancied himself to be—and liked, in turn, to deal with. So taken was he with his new acquaintance and business partner that he readily agreed to share Spencer's hotel room rather than stay on in his own: when Spencer told Norfleet he was staying in a double room at the nearby Jefferson, foolishly stuck with a needlessly large accommodation after the friend he was to share it with had been detained at the last moment, it seemed a natural decision. The reasonable and frugal thing to do—Norfleet was always careful about money; you didn't get to where he was if you weren't. And besides, he really liked Spencer. He welcomed the chance to get to know him better. Plus, it was a buffer against the city loneliness.

Later that day, the two men made their way to the Adolphus Hotel to meet with Spencer's boss and see if they couldn't come to an understanding about the land. It was there that Norfleet was sitting as he leaned contentedly into the chair.

Something disturbed his back. A stray magazine left behind by a careless reader, he thought, and shuffled forward to remove it. But it wasn't a magazine at all. It was a wallet. It was fat, filled with cash—over $200, in fact, no mean sum at all—and alongside it, a copy of a shockingly large bond, for $100,000. In the front, there was a Masonic membership card. J. B. Stetson, it read. The rest of the contents seemed to confirm that this was Stetson's wallet. There was the membership card for the United Brokers. And on the bond, a promise of guaranteed performance by the same Stetson. Norfleet was an honest man. He set about trying to return the property, whoever Stetson might turn out to be.

He tried the front desk. Indeed, there was a Mr. Stetson registered, and he happened to be in his room at the moment. Norfleet and Spencer made their way up. Frank knocked on the door. "Excuse me," he asked as the door opened a slit. "Have you lost anything?"

"No," came the curt reply. The door slammed in Norfleet's astounded face. He turned to go back to the elevator.

As he and Spencer reached the end of the hallway, a voice cried out after them. "Gentlemen! Gentlemen!" it said. "I have just discovered that I have lost a very, very valuable pocketbook." The men returned. Stetson invited them in.

First, he wanted to apologize. He had mistaken them for reporters. The bloody bastards had been hounding him all afternoon. But he was beyond ecstatic to make their acquaintance. The cash was good to get back, sure, but the real prize was his Masonic membership card. He was so very happy to have it once more safely in his pocket. Norfleet understood. He was a fellow Mason.

So glad was Stetson to be reunited with his property that he offered both men a hundred-dollar reward. Spencer eagerly pocketed the cash, to Norfleet's surprise. Norfleet politely refused. Sure, it was a lot of money, but he was only doing his duty. The pleasure of seeing Stetson's relief was reward enough. But Stetson insisted; he wanted to show his gratitude. You know what he would do? He would take the hundred dollars and invest it on the rancher's behalf. It was his profession, he made huge returns, and normally his investment advice came at a high price. But in this case, he would make an exception. He had just received a tip, and he could act quickly. Would Norfleet take any winnings from his investment? Norfleet agreed. It seemed a good compromise. Stetson left to place some calls and make some bets.

Spencer lounged behind Stetson's vacated desk. Norfleet paced the room and took stock of their surroundings. Several impressive-looking wardrobes, overflowing with fine garments and shoes. A solid desk, stacked with papers and stock reports, cryptograms and keys—Stetson had explained earlier that much of the information he received was sensitive and confidential; he and his company had developed a stealthier way to communicate. They were very lucky, Spencer offered, unprompted. They'd chanced on an acquaintance with a very powerful man indeed.

Shortly, Stetson returned. He handed Norfleet a pile of bills. Eight hundred dollars. His winnings, he said, from a successful foray into the markets. This time, Norfleet took the money. And why not? It was a return from a well-placed investment by a new friend. He was on his way out the door, cash in hand, when Stetson made a motion to stop him. Hand on his shoulder, he inquired whether Norfleet might consider returning the following morning. He was expecting some news from the cotton markets and would love to continue their acquaintance and perhaps make a small proposition. After all, Norfleet *had* saved his investment and reputation. Norfleet acquiesced.

Later that afternoon, he went to visit Captain Dick Slaughter, the man who owned that choice tract of land. They drew up a contract. Things were going well for Norfleet: a buyer for his land and the potential for some successful investments, all in one. He would, he confidently told Slaughter, be able to pay the full $90,000 in forty-five days. For today, he put down a $5,000 deposit, shook hands, and went to enjoy the rest of the day. The streets of Dallas seemed friendlier by the minute.

Early the next morning, Norfleet and Spencer returned once more to the Adolphus. While Spencer went to buy the morning papers, Stetson made Norfleet a proposition. On certain days of the month, he explained, his company controlled the market for certain stocks. They would advise him on the optimal moment to buy and sell—and if he executed everything properly, he would make a large sum of money. All he needed was a smart, discreet, honest, and straightforward man on whom he could rely, to use his name to make the trades. And Norfleet— well, he was a fellow lodge member. What more could you require?

Norfleet had never had anything to do with the markets before. The mechanics of the thing seemed close to gibberish. But he was a good businessman, and he knew that, in the business world, getting something for nothing simply didn't happen. And if you got something by knowing something someone else didn't—well, in some cases, you were smart. In others, you were shady. "Is this legitimate?" he asked Stetson. He wanted no part of anything that was even remotely gray.

"Absolutely," Stetson assured him. "It's strictly business. We do it every day."

Norfleet agreed. He felt he could trust Stetson. The bonds of brotherhood run deep. There was only one problem. "I have no money," he told the two men. (By this time, Spencer had returned, papers in hand, and been apprised of the business dealings.)

Not a problem at all, Stetson assured him. No money was needed. His membership in the United Brokers, which allowed him to trade in the stock exchange, was backed by $100,000.

The stock exchange was impressive. A large stone building with multiple offices, hallways, people milling around, and money flying about. The men approached a glass window. Here, explained Stetson, was where buy orders were placed and money returned.

Norfleet felt a hand on his shoulder. "Excuse me," an official-looking man said. His name was E. J. Ward. He was the stock exchange's secretary. "Are you a member of the exchange?"

Norfleet was not.

"I am very sorry to do so, but I shall be forced to invite you outside, as only members are allowed here."

Norfleet quickly made his exit; he didn't want to run afoul of any regulations, he assured the secretary. Wait in my hotel, Stetson instructed him. Norfleet demurred. He wanted to drop out; it just didn't seem right.

Spencer chimed in. He understood how the markets worked. He'd accompany Stetson. All Norfleet would have to do was wait. In fact, Stetson immediately offered, how did Norfleet feel about investing his $800 winnings?

The day drew to an end. Norfleet had spent the better part of the afternoon wandering the town, seeing some cattle, eyeing the competition. He was now back at the Jefferson, lounging by the window, thinking back on the wondrous few days he'd had. New friends. New experiences. A new type of finance he didn't quite grasp but that seemed awfully impressive. The door burst open.

Spencer was ebullient—$68,000, cash. He threw it on the bed. Stetson, ever the more composed, simply smiled. Meticulously, he counted out Norfleet's share from his $800: $28,000. This was truly cause for celebration.

Norfleet was shocked. Pleasantly so. All he'd done was behave like a decent human being, and yet here he was, a far richer man than he'd been a mere twenty-four hours earlier. It was a fortune.

Someone knocked on the door. It was Ward—the man who'd just that morning ejected him from the exchange building. Had they had, he asked, sufficient funds to cover the orders in the event the market moved against them? As nonmembers, they had to guarantee all trades in advance.

No, they both replied. They didn't have the requisite cash.

Stetson rose from the chair. According to the exchange rules, he told the secretary, they had until the following Monday to come up with the call money.

Ward agreed. In the meantime, though, he'd need to hold on to the cash they'd won. They would get a receipt, but the money itself would have to wait.

The three friends conferred. How to raise the funds? In the end, they came up with an agreement. Spencer would raise $35,000. His agency business was thriving—"Not so bad for a young man just out of the army, huh?"—and he could come up with it in short order. Norfleet's share: $20,000. Stetson would supply the remainder.

The next day, Norfleet left for home, accompanied by Spencer— Spencer's money was already on the way, and he'd take the opportunity to inspect the farmland. Norfleet, on his end, would need to borrow money from his bank, where they knew him and trusted his word.

Three days later, he was ready to reclaim his winnings.

It was at the Fort Worth Cotton Exchange that their fortunes took a downward turn. Or, rather, that stupidity got the best of the moment. For when Stetson instructed Spencer to sell "Mexican petroleum" at a two-point margin, Spencer mangled the instructions. He'd lost Stetson's original note, and when he re-created it from memory, instead of selling, he had placed an order to buy. Stetson's information was good; Spencer's execution was shoddy.

For the first time in their weeklong acquaintance, Norfleet saw Stetson lose his cool. "Spencer, you have ruined us!" he screamed, flinging the receipt in his face. His skin was red, almost purple. His eyes bulged. Rage seemed to radiate from every pore. "You have lost every dollar we have and that we had coming to us."

Spencer became hysterical. He'd lost his mother's estate, he cried. He was ruined. Norfleet couldn't quite grasp it. Twenty thousand dollars—gone. All because of a stupid, stupid, stupid error.

After a while, Stetson calmed down. He'd make things right, he vowed. He would go back to the exchange and try to hedge the loss.

The two men waited in silence. They were both ruined. And it seemed an awful lot to hope for that Stetson would succeed.

But again, their luck seemed to have turned. Stetson returned, triumphant. He had gotten in a sell order, and their losses were covered. Indeed, shortly after, the exchange secretary arrived; $160,000 was theirs—their initial capital, and then some. But, as before, a cash guarantee was required.

On the morning of November 20, Norfleet again rode for home. He had lost $20,000, true, but if he now raised an additional $25,000, he would recoup all losses and even come out ahead. His credit tapped, he turned to his brother-in-law.

* * *

There's a sense in which any decision of any weight concerning the future is a gamble. It's inherently risky because the future is inherently uncertain. And so, in the interim—the period after we've made our choice but before we know the final outcome—we wait, we look, we evaluate the evidence, we calculate the odds that things will turn out as expected. In other words, we form what is known as an expectancy: an expectation of how things will progress. It can range from the very basic—I've settled on a restaurant for this evening and expect my meal to be delicious—to the more complex—I've decided to invest in this real estate venture and expect building to commence in 2015, conclude by the end of the year, cost $20 million, and, by 2017, bring in $10 million a year. (Clearly, I've never invested in real estate in my life.) That initial set of expectations will in turn affect how we think, feel, and act as new evidence comes in. It will, as well, affect how we interpret and evaluate that evidence in the first place.

When we committed to the confidence game, we had formed a very particular expectancy: that of eventual success. And at this stage in the game, everything has been going according to the exact expectations we've set out; our plans seem to be well laid indeed. We're coming off some heady wins. We have money in hand. We have fine lab results. We have a solid piece of reporting. We have a rare, genuine bottle of wine or work of art. We've established a bond of trust with our deceiver—he's been good to his word so far. The convincer has done its work. We think we're in the home stretch; just a little more of the same, and our initial confidence, trust, and judgment will be completely verified.

From the confidence man's perspective, this is the ideal moment to make a killing: pull the plug just when your mark is at his most convinced. The mark has already tasted victory and lauded himself on his discernment and prowess. He's already hooked. If the grifter lets him keep winning, it doesn't do him any additional good. Everything that goes to the mark, after all, is less for the confidence man. Instead, what if the grifter now makes the mark lose? At least a bit? In other words, what do we do when reality suddenly doesn't match the expectancy we've built?

That's the question at the heart of the breakdown, the moment when the con artist sees just how far he can take us. In the put-up, he picked us out of the crowd with care. In the play, he established a bond through some emotional wrangling and expert storytelling. In the rope, he laid out his persuasive pitch for our already-willing ears. In the tale, he's told us how we will personally benefit, relying on our belief in our exceptionalism. In the convincer, he's let us win, persuading us that we'd been right in going along with him. And now comes the breakdown. We start to lose. How far can the grifter push us before we balk? How much of a beating can we take? Things don't completely fall apart yet—that would lose us entirely, and the game would end prematurely— but cracks begin to show. We lose some money. Something doesn't go according to plan. One fact seems to be off. A figure is incorrectly labeled. A wine bottle is "faulty." The crucial question: do we notice, or do we double down? High off the optimism of the convincer, certain that good fortune is ours, we often take the second route. When we should be cutting our losses, we instead recommit—and that is entirely what the breakdown is meant to accomplish.

Leon Festinger first proposed the theory of cognitive dissonance, today one of the most famous concepts in psychology, in 1957. When we experience an event that counteracts a prior belief, he argued, the resulting tension is too much for us to handle; we can't hold two opposing beliefs at the same time, at least not consciously. "The individual strives," Festinger wrote in *A Theory of Cognitive Dissonance*, "toward consistency within himself." True, here and there one might find exceptions. But overall, "It is still overwhelmingly true that related opinions or attitudes are consistent with one another. Study after study reports such consistency among one person's political attitudes, social attitudes, and many others." He continued, "There is the same kind of consistency between what a person knows or believes and what he does." If we believe in education, we send our children to college. If a child knows something is bad but can't quite resist it, she'll try to avoid getting caught if she does it. So when something goes awry—someone knows smoking is bad for him but smokes anyway, for instance—we work to reduce the tension, through a process Festinger called dissonance reduction.

Festinger first observed the tendency not in a lab, but rather in the actions of a cult he had been following, which believed that an alien-led rapture would, on a certain date, at a certain time, lead the members to the alien world as a reward for their goodliness. When the date and time came and went, though, and no aliens were forthcoming, Festinger expected the cult would disperse. Instead, the group promptly reformulated their understanding of the alien plan.

While Festinger was surprised, the behavior wasn't a new one—and was actually to be expected of the mind that has fallen sway to a con as strong as the cult. Writing several centuries earlier, Francis Bacon wouldn't have been at all shocked. He would have likely anticipated correctly just how the whole thing would play out. "And such is the way of all superstitions, whether in astrology, dreams, omens, divine judgments, or the like," he wrote, "wherein men, having a delight in such vanities, mark the events where they are fulfilled, but where they fail, although this happened much oftener, neglect and pass them by." In other words, they work to minimize the discord in their minds—the exact tendency Festinger would term dissonance reduction.

To reduce dissonance, Festinger argued, we can do several things.

We can revise our interpretation of the present reality: there actually isn't any inconsistency; we were just looking at it wrong. We achieve this through selectively looking for new, confirming information or selectively ignoring disconfirming information. The study on smoking was flawed. The sample was biased. It doesn't apply to me. We can revise our prior expectation: I thought this would happen all along, so it's actually not discordant. I always knew they would try to convince me smoking was bad, so learning that fact isn't actually jarring. I was prepared all along and made the decision anyhow: I think my experience will defy the odds. Or we can alter the reality itself: stop smoking. Generally, the first two approaches tend to be easier to accomplish. Changing your perception or your memory is easier than changing behavior. It's easier to change what we believe about smoking than to actually quit.

Even as conflicting evidence comes in, expectancies tend to be sticky, especially when they've been confirmed in the past. "Once useful expectancies have developed," write psychologists Neal Roese and Jeffrey Sherman, "our cognitive system is rather conservative about altering or replacing them." We don't altogether ignore new inputs—that would be maladaptive and stupid—but we err on the side of what we've already decided was true. After all, we did a lot of work to get to that point. And what we've already decided was true can color how we view the new event: even as a conflicting piece of information is coming to our attention, we are already revising our interpretation of it to fit with our expectancy.

Our prior expectations act as a heuristic of sorts: they give us a basic cognitive road map for how we should look at what's going on, so that with every new piece of information we don't have to reinvent the wheel. The stronger the expectation and the greater the opportunity for ambiguity, the more likely we are to experience the so-called expectancy assimilation effect, that is, assimilating new data to fit old views rather than revising the old views themselves.

"When men wish to construct or support a theory," wrote Charles

Mackay in *Extraordinary Popular Delusions and the Madness of Crowds*, his popular 1852 exposé of hoax-like behaviors among his more devious-minded compatriots, "how they torture facts into their service!" Psychologists have since termed that tendency the confirmation bias, our predisposition to take in and sift through evidence selectively, so as to confirm what we're already expecting to be the case. Our desire to avoid dissonance in the first place has an in-the-moment impact on how we evaluate what's happening—and what we choose to evaluate or ignore in the first place. It's a sort of unconscious equivalent to what a lawyer does as part of his job description: collect evidence and present it in a way that sheds the best possible light on your side of the case, one very particular, and particularly selective, version of events that presents the cleanest and most convincing picture.

Franz Friedrich Anton Mesmer was used to performing miracles. A physician by training, he had over the years developed an approach to therapy that could cure the trickiest, most intractable of ailments. It was based on the theory of animal magnetism. Naturally occurring magnetic fluids, Mesmer argued, could be used to cure both body and mind. His first therapeutic breakthrough came in the case of Franzl Oesterline. She had a "convulsive malady" that necessitated around-the-clock care, and no traditional remedies seemed to work. Mesmer decided to test his theory: he set up a magnet that would alter the "gravitational tides" that were having such a severe effect on the young woman. The cure worked. It was as if a fluid had drained from her body, Oesterline recounted. She recovered almost instantly. In short order, Mesmer's Vienna practice became known for its incredible cures. A blind pianist was once more able to see. A paralytic was able to walk.

Next Mesmer took his trade to Paris, where he became a favorite of Marie Antoinette and Wolfgang Amadeus Mozart. His mesmerizing salons were the talk of the town. Sometimes he used magnets. Other times he would ask visitors to sit in magnetized water or hold a magnetized pole. He could mesmerize a roomful of people at a time: they would faint, have epiphanies, be cured of whatever ailed them. A Magnetic Institute soon followed.

King Louis XVI, however, had his doubts. He appointed a commission from the French Academy of Sciences to investigate Mesmer's claims. Benjamin Franklin, Joseph Guillotin, Jean Bailly, Antoine Lavoisier: the prominent men of Paris set about verifying the practice of "mesmerism." At the time, Franklin was quite ill. The tests, it was decided, would be held at his residence. Rather than go himself, Mesmer sent an assistant—or, if you will, a possible scapegoat should things not go according to plan. It turned out to be a rather shrewd move. The assistant "magnetized" a tree to see whether a blindfolded twelve-year-old could tell it from the other trees. He could not. There was no basis for animal magnetism, the commission reported back. The whole thing was a sham—at least from a scientific standpoint.

From what standpoint was it not? If it was all a con, how had it had physical effects on so many people? Mesmerism is one of the earliest examples of the power of our beliefs to change reality: the placebo effect, or dissonance reduction at its finest, in full action. We want to believe something works, and so we will it to work. Our mind literally changes the reality of our body's health. Mesmer clearly possessed strong powers of suggestion, and people really did get better in his presence. Scientifically, what he was doing was worthless. But people latched on to his purported claims, and the more popular were his successes, the more they conveniently forgot those patients he wasn't able to help. His reputation grew stronger apace.

One of the earliest scientific demonstrations of the power of belief to change reality came again not from a lab, but this time from the classroom. In 1965, Harvard psychologist Robert Rosenthal joined with an elementary school principal, Lenore Jacobson, to determine whether how a teacher expects a student to perform would, in turn, affect how she would see the student's performance. At the Oak School, Rosenthal and Jacobson gathered together a small group of elementary school teachers and told them about a test that measured intellectual capacity, the

Harvard Test of Inflected Acquisition. They had given the exam, they said, to Oak School students. Now they would share the scores, so that the teachers had the added information to better teach their classes. Some students, the researchers said, were "growth spurters." They could be expected to show significant improvements that year. The "spurters," of course, were actually chosen at random; the Harvard test in question did not even exist.

All the same, the teachers were soon seeing evidence of great intellectual promise from their "special" students. They were more curious, caught on to things faster, made fewer mistakes. In what Rosenthal and Jacobson then named the Pygmalion effect, now known as the self-fulfilling prophecy, by the end of the year, the spurters had indeed spurted past the other children. They were expected to do better, the teachers put more energy into teaching them—and, miracle of miracles, they did do better.

While Rosenthal's results are most often cited in the literature on self-fulfilling prophecies rather than confirmation bias, they illustrate one of the reasons the bias persists. First, it was selective information processing—classic confirmation—that caused the teachers to see students who were actually no different from their peers as somehow exceptional. It was all too easy for them to gather confirming instances of that superiority, and promptly forget the disconfirming ones. But then, the confirmation bias *actually changed reality*. The teachers managed to first reduce dissonance—between the students' actual performance and their purported talent—by selectively analyzing information, and then to do what dissonance reduction almost never can: change the resulting actuality. In this case, their altered behavior was enough for things to shift in their expected direction: the world accommodated their false expectancy and made it true. Children at a malleable point in their intellectual development respond to the most minute nuance in their environment in seemingly outsized ways. Pay more attention to one, and she thrives. Ignore the advances of another, she wilts. Teachers expected spurters to be special; they singled those spurters out, to the detriment of the rest of the class; and so belief changed reality. Because, in some instances, how we act does indeed end up affecting how we do, the confirmation bias persists despite its tremendous destructive potential. After all, thinking can indeed sometimes make it so.

Was it so crazy for Norfleet to think he could make back his investment? He had just been so successful, and Stetson was so good with the markets. It was all but a sure thing. That momentary loss was swiftly forgotten. The piles of ready cash loomed large.

In the case of first and second graders, it can be relatively simple to read into behavior: it's ambiguous enough, and they are still quite malleable. Tests aside, it can indeed be a matter of judgment as to who has higher potential—highly subjective judgment, but judgment all the same. Besides, for a teacher, being accurate in her evaluation of students isn't inherently at a high premium. It's not like she has money at stake. (The children, of course, are a different story. What was harmless for teachers was pernicious for them. One has to wonder how the non-spurting children turned out.) But what about more difficult cases, where the evidence is both clearer and more personally important? Do people then really do the same thing—selectively evaluate evidence and declare themselves confident in their own accuracy despite contravening evidence? How is upping the ante even possible—if you make a mark lose, don't you lose him for good? The breakdown seems doomed to fail by its very intent. As the saying goes, fool me once, shame on you; fool me twice . . . How, then, does it manage to succeed so spectacularly?

In 1994, a group of psychologists at Columbia University decided to test a case where the accurate reading of evidence was the whole point: the reasoning of juries. Here's what we hope happens as a jury decides a case. Jurors come in with a completely open mind and no prior knowledge of the case. They listen to the evidence, piece by piece, making notes on each separate fact they hear. Then they look at all the facts together and see what story—the defendant's or the prosecutor's—seems to have the most support. But even then they're not done. Next, they focus in on the supported story, review every piece of information that *doesn't* support it, and make sure none of those facts are game changers: the exclamation points in favor of the verdict still outnumber the possible question marks. Only then do they reach a decision.

In reality, Deanna Kuhn and her colleagues found, events unfurl in a quite different way. First, members of a mock jury listened to an audio reenactment of opening and closing statements, witness and defendant cross-examination, and judge's instructions to the jury for the case of *Commonwealth of Massachusetts v. Johnson*. Frank Johnson stood accused of first-degree murder. One afternoon, he had quarreled in a bar with Alan Caldwell. Things got heated. Caldwell took a razor from his pocket and made a threat: Johnson had better watch himself. Later that day, as afternoon wore into evening, the two men found themselves back at the bar. They decided to take things outside. No one is quite sure what exactly went on out there, but the outcome was clear: Johnson knifed Caldwell, and Caldwell was dead. Had Caldwell again pulled out his razor? Did Johnson actively seek to stab him, or had he merely pulled out a knife to show he, too, was armed? Had Johnson gone home in the interim with the explicit intention of getting his knife—and why had he decided to return to the bar? Why did the two men go out together in the first place, after an earlier fight? The questions loomed large.

What verdict did the supposed jurors favor? the judge's instructions asked. What factors had gone into the choice? Was there any particularly influential evidence? How sure were they of their decision? And was there any evidence to suggest this verdict might not be the right one after all?

The reasoning process, Kuhn found, was often the exact opposite of the ideal. Almost immediately, each juror had constructed a plausible story out of the events, spontaneously filling in uncertain holes to fit into the resulting narrative. Their "facts," it turned out, diverged quite substantially. "Caldwell first hit him in the face and he [Johnson] fell to the floor and then Caldwell took out his razor," wrote one juror. "So he [Johnson] thought he [Caldwell] would stab him, so he had to take out his fishing knife to defend himself." Or another: "Because Caldwell was threatening him before and later during the day and attacked him in the evening. So what he was trying to do was to defend himself from that. He just walked with the knife like he was going fishing or something like that. So, since he drew out the razor from his pocket and started to ... you know, he was trying to defend himself so he takes a knife to defend himself." They had supplied a lot of those "facts" themselves, where actual factual evidence was scarce. But in their minds, their story was the story.

Fewer than 40 percent of the mock jurors had even generated any spontaneous counterargument for their position—and the counterarguments, both spontaneous and prompted, were, in the majority of cases, not even real counterarguments. Two thirds simply presented evidence for another verdict, rather than evidence against this particular one. In other words, truly disconfirming evidence wasn't even considered in the vast majority of cases.

What's more, even though there was no clear consensus as to the proper verdict—that is, the data were ambiguous enough that multiple decisions were possible—most jurors were highly confident of the fact that they'd chosen the "right" one. Support for the verdicts was just about evenly split, with 50 percent of jurors opting for either first-degree murder or self-defense, and 48 percent for manslaughter or second-degree murder. Yet confidence ran high: just about two thirds of the jurors reported either high or very high certainty in their choice.

Kuhn's subjects had included a wide range of ages, educational levels, backgrounds, communities, and professions. Yet for all of them, the confirmation bias loomed large: a plausible story, followed by selective weighing of evidence, with pieces that fit the bill carefully inserted into their proper place, and those that didn't promptly discarded. In a jury, the motivation to be accurate couldn't be higher: lives are being made or broken by your actions. But the person who wins the case need not have the best evidence, simply the best story, the story that most vividly catches a juror's fancy. A good enough story—or one that successfully shows why the other guy's yarn just doesn't hold up—can trump any evidence that might later follow. That's why the well-executed breakdown, instead of ending the game then and there, actually takes it to the next level. We've already heard the tale, and so, hot off the convincer, our confirmation bias is going strong: the evidence seems off, but our confirmatory tendency dismisses it and we commit ourselves to the story even further. We are simply too far along to perform an objective evaluation.

Moe Levine was a legendary trial lawyer. Throughout the 1960s, right up until his death in 1974, he represented dozens of clients in injury lawsuits, using an approach he termed the "whole man." You cannot injure a part of a man, the logic goes; you only injure the whole man. A life is simply never the same after a serious injury. That philosophy colored his entire approach to trials—and earned him a reputation as one of the best speakers of his time. In a famous double-amputation case in which he was trying to win compensation for his client, he ended his closing argument with the following thought:

> As you know, about an hour ago we broke for lunch. I saw the bailiff come and take you all as a group to have lunch in the jury room. Then I saw the defense attorney, Mr. Horowitz. He and his client decided to go to lunch together. The judge and court clerk went to lunch. So, I turned to my client, Harold, and said, "Why don't you and I go to lunch together?" We went across the street to that little restaurant and had lunch. (Significant pause.) Ladies and gentlemen, I just had lunch with my client. He has no arms. He has to eat like a dog. Thank you very much.

According to reports at the time, he won one of the largest settlements in New York history.

And *that* is how the breakdown is possible. It isn't about the objective evidence in front of you, whether it's determining whether a financial loss is evidence of a scam or whether or not an injury qualifies for compensation. Moe Levine could have rebutted many a fact on the emotional strength of this story, just as Stetson and Spencer could explain away any loss through a compelling narrative. Confidence men are master storytellers, so by the time things appear to be getting dicey, they are perfectly placed to make us believe ever more strongly in their fiction rather than walk away, as we by any sane estimation should. They don't just tell the original tale; they know how to make even the most dire-seeming evidence against them look more like evidence in favor of their essential trustworthiness and their chosen scheme's essential brilliance.

In the case of Norfleet, what he already knew about Stetson and Spencer—that they were honest, had helped him in the past, had made him money, and had offered to buy his land—affected how he would see the first of what could, only in retrospect, be called red flags: the moment when Spencer not only lost Stetson's ticket, but then made an elementary error in writing a new one. Norfleet had already formed a very specific expectancy: Stetson is a financial wizard and has fail-safe ways to earn me money—and he has asked for nothing in return. And Spencer is a man very much like himself, who has charmed his wife, told his boy he was buying the farm, and put in a good-faith show with cash of his own. So was this likely to be a ploy or an honest error, one that Stetson would now honestly try to fix? The story seemed solid enough, unlikely to change in midstride. After all, it was so persuasively told, with plenty of evidence to back it up from the start.

"The human understanding when it has once adopted an opinion (either as being the received opinion or as being agreeable to itself) draws all things else to support and agree with it," wrote Bacon. "And though there be a greater number and weight of instances to be found on the other side, yet these it either neglects and despises, or else by some distinction sets aside and rejects; in order that by this great and pernicious predetermination the authority of its former conclusions may remain inviolate." As the scientific evidence has come in, it has only made his point all the stronger.

* * *

Back in Fort Worth, the men reconvened. They had collectively raised $70,000, still $10,000 short of their $80,000 guarantee. Not to worry. Stetson would just run this over to the exchange against their debt.

But here, Norfleet paused. He was no sucker. He was not parting with his money until it was all there and he knew for a fact where it was going. Stetson reassured him, tucking the money under his arm and walking out the door.

Not so fast. Now Norfleet drew a gun. A double-action Smith & Wesson. This was real cash. He was not about to watch it walk out the door in circumstances he didn't fully grasp.

This was not how Stetson conducted business. Disgust painting his face, he threw the money back on the bed. "Take the money and go to hell with it," he spit out, "if you can't stand by the agreement we made."

Norfleet was never one to bail on a deal. His word was good. Theirs, however, he was beginning to doubt. "You're partners," he told them. "And crooks of the first class."

Spencer began to sob. Stetson, meanwhile, looked Norfleet straight in the face and made a gesture: the grand hailing distress sign of a Master Mason. Not a sign to be used lightly. Norfleet replaced his gun.

"Brother," Stetson addressed him, a smile on his face. "You know I have trusted you with $60,000 and $70,000 in your room overnight, and not once did I question your honesty." He continued, "When I started away with this money I only thought I was doing what had been agreed on."

Spirits calmer, the three men once more sat down. Spencer would raise the $10,000 balance, they agreed. He'd wire the amount to Norfleet. And together Stetson and Norfleet would go to the exchange and collect the $160,000. That settled, Spencer departed for Austin, where he would sell some Liberty Bonds to raise the missing cash, and Stetson,

$70,000 in tow, departed for Dallas, to give him time to confirm the bid at the Dallas exchange. He was to meet Norfleet at ten sharp the following morning, at the Cadillac Hotel.

Norfleet arrived at half past nine; he didn't want to miss Stetson. Ten o'clock came and went. Eleven. Norfleet grew anxious. Leaving a note with the clerk, he walked from hotel to hotel in his search for Stetson. Maybe he had somehow ended up in the wrong place? He returned to the Cadillac. No, sir; no one answering to Stetson had called in the meantime. It was then that Norfleet realized that he'd lost not only his life savings, but, too, the buyer of his land. He wasn't just $45,000 poorer; he was also in debt to the tune of $90,000. How would he pay Slaughter for the ranch? He'd been swindled not once, but twice—even when his gut had told him something might be off. How could that happen to a man like him? How could someone so famed for his business acumen have become a laughingstock—one the press would soon dub the "Boomerang Sucker," the one who got suckered not once, but twice? It was the breakdown at its finest.

* * *

When reality pulls a one-eighty from expectancy, being selective in our perceptions isn't the only strategy open to us. As Festinger argued, we can also change our prior beliefs. We can, in essence, revise history.

Hindsight is always twenty-twenty, as the saying goes. And even though we often utter those words with a wry smile to justify a silly-seeming error, we don't tend to realize that, just as often, we revise our own memories of what came before so that it's not just hindsight that's twenty-twenty; it's as if we'd expected events to unfurl in a certain way all along. I knew she was up to no good. I knew he was pulling my leg. I knew he was going to call that shot. I knew, I knew, I knew. Yet if we had actually known, wouldn't we have acted quite differently? "Within an hour of the market closing every day, experts can be heard on the radio explaining with high confidence why the market acted as it did," says Kahneman. "A listener could well draw the incorrect inference that the behavior of the market was so reasonable that it could have been predicted earlier in the day."

It was the fall of 1972, and President Nixon was in the final stages of preparation for his trip to China. It would be a historic moment, all knew, but no one was sure precisely how. The media was filled with various predictions. Would the visit be a success? What would be accomplished? What would be discussed? For Baruch Fischhoff and his Hebrew University colleague Ruth Beyth, this was just the opportunity they had been waiting for. For several years, they had been studying the nature of our judgments before and after the fact. They'd found something they called creeping determinism—a determinism that crept backward from knowledge to prior belief. Never before, though, had they had a chance to conduct such a precise test of their theory, where not only could predictions be made in real time, but they could then be verified, and memory retested.

One afternoon, the two psychologists asked students in their classes to make a few predictions. President Nixon was about to go to China, they explained. Here were a few possible directions the visit might take: the United States will establish a permanent diplomatic mission in Beijing, but not grant diplomatic recognition; President Nixon will meet Mao at least once; and so on. How likely did they think each of them was to happen, from zero (no chance) to one hundred (certain to happen)? Two weeks later, Nixon's trip now concluded, they again handed out some questionnaires. Now, though, they asked the students to do something slightly different: reconstruct their earlier answers—that is, pick the same likelihood for each event that they had two weeks prior. They also asked them how closely they had been following the news, and, for each event, whether they knew the actual outcome.

The second time around, three fourths of the students reported having given greater probabilities than they'd actually done to the events that they subsequently believed had taken place. Fifty-seven percent reported lower after-the-fact probability judgments for events that hadn't actually happened.

Fischhoff and Beyth, moreover, hadn't simply been looking at a single group of students in isolation. Instead, they'd given the questionnaires to different classes, at different times (and some had been asked about Nixon's trip to Moscow instead of China). For some students, the elapsed time from the first to the second was indeed two weeks. For others, though, it could be anywhere from three to six months. Over time, the psychologists found, memory got even worse: fully 84 percent of those in the three-to-six-month group showed faulty recall. They termed the tendency the hindsight bias. In hindsight, we don't just say we should have known it. We say we did, in fact, know it.

So what could Norfleet do, once his initial money was lost? Either he could admit he'd been wrong, that he'd fallen for the magic wallet scam—one of the oldest in the book—or he could say he'd known there was risk all along, but that he had made the investment because, fundamentally, the plan was sound. And if the latter was true, then why not continue to show support by giving over even more money? In hindsight, he was being daft. In the moment, he was exhibiting a hindsight bias of the strongest kind.

Stetson's show of indignity made it all the stronger: it activated the memory of their shared Masonic bond, of everything that came with fellowship and trust. Of the many good turns he'd done Norfleet, and the many ways he'd trusted him with astronomic sums. Stetson did, in other words, what con artists do best: selectively draw our attention to the things they want us to remember so that we conveniently forget the things that cast them in a bad light—like the fact that Stetson had just walked out with the cash. Besides, everything can be reinterpreted in a positive light, can it not? He was just, he thought, acting according to instructions. How could Norfleet be so untrusting?

When he handed over his cash for the final time, putting away his gun and letting Stetson depart, Norfleet attempted the third of Festinger's change strategies: act in a way that attempts to change reality. The reality was that he'd lost money. But how could that be if he'd made a sound investment? It was an accident, a mere fluke. A spot of bad luck.

And there's nothing better to change some bum luck than a little extra financial greasing. Doubling down: it's exactly the sort of reasoning a con artist relies on as he executes the breakdown.

In 1796, the Marquis de Laplace observed in his *Essai philosophique sur les probabilités* that "it is principally at games of chance that a multitude of illusions support hope and sustain it against unfavorable chances." This became the first known formulation of a bias that in more recent years has become one of the most widely studied tendencies in cognitive psychology: the gambler's fallacy. The name comes from that temple of chance, the casino. A gambler has just lost a hand. Now another. And another. Why does he keep playing? Why doesn't he just cut his losses and walk away while he's not too far behind? We tend to believe that chance has a way of evening things out. If a coin has landed on tails eight times, the next one *must* be heads. It's hard for us to wrap our heads around the fact that probability doesn't care about timing, doesn't care about what we think, and doesn't care about what came before. Each event is entirely independent of the one before, and will in no way affect the one after. Still, the gambler insists that the next one will be the lucky winner. It's been a long time coming, but it's right around the corner, in the next toss of the die, turn of the wheel, flip of the card.

Life is not a casino, and often the gambler's fallacy isn't a fallacy at all. It's an accurate adaptation to changing events. As Harvard University psychologist Steven Pinker notes in *How the Mind Works*, "It would not surprise me if a week of clouds really did predict that the trailing edge was near and the sun was about to be unmasked, just as the hundredth railroad car on a passing train portends the caboose with greater likelihood than the third car." And so, when it comes to events that really *are* chance, from gambles on craps tables to gambles in stocks, and events that, while not completely chance, are governed by a high degree of uncertainty, like financial investments, our gambler's fallacy (now properly fallacious) is all the more likely to persist: after all, at times it's not a fallacy at all.

In 1951, Murray Jarvik, a psychopharmacologist at UCLA—who also happened to invent the nicotine patch and test out some of the earliest versions of LSD—asked people to try to do their best to anticipate the future. Every four seconds, he would say either "check" or "plus," the first to signal the sign for a checkmark and the second for a plus sign. Before each word, he would first say, "Now!" At that point, each subject would need to draw one of the two signs on the page, a best guess for what would come next. Jarvik would then give them the "correct" answer, which they were to note down right next to their guess.

Jarvik had three groups of students. In each group, the number of checks and pluses wasn't actually at chance. Instead, checks were relatively more frequent. What differed was that relative frequency: 60, 67, or 75 percent. If people were learning based on actual probabilities and feedback, they should have quickly realized that they should be guessing "check" more often than "plus."

Indeed, overall, that's precisely what happened. The higher the frequency of checks, the faster the learning. But there was one major exception: whenever a participant came across a streak of more than two checks in a row, the guesses for subsequent checks plummeted. No matter the group and no matter the overall frequency of the check, people simply couldn't believe that runs could go on indefinitely. The next one would surely be a plus; it was about time. Jarvik called this the negative recency effect. "The interference of the negative recency effect with the overall trend of probability learning is so great after three to four 'checks' for the various curves that all gains are temporarily obliterated," he wrote, "and after four or five 'checks' the preponderance of anticipations is in the opposite direction, that is, of plusses to come."

The negative recency effect was the first experimental demonstration of the gambler's fallacy in action. Even with strong probability, it overshadows logic. In the decades since Jarvik's work, it has been demonstrated in situations like actual gamblers' behavior in casinos, state lottery games, card games, heads-tails guesses, and stock market trading.

Norfleet had just lost $20,000. But with just one more investment, one more play, he could make it all back, and then some. And so, like all gamblers, even the most rational-seeming ones, he took the plunge.

A loss, a good confidence artist knows, doesn't spell the end: that's why the breakdown sucks the mark in further rather than letting him off the hook. Under the right circumstances, a loss can signal a deepening of commitment. There's evidence that if we experience a particularly painful situation—the loss of a lot of money, for example—and then successfully overcome it, or think we've done so, say, by deciding to give more money, we feel a great sense of accomplishment—and, a bit perversely, a greater sense of loyalty to the cause of our pain. In one early study, Harold Gerard and Grover Mathewson found that people who had to undergo a severe electric shock to be admitted to a group subsequently rated the group as more attractive. We may have lost, but it was all worth it: we become more loyal by virtue of pain, be it physical (shock) or emotional (financial loss).

Consider how loyal Robert Crichton remained to Demara over the years. He had been fooled by him multiple times, when he vouched for the great impostor's "genuine reformation," only to have it blow up in his face. He'd put his reputation on the line for Fred's new escapades, only to have that reputation tarnished when those escapades went south, as they inevitably did. He invested thousands of dollars in helping Fred "make good," despite no return on investment—and several lawsuits where Fred claimed he'd been "duped" and was owed massive amounts of money. Time and time again, Demara took advantage of Crichton—and time and time again, Crichton remained loyal to him and believed in their friendship. Fred was masterful at playing the breakdown over and over: another loss, but *this* time, I swear I'll make it right, if only you stay committed. How could you say no?

Unfortunately for us, the worse the losses get, the more we are likely to stumble. Positive illusions, psychologist Shelley Taylor notes, are often defensive mechanisms to a threatening circumstance. Even if we don't realize our worldview is under fire, we already start overcompensating to protect it. We don't yet understand we're being conned, but already, we are buying into the game all the more, to try to protect our certainty that everything will turn out for the best.

* * *

Not all marks are created equal. Twice suckered was two times too many for Norfleet. He vowed to get revenge. Over four years and thirty thousand miles, crisscrossing the country, traveling into Mexico and Cuba, scouting up into the wilds of Canada, he meticulously tracked down every single member of the vast gang that had conned him out of wealth and reputation. "Go get those miserable crooks," his wife had told him. "Bring them in alive." And that's precisely what he did.

By the time Norfleet died, in October 1967, he was no longer the Boomerang Sucker. He was the "Little Tiger of Hale County," the one who single-handedly took down one of the largest organized crime rings in the nation.

CHAPTER 8

THE SEND AND
THE TOUCH

Contrary to popular opinion, the hustle is not a new dance step—it is an old business procedure.

—Fran Lebowitz

For close to twenty years, the modern art world witnessed an influx of never-before-seen masterpieces from some of the most acclaimed Abstract Expressionist—AbEx—artists of the twentieth century. Jackson Pollock. Mark Rothko. Robert Motherwell. Clyfford Still. Willem de Kooning. Barnett Newman. Franz Kline. Sam Francis. The scope was tremendous, the quality undeniable. The dealer who brought them to the public eye, Glafira Rosales, had exclusive ties to an anonymous collector who had received a large art inheritance from his father; it was from his collection that the paintings now came. And the gallery responsible more than any other for bringing them to the public eye: Knoedler & Company, the oldest art gallery in Manhattan.

The buyers spanned a who's who of art collectors, from prominent business moguls to actors to people who simply loved art. The Abstract Expressionist masterpieces made their way around the world. Local exhibitions. The famed Fondation Beyeler. A Guggenheim show.

Experts rendered their opinions. David Anfam, the historian who had authored the catalogue raisonné—the definitive, official compendium of an artist's work—for Mark Rothko's works on canvas declared the Rothkos breathtaking. The National Gallery, then in the process of compiling the catalogue raisonné for Rothko's works on paper, declared its intention to include a Rothko from the collection in its final pages. "This belongs in the Metropolitan Museum," one expert wrote about a Pollock. But from whence had this treasure trove come?

Glafira Rosales was a relatively recent arrival in the United States. Born in Mexico, to a prominent Catholic family, she had grown up surrounded by the crème de la crème of society. Artists, collectors, leaders congregated in the Rosales household, chatting with the little girl, asking her uncle, the bishop, for advice. Among those friends was an older couple, European Jewish émigrés, she recalls. They were avid art collectors, and she listened in rapt fascination as they described the artists they'd met and the paintings they'd bought. This, thought Glafira, was what she wanted to do with her life.

She grew up. She traveled the world. In Spain, she met a man and promptly fell in love. His name was Jose Carlos Bergantiños Diaz, and he promised he would take care of her always. Together, they decided to try their fortunes in the United States, the land of opportunity for immigrants. They bought a house in the suburbs. They had a daughter. At long last, she opened the art gallery she'd always wanted: King's Fine Arts. Glafira immersed herself in her art. Jose Carlos took up some philanthropic and humanitarian pursuits. Life was going well. Better than she'd ever hoped. In 1986, she was granted permanent residence.

It was sometime in the early 1990s that the news reached her from Mexico: her old family friend, the art collector, had died. And unlike him, his children had no interest in painting; they wanted nothing more than to get rid of the things. They were only taking up space in storage. To them, they were worth far more sold. They'd heard that Glafira was now in the art world herself. Would she help find the canvases a good home? The price was unimportant—she could determine the market value herself. That's what they were hiring her for. That, and her discretion. Since she was a family friend, they knew they could count on her silence.

It was of paramount importance, the son stressed, that the paintings' origin not become known. It wasn't much of a secret that their father had been a closet homosexual—and the paintings, well, they had been acquired under the radar, with the help of a certain like-minded special friend of his, who worked closely with the artists and was able to move unmolested from one studio to the next, picking up pieces that wouldn't be inventoried, wouldn't be officially catalogued, and so wouldn't be subject to those pesky tax regulations. For family pride— they didn't want to officiate that he was gay—as well as family decency— they couldn't be seen as tax evaders—it was crucial, he couldn't repeat enough, to maintain complete anonymity.

Glafira was only too happy to oblige. But one question remained: how would she sell the paintings? Her own gallery was far too small and unimportant for such a large trove of masterpieces. Besides, AbEx art wasn't her specialty. She didn't rightly know what the works were worth or who the key collectors would be. For that, she needed a specialist.

Since the mid-1980s, Rosales had been making her way around the New York art scene. She attended auctions, socialized at openings, could be seen smiling, a glass of champagne in hand, at events and parties throughout the city. It was on one of these evenings that she'd met Jaime—Jimmy—Andrade. They'd hit it off at once. Like her, he spoke Spanish. He was older, elegant, a gentleman of the classic school. His partner, too, she liked immensely—Richard Brown Baker, a contemporary art collector famed for his eye and his largesse. Whenever she and Andrade saw each other, they met like old friends. Air kisses, fond words, endless smiles all around. And Andrade, she knew, had for decades worked at the Knoedler Gallery—just the kind of place, with just the kind of reputation, that she now needed for her newly discovered collection.

Glafira called Jimmy. He'd already arranged to have her come to the Knoedler once before, when Glafira had come into possession of some sketches by Richard Diebenkorn, but this time she had something far more substantial, she told him. Would he arrange an introduction to Ann Freedman, the gallery's director? There was a painting she would want to see.

Ann Freedman doesn't recall the first time she met Glafira Rosales. It hadn't seemed important—some friend of Jimmy's bringing in some Diebenkorns that, in the grand scheme of things, weren't worth all that much. Back in 1991, 1992, maybe even 1993? She couldn't rightly be sure. Someone had brought the prints. She'd sold them. That was that.

But this meeting—this meeting she recalls well. It wasn't Glafira Rosales who made an impression. It was the painting she held out in her arms. A pale pink-peach background. Two clouds of color. "Breathtaking. It was a beautiful Rothko," she tells me, closing her eyes. Freedman is tall and thin, a mass of short gray curls lining an angular face, rimless glasses, a penchant for sneakers over heels that does nothing to mar the elegance of her outfits. It's a painful subject for Freedman to revisit. That meeting, after all, led to what some might call her downfall: being dismissed from Knoedler, accused of fraud, watching her beloved gallery shut its doors. (Rosales did not implicate her in her confession; legally, Freedman is innocent, as of this writing.) Losing friends. Losing clients. Losing the faith of the people who had once held her in high regard. She could not have predicted it, not for a moment. The art was just so compelling. How could it have been fake, or "wrong," in the preferred language of the art world?

Freedman asked Rosales where the painting had come from. It was beautiful, true, but it needed a provenance. Paintings don't just appear out of nowhere. A private collector, Rosales explained. Somebody who wished to remain anonymous—she had promised the family. It had been purchased under private circumstances, never recorded, and had been in storage for decades. For half a century or more, the art had been languishing away. All Rosales was willing to say for certain was that a certain Mr. X had, back in the heyday of Abstract Expressionism, grown chummy with some artists destined for future greatness. He dealt in cash, off the record, directly from the artist to his home. No official paper trail existed because no official paper trail had ever been made. Any receipts that did pass from hand to hand, Rosales said, would likely have been thrown out by Mr. X's daughter after his death. His son was the one who was now parting ways with the art.

And what did Rosales reveal about the son? He was of Eastern European descent, with residences in Switzerland and Mexico. Around 2001, after years of working with Freedman, who relentlessly badgered her for more information, Rosales would finally provide Knoedler with a family name. It was the same as the name of a Mexican painter of European ancestry who had lived in Switzerland and died in Mexico. His sons had managed his art collection since his death. None of the artists Rosales had dealt in, they later claimed, had ever passed through their father's collection. That, however, came much later.

For now, all Glafira was willing to say was that Mr. X had children, and those children did not like art. Freedman told her she'd need more information before she could proceed, and asked her to leave the painting with her for evaluation. Rosales left.

As luck would have it, David Anfam, the world's foremost Rothko specialist, was in town from England. He came over to take a look. He declared it a beautiful example of Rothko's style and assured Freedman it was "right," confirming her initial impression. Of course, one opinion does not a provenance make, but the same assurances soon came from others: Stephen Polcari, an art historian and AbEx specialist who had previously served as director of the Archives of American Art at the Smithsonian. E. A. Carmean, a former curator of twentieth-century American art at the National Gallery and director of the Modern Art Museum of Fort Worth. A slew of experts passing through the Knoedler. Rothko's son, Christopher, loved it. The experts loved it. And though the collector was anonymous, that wasn't all that uncommon. The art world is a murky place, with many opting to remain unknown, and bills of sale often elusive. Glafira did provide a signed statement that she was legally authorized to sell the art, and Freedman's team of researchers had not uncovered any indication to the contrary. Backed by the weight of expert opinion, Freedman decided to proceed with a sale.

More paintings from the collection began to appear. One by one, Rosales said, the accidental owner wanted to get rid of them all. Freedman was thrilled—each one passed close inspection—but, she said, she needed a better sense of the history. "Anonymous" and "Mr. X" simply wasn't good enough. A name was suggested, Freedman can't rightly recall by whom. It might well have come originally from her own researchers: Alfonso Ossorio, himself an Abstract Expressionist who had advised many a client on potential purchases. Ossorio fit the timeline and the artists, and the story seemed to hold. Rosales said she would check with the owner.

Indeed, she came back to Freedman, Ossorio had been involved. It was soon after, Ossorio's name now in the provenance, that a buyer, Jack Levy, asked for his prospective purchase, a $2 million Jackson Pollock, to be checked by the International Foundation for Art Research, IFAR. The sale would be conditional on the painting's authentication. Freedman readily agreed. The art, she knew, spoke for itself.

But IFAR wasn't as confident. The provenance, the report said, just didn't add up. Ossorio could not be the dealer. Because of the gaps in provenance, IFAR's area of expertise, the foundation could neither confirm nor deny the painting's authenticity. The sale fell through.

Freedman showed the report to the experts. Bollocks, they said. It made no sense. They would disregard it. It cast no material light on the painting itself; everything hinged on the likelihood of Ossorio's involvement. Read the actual report: no one had any material doubts as to the Pollock's authenticity or quality. Some of the reviewers said they couldn't render a firm opinion, true, but the majority of the doubts hinged on the dubious provenance. Convinced, Freedman bought the painting back herself, splitting the cost with David Mirvish, a prominent Canadian collector. Her belief was strong. She would take the financial risk. Mirvish, too, read the IFAR report. He went along with Freedman; her take seemed the correct one.

What about Ossorio? Freedman asked Rosales. He had been involved, Rosales said, but wasn't the actual dealer. There had been a miscommunication.

Soon, another name surfaced, this time most likely from Knoedler itself. David Herbert. A prominent dealer who knew many of the painters personally, gay like Mr. X, secretive: he was the perfect link. Rosales confirmed the find. Yes, David Herbert had been an adviser.

The story made sense. E. A. Carmean dug into the research. The threads came together. Herbert was in all the right places at all the right times. They had found, they thought, the missing link.

The paintings kept selling. Knoedler continued to profit nicely from the sales—as did Julian Weissman, a former Knoedler employee who had left in 1997 to start his own gallery and to whom, unbeknownst to Freedman and Knoedler, Rosales was also feeding works from the collection. Knoedler received over $63.7 million, and Weissman over $17 million. Rosales's share grew, as well. Between 2006 and 2008 alone, Rosales netted some $14 million from the sales of her prize collection. Between 1994 and 2008, she'd sold sixty-three paintings, forty through Knoedler, twenty-three through Weissman's gallery. Rosales claimed that she'd held on to only a portion of the commission; the rest had gone to the client.

Push as she might for more information, Freedman kept coming up against a dead end. Could she go to Mexico to meet Mr. X? she asked. She bought a ticket for her assistant and put him on a plane. Rosales was mortified. How could Freedman betray her trust? No, a meeting was not possible.

In 2009, just after Rosales became a U.S. citizen, the Dedalus Foundation, dedicated to Robert Motherwell's work, issued a report on the Rosales Motherwells. Originally, its experts had declared the Motherwells authentic. But as more paintings came to the surface, they began to voice doubts. The report stated, flat out, that Dedalus could no longer stand behind the work. In their opinion, it was not by Robert Motherwell.

The same year, the FBI began its own probe into some art that did not seem altogether right. It took time, but when, in 2012, Eric Jonke, a special agent with the IRS Criminal Investigation division, was charged with investigating, he dug quickly and efficiently to the root of the problem.

In the end, Rosales was charged simply with tax evasion, joining the long list of criminals like Al Capone who'd gone down on the same charge. In the initial complaint, Rosales was charged with failing to disclose all of her sales income from Glafira Rosales Fine Arts LLC on her tax returns and understating her overall income. She had also failed to disclose a foreign bank account, at Caja Madrid—a legal requirement in the United States if the account in question held over $10,000, as this one did. Most of the proceeds of the sales, in fact, had gone directly overseas, without so much as a disclosure. For the 2006–2008 period, during which she'd earned $14.74 million, she had failed to report at least $12.5 million to the U.S. government. Rosales was promptly arrested.

Lawsuits appeared. Pierre Lagrange, who had bought a Pollock from Knoedler back in 2007, for $17 million, was now demanding a refund. A forensic specialist, he said, had declared it a forgery. Freedman was dismissed. Knoedler Gallery shut its doors. But Ann Freedman stood firm: the art was good. "I had every confidence that, one day, I'd be vindicated. They'd be the foolish ones," she told me. "I believed in those paintings with all my heart."

And then came the bombshell. Glafira Rosales confessed. She'd done it: passed off fake paintings as real, with the help of Bergantiños, his brother, and an elderly Chinese immigrant in Queens, Pei-Shen Qian—the painter. He had created every last one of the AbEx masterpieces, and they were all blatant forgeries.

As she would later admit, Rosales had known all along she was committing fraud. She "then and there knew the Rosales works were fake and were not by the hand of the artists that Rosales claimed they were."

* * *

How is it possible that some of the most respected names in the art world were taken in for so long by a fraud of such magnitude? How did no one spot the stream of impostor paintings that was slowly making its way into reputable collections?

The send is that part of the con where the victim is recommitted, that is, asked to invest increasingly greater time and resources into the con artist's scheme—and in the touch, the con finally comes to its fruition and the mark is completely, irrevocably fleeced. It's Glafira Rosales bringing more and more paintings to Ann Freedman without any further clarity on the murky provenance that Freedman finds problematic (the send), and getting her to sell all of them, for more and more money, while Rosales herself makes plans to quietly disappear from the stage, leaving Freedman and Knoedler to deal with any fallout (the touch; here, of course, it didn't quite go according to plan. Rosales hung on too long and was unable to leave as cleanly as she might have done a few years earlier). And while it would seem a difficult task to get people to give more where they've already given without return, commit more where they've already committed without evident reciprocity— Freedman continuing to sell the paintings even though the information she has repeatedly requested is not forthcoming, and ignoring any red flags in the process—it ends up being far simpler than it looks. Once the send is in motion, with the mark recommitted to raising the stakes, the touch—the con's end—is inevitable. Once we are in, well and good, we are all in.

On the evening of June 3, 1976, personnel from the Teton Dam project in eastern Idaho were going through a routine inspection when they noticed two small leaks, one 1,300 feet and one 1,500 feet downstream of the toe of the dam. Clear water was rushing out from the two seeps, at sixty gallons and forty gallons per minute. Concerned, the inspectors reported back. The leaks, the managers concluded, were not serious. Besides, as of nine in the evening on the following day, there hadn't been any additional reports.

Early the next morning, about seven, some contractors from Gibbons and Reed who'd arrived to work on the dam noticed water flowing from one of the abutments. At seven forty-five, a group of surveyors from the Bureau of Reclamation arrived at the site. There, at the toe of the dam, was another leak. And a bit higher up, another one. Immediately, they informed their supervisor. By quarter past eight, the project construction engineer and field engineer, Robert "Robbie" Robison and Peter Aberle, had both been notified. By nine, they were at the dam in person. Another leak from the abutment, this time into the embankment's rock fill. The men gave instructions for the leaks to be properly channelized.

By half past ten, the dam's downstream face had turned dark: a wet spot that spread slowly outward. A deafening sound, like a crash or explosion, a "loud roar," Robison later said. What they heard next sounded like a waterfall. A massive one. The water was flowing rapidly, taking the embankment materials down with it. Quickly, two dozers were dispatched to the site, to push rocks into the fast-eroding holes. Robison looked inside: a tunnel some thirty, maybe forty feet long, six feet across, all the way into the embankment. "The water was flowing extremely muddy," he recalled, "exiting from the hole in the embankment about fifteen to twenty feet from the abutment." The dozers had only been working some twenty minutes before the soil became too slippery. Soon, one after the other, they tumbled over the edge, and downstream.

A whirlpool began to form on the water's surface. Like a slow-motion horror film, it slowly spread, widening and quickening as it went. They tried to stop it with rocks, but nothing seemed to help. Then the sinkholes started appearing. The embankment crest collapsed. At 11:57, three minutes before noon, the dam was breached. It had taken only five hours from that morning's leak for the whole thing to come crashing down.

The Teton Dam failure was one of the costliest in the nation's history. The dam had cost $85.6 million to build. In a five-hour span, the damage topped half that, $40 million, at the site alone. But the destruction went much further. About three hundred square miles, eighty miles down the Teton and Snake rivers, all the way to the American Falls Reservoir, had been flooded. Eleven people died, and twenty-five thousand more became homeless. In the towns of Rexburg and Sugar City alone, somewhere between sixteen and twenty thousand livestock were lost to the rapidly flowing water—about the strength of the Mississippi River at peak flood—and over one hundred thousand acres of farmland were now unusable, covered by floodwater that showed no signs of receding. By March 16, 1977, the damage claims topped a quarter of a billion dollars. The total claims, however, were expected to rise to $400 million—not counting the damage to the dam and its structures. Eventually, about $300 million in claims were paid out, and the total cost of the damage, by some estimates, was a full $2 billion. In short, the cost of failure was over twenty-three times that of the project itself.

What went wrong—and could it have been averted? In August 1976, Congressman Leo Ryan, appointed as the head of the House of Representatives committee set up to investigate the events at Teton Dam, initiated hearings into the failure. It was there that some alarming evidence came to light. There had been questions about the appropriateness of the site, about the structure of the dam itself, about how construction was progressing. Robert Curry, a geologist at the University of Montana, pointed out that the Bureau of Reclamation's study, back in 1961, had barely mentioned permeability—though the high permeability of the geologic material at the site would have certainly contributed to the dam's collapse. In his mind, the data for the project to move forward was "inadequate" at best. Harold Proska, a geologist for the U.S. Geological Survey, went even further: the site was in a "young and unstable" area. In fact, he pointed out, back in January 1973, over three years before the disaster, the U.S. Geological Survey team had sent a memo to the Bureau of Reclamation saying that the "safety of Teton Dam project is of immediate concern." Construction, though, had already been started. The memo was summarily dismissed. The director of design and construction, Harold Arthur, did admit that there had been problems "with extensive jointing, the fractures or potential fractures in the rock." But they weren't deemed serious enough to halt the building.

The committee chair had a theory as to what, precisely, was going through people's minds as they pushed forward despite the obstacles. He called it "momentum theory" and wondered whether *anything* would have caused the halt of construction once it had already gotten under way—"that is, the inclination on the part of the Bureau of Reclamation to continue dam construction, once commenced, despite hazards which might emerge during the course of construction," he explained. Arthur was adamant: that would never be the case, be it at Teton Dam or anywhere else. Safety was their first concern. When Ryan pushed, however, Arthur did admit to one thing: not once in the history of the Bureau of Reclamation had a project been stopped once ground on the construction had been broken.

The Teton Dam seems far removed from the world of the confidence game, except for one key similarity: once we've invested heavily in something, we no longer see it clearly, no matter the costs. Things that are red flags in retrospect are dismissed as irrelevant once we've already sunk sufficient resources—money, time, reputation—into an endeavor. It doesn't matter if we're dealing with artwork or something as serious as losing human lives, taking away people's livelihoods, creating billions in damage, and setting back the environment of an entire region by decades. One would think that nothing is as important to get right as a massive infrastructure project that has an equally massive potential to inflict harm. How could they not have known? How could they not have seen? How could they not have taken note of the warnings? The fact that they don't see or know, of course, is the reason that the send and touch are able to unfold as they are: we are so invested that we become blind, and so we raise our commitment right until the moment when the whole thing comes crashing down, be it literally (the dam) or metaphorically (an art gallery).

To victims of the Teton Dam disaster just as to victims of the Rosales art fraud, it seems obvious that *people should have known*. Look at the IFAR report, the Dedalus report, the shady Mr. X. You'd have to be daft not to realize you were dealing with fakes. Look at the geological reports, the warning letters. Construction should have been ended. Ann

Freedman should have realized, if not immediately, then at least once the paintings just kept coming, that something wasn't right. Because the flags. They are there. They are waving. And people aren't blind, right? Except they absolutely are. And the more they have invested, the blinder they become.

In the early 1980s, Paul Slovic and Richard Thaler were discussing the crazy things people do as they make decisions to buy and sell, invest and divest, in ways that seem completely illogical to an outside observer. Why, for instance, would a family drive sixty miles through a snowstorm to get to a basketball game they don't even particularly want to see? Well, Teton Dam, Slovic offered. Teton Dam was the perfect case in point. The family had spent money on those tickets. If they'd been free, maybe they would have stayed home and avoided hours of frustration. But the weight of the cost made it seem too important to let the tickets go. They had to make the three-hour drive. They'd already committed. And the builders at Teton Dam: maybe had they not greenlighted the project, they would have stopped on those same warnings. But the weight of the cost loomed too heavy after ground was first broken. As one senator put it in discussions of another project, the Tennessee-Tombigbee Waterway, "To terminate a project in which $1.1 billion has been invested represents an unconscionable mishandling of taxpayers' dollars." Thaler termed the phenomenon the sunk-cost fallacy.

The sunk-cost effect gives us a continued, strong motivation to believe in something even when the landscape has changed significantly since we first invested ourselves in it. In theory, we should only care about new, incremental costs. What we've already put into something shouldn't matter: it's lost anyway, whatever "it" happens to be—time, money, energy, whatever else. We should stick with it only if it still seems worthwhile in light of new evidence. We should abandon a dam if we see signs that the available data have changed since we authorized it. The money has already been spent, true. But if the signs are accurate, we are heading for disaster. Why throw good money after bad? We should abandon a partnership with a collector if we see signs that he's not what we first thought him to be. The paintings have already been sold, true. But if the signs are accurate, we are headed for an even greater hit to our reputation. Why not admit you were wrong, and emerge ahead of the inevitable scandal?

Alas, that is not at all how our minds work. The more and the longer we've invested in something, the more likely the sunk-cost argument is to get the better of both our reason and our perception. We don't ignore red flags. To us, they simply aren't there. They might be right in front of us, but we literally don't even see any signs of danger. In a famous study on inattentional blindness, Daniel Simons and Christopher Chabris found that a majority of people fail to perceive a gorilla pounding her chest in the middle of a basketball game when they've been instructed to count the number of basketball passes between certain players. So busy are they with their task that they fail to see something much more glaring. The exact same thing happens by the time we get to the send and the touch: when we should be running away, we don't even see the danger, committing ourselves further and further until we have nothing left. To a disinterested observer, with nothing invested and no preconceived notions, the gorilla is there, plain as day. To someone invested in a specific task or engrossed in the drama of the confidence game, it is essentially invisible.

In 1985, Hal Arkes and Catherine Blumer published a series of ten studies to illustrate sunk costs in action and thus shed light on what was driving the irrational-seeming behavior. What if they spelled it all out and made the red flags and errors clear? What did the sunk-cost fallacy mean in a practical scenario? It would be the equivalent of pointing the Bureau of Reclamation's leader at every bit of evidence and calling out the potential for trouble, or laying out a list of reasons, complete with documentation, for Ann Freedman as to why Glafira Rosales might not be what she said, and then looking to see if their behavior would change.

The researchers began with a classic behavioral economics problem. People were told that they have tickets for two ski trips, one to

Michigan for $100 and one to Wisconsin for $50. The trip to Wisconsin is likely to be the more enjoyable one. Alas, it ends up that the tickets are for the same weekend and neither is refundable. Which do you keep? Over half the participants elected to stick with the more expensive trip—even though they knew they would enjoy the other one more. The result held even when no actual money was spent and the tickets were a gift from a radio promotion.

Arkes and Blumer then enlisted the help of a local venue, the Ohio University Theater. Would the theater, they wondered, be willing to help them with an experiment: sell some randomly selected season ticket purchasers discounted tickets? The theater was happy to oblige, billing it as a select promotion. That season, some season ticket holders had their usually priced seats, at $15 a ticket; others had gotten a $2 discount per ticket; still others got a $7 discount. The tickets were color-coded so that once they were collected at each performance, you could count how many of each had been used.

Over the course of the 1982–1983 season, Arkes and Blumer tabulated the receipts. Did people who'd paid more also attend more performances? As it turns out, they did. For six months after the purchase, those who'd paid full price were reliably more likely to be seen in the theater than those who'd received a discount. On average, they attended 4.1 of the five performances, as compared to the 3.3 performances seen by the two discount groups.

What if the price were in millions? It didn't matter. People were told to imagine they were the president of an airline that had spent $10 million on the development of a plane undetectable by radar, only to find, with 10 percent of the project left to go, that a rival had released a superior model. They still overwhelmingly advised their company to finish the project rather than spend the remaining funds on something else. A full 85 percent suggested the wisdom of seeing it through to the end. What's more, they not only insisted on continuing to invest, but thought that the likelihood of financial success despite the odds was still 41 percent—significantly more than the odds given by a disinterested observer. The researchers tested another scenario in which you were either advising a different company or the project hadn't yet been started; to such third-party observers, the foolishness and chance of failure were apparent. But to the people in the actual scenario, the chance of success was seen as far more certain.

Arkes and Blumer observed this effect in scenario after scenario, going so far as to give the tests to economics students who had already studied the very effect the tests were getting at. Their results were indistinguishable from those of naïve participants who knew nothing of sunk costs. To the psychologists, the results were clear: cutting losses would mean admitting a mistake, and the psychological costs of doing that were simply too high. "The admission that one has wasted money would seem to be an aversive event," they wrote. "The admission can be avoided by continuing to act as if the prior spending was sensible, and a good way to foster that belief would be to invest more." Indeed, in an unrelated study, Northwestern psychologist Barry Staw found that even telling someone flat out that an investment decision was bad wasn't enough to get them to reverse it. Business school students who felt responsible for a bad investment continued to put money into it—significantly more than in any other option.

The thing is, just as with most fallacies, the psychology of sunk costs—continuing to wait it out despite a stream of losses—isn't always irrational. In the entrapment effect, people undergo steady, small losses as they await an eventual goal—like commuters who've already spent an hour waiting for the bus and remain reluctant to call a cab because the bus *might still come*. And indeed, at times, come it does. We are willing to take on increasingly greater risk for a reward that is potentially even greater. A dam in an area that has long needed it, leading to billions in economic gains. An art legacy that will cement your role as a discoverer of a key trove of important paintings, a part of the legacy of Abstract Expressionism. The only problem is, we fail to see the picture for what it is, and in so doing, both underestimate the risk and overestimate the chances of success. The longer we remain in the confidence game, and the more we have invested and even lost, the longer we will persist in insisting it will all work out: in the breakdown, we've lost, and it seems like we should rightly quit, yet here we are in the send, reupping our commitment so that the actual touch goes off without a hitch.

Not only do we become blinded to risks, but the past starts to look infinitely better in retrospect. Writing in the *Harvard Law Review* in 1897, future Supreme Court justice Oliver Wendell Holmes observed, "It is in the nature of a man's mind. A thing which you enjoyed and used as your own for a long time, whether property or opinion, takes root in your being and cannot be torn away without your resenting the act and trying to defend yourself, however you came by it. The law can ask no better justification than the deepest instincts of man." In psychology, that idea is called the endowment effect, first articulated by Thaler in 1980. By virtue of being ours, our actions, thoughts, possessions, and beliefs acquire a glow they didn't have before we committed to them. Sunk costs make us loath to spot problems and reluctant to swerve from a committed path. And the endowment effect imbues the status quo—what we've done—with an overly optimistic and rosy glow. It makes us want to hold on to it all the more. Those mysterious paintings start looking all the more real once they've been hanging on the walls of your home— Freedman herself purchased two, hanging them prominently in her entryway. Of course you weren't wrong about them. Just look at how beautiful they are. The proof, as they say, is in the pudding.

In 1991, Daniel Kahneman, Richard Thaler, and Jack Knetsch offered a compelling example: the case of one of their economist colleagues. Years earlier, he'd bought some cases of Bordeaux—he was a fan of French wines. At the time, they were $10 a bottle, right in his price-point sweet spot. On principle, he tried not to buy wine over $30 a bottle. In the intervening years, though, his cases had grown substantially in value. Now each bottle would bring over $200 at auction. The friend had been approached by potential buyers, willing to give him quite a bit of cash to part with the wine. He had refused—although he'd equally refused to buy any additional bottles at the new, "crazy" price. He wasn't going to get that much additional enjoyment out of them—he simply didn't think a wine could ever justify such a price tag. He was, the behavioral economists concluded, suffering from both an endowment effect—to him, the bottles were worth even more than $200 simply because they were *his*, though the exact same wine bought anew would be worth substantially less—and a status quo bias—the tendency to leave things as they are, neither buying nor selling, but simply continuing on as is.

Experimentally, the endowment effect is remarkably well documented. Repeatedly, people who don't own something—say, a pen or a mug, two items often used in these studies—will be willing to pay less for it than they would to sell the exact same object. Take this example, from one of Kahneman and Thaler's many studies. I give you a list of prices, from $0.25 to $9.25. I ask you one of three questions. In one case, I've already given you a mug from your college. Now I want to know whether you'd be willing to sell it for each of the range of prices (the "sellers"). In another case, I ask you whether, at each price, you'd be willing to buy a mug (the "buyers"). In a final case, I ask you whether, at each price, you'd rather have the cash or the mug (the "choosers"). Objectively, the sellers and choosers are in identical positions: getting either cash or mug, at a price of their choice. But what the researchers observed was that the choosers actually behaved much more like the buyers, willing to spend, on average, up to $3.12 on the mug (compared with the buyers' $2.87). Above that, they wanted the cash. The sellers, in contrast, wouldn't part with the mug for less than $7.12. Once we have something, its value increases by virtue of that ownership. We no longer look objectively; we look with the eyes of someone who has put down a stake.

Small children do the same thing instinctively: the toy they have becomes more valuable than the toy they didn't get. It's the grass is greener turned on its head. We quite rationally decide that we might as well enjoy what we own. And so its value rises in our minds.

The status quo bias only makes things worse. We like things as they are. Children already know the toy they have is fun. Why risk exchanging it only to find the new one isn't as good? The new path is uncertain. The one we're on, we've already charted out and experienced. Just ask the executives who came up with New Coke. They'll tell you how deeply we cling to the status quo. From toys to elections (the incumbent effect) to jobs and relationships that coast along on inertia, the status quo is supremely attractive. As Samuel Johnson once said, "To do nothing is within the power of all men." Once we're in the home stretch of the confidence game, our investment renders us unable to be objective about the past evidence; we ignore the breakdown and open the way for the send because we refuse to admit we could have been wrong. We persist in acting as we did before, despite the growing evidence that we should change course. And so of course the con is successful: the touch goes off without a hitch, and we're left completely fleeced.

In one of the first demonstrations of the effect, William Samuelson and Richard Zeckhauser had people role-play a layperson, a manager, or a government policymaker. In one scenario, approximately five hundred economics students pretended to be, while financially literate and interested in the markets, inexperienced in investment—until now, when a relative has left them a large inheritance. How would they invest it? People left to their own devices chose substantially different investments from those who'd been told that a good chunk of the money had already been invested in a certain company. Independently, the company hadn't been very popular or a particularly attractive option. But when a good amount of the investment was already in it, many elected to keep it that way.

The same pattern held even when the data were very clearly against the status quo. This time, students were top managers at a regional airline and had to decide on the number and type of aircraft they would fly in each of two years. They could, the experimenters told them, switch leases for year two at absolutely no cost. At each decision point, for the first and second year, the students received a forecast for predicted economic conditions. The forecast was either good (stable airfares, high demand) or bad (price wars, lower demand). Some students received a good followed by a bad forecast, while for others the forecasts were reversed.

Rationally, someone with a good forecast should lease a larger fleet. Someone with a bad forecast should commit to a smaller one. If the forecast changes, the first manager should cut back, and the second expand. That's not, however, what their subjects did. In the first scenario, 64 percent of the students had chosen the larger fleet to begin with—and a full 50 percent stuck with it for year two. That is, 79 percent overall stuck with the status quo. In the second scenario, 57 percent started out with a smaller fleet—and despite the lost economic opportunity, 43 percent stuck with it in year two. That is, 86 percent overall sticking to their guns despite the changing landscape and the new information. The status, in other words, had changed markedly. The status quo, however, had not.

Samuelson and Zeckhauser went on to replicate the effect in actual behaviors, first by looking at the default options in Harvard University employee health plans, and then by examining retirement plans for the Teachers Insurance and Annuity Association. In both cases, a very strong status quo persisted. Despite new, better plans becoming available, people tended to stick with what they knew. "The individual," they concluded, "may retain the status quo out of convenience, habit or inertia, policy (company or government) or custom, because of fear or innate conservatism, or through simple rationalization." Whatever the reason, their strong bias was to hold on to it no matter what. And when they tried to explain the logic to push people to change? "Most were readily persuaded of the aggregate pattern of behavior (and the reasons for it), but seemed unaware (and slightly skeptical) that they *personally* would fall prey to this bias."

In the confidence game, the status quo favors the grifter and leaves the mark in the cold. It's a question of perception. I, Ann Freedman, have already put my reputation on the line for these paintings. I've been selling them. And buying them myself. And exhibiting them. Clearly, I believe in them—and others know I do. If I swerve from the path now, what will it look like? And anyway, there's no reason to worry. The longer we're committed to one path, the more right it feels. Fool me for a day, shame on you. Fool me for months, years, or decades, well, that's a different story. I'm not that gullible. I couldn't possibly be fooled for that long. That's the exact kind of reasoning that makes us so susceptible to the send: we give more and more to justify our "objectivity." And by the time we realize something is off, if we ever do, the touch has already gone off and the meat of the confidence game is done.

Once we're in the game, it's easiest to follow the path of least resistance. It justifies what we've already done and reduces the effort we need to make going forward. The deeper we get, the more difficult psychologically it becomes to extricate ourselves, or to see that we're even in need of extrication. All of the factors are aligned against us.

Remember Demara's escapade aboard the *Cayuga*? Even after news came that he was an impostor and not the doctor he'd been letting on, the captain didn't believe it. He thought the other Dr. Cyr was the liar. He couldn't have possibly been inveigled by Fred's wiles. He'd have him back as staff surgeon any day of the week, he said as they parted ways. He trusted completely in Demara's surgical skill.

Besides, we tell ourselves, the moment I see a red flag, I'll get out. I can always get out. This is my choice, my situation, my life, and I am in control. The reason I haven't gotten out up until now is that there have been no red flags and no reason to do anything other than what I've been doing. I can change my mind whenever I want, if I see a reason to change it. I am, after all, smart, successful, and naturally skeptical.

That certainty, alas, is an illusory one. It's the belief that you can always control your exit, a subset of a broader category of beliefs in your ability to control events even when they've gone beyond your reach—the illusion of control. We recommit and are taken for all we're worth, victims of send and touch at once, because we never get out of any situation in time. We always think we're in control, and so we never realize when we should cut and run.

In 1975, psychologist Ellen Langer tried a simple experiment: have people flip a coin and predict how it would land. The coin, however, didn't just land randomly. Langer had carefully engineered the sequences. Some people ended up making a lot of accurate calls right off. Some people would be wrong most of the time, until near the end, when suddenly they became more accurate. And for some, the calls were basically random. In each case, the number of each type of call was the same. What changed was the order in which it came.

Coin flips are based entirely on luck. Unless you're playing with a loaded coin, you always have a fifty-fifty shot at guessing correctly. It's not an outcome you can control, not a skill you can improve, not something you can be good or bad at doing. It's simply that. A flip of a coin. That's not, however, how people perceived it. Those who made a lot of accurate calls early on said that they were simply good at predicting coin tosses. They treated it like a skill instead of dumb luck and said that, with practice, they'd even improve over time. When Langer asked how many correct guesses they'd gotten before, they vastly overestimated their success. She called this tendency the illusion of control: we think we are in control even when there's no way we can be—and even if, somewhere in the back of our minds, we know we're dealing with a game of chance. As Langer put it in the title of her paper: "Heads, I Win; Tails, It's Chance."

We overestimate the extent to which we, personally, are the designers of our success, as opposed to it just happening all on its own. When something goes wrong, we're only too eager to blame ill fortune. Not so when it goes right. In several studies, teachers accepted the credit for student improvements but blamed the students if they continued doing poorly. Likewise in investment behavior: if we pick a stock and it goes up, we think we're the cause; if it goes down, stupid markets.

And the deeper we're enmeshed in something, be it a confidence scheme or a more benign sort of game, the stronger the illusion grows. In one of her subsequent studies, Langer found that the more information individuals had about a pure chance lottery, the more confident they were in their ability to win—to the point that they actively refused a chance to trade their original ticket for one where the objective chances of winning were better. What's more, when participants were given time to familiarize themselves with and practice on a task of pure luck, they rated their confidence in their ability to succeed in that task significantly higher—even though the chance nature of the task had not changed in any way. They further thought they had more control if, in a dice game, they, and not someone else, were the ones doing the throwing.

Here's the most pernicious part: when you try to be reflective, you only tend to polarize your existing beliefs. Langer found that initial optimism grew only stronger with some "rational" thought. Yes, people seemed to decide. I really am that good. In other words, if Ann Freedman were to stop and reflect on her tremendous commercial run in Abstract Expressionism, she would become more likely to conclude that she was an exceptional gallery director and judge of quality—*not* that she might be the victim of a massive fraud. And so she would play right into the send, selling more and more paintings, until the touch left her with all the downside and no one to blame.

And it's not just gambling. In one classic demonstration of the effect, clinical psychologists were asked to give confidence judgments on a personality profile. They were given a case report in four parts, based on an actual clinical case, and asked after each part to answer a series of questions about the patient's personality, such as his behavioral patterns, interests, and typical reactions to life events. They were also asked to rate their confidence in their responses. With each section, background information about the case increased. As the psychologists learned more, their confidence rose—but accuracy remained at a plateau. Indeed, all but two of the clinicians became overconfident, and while the mean level of confidence rose from 33 percent at the first stage to 53 percent by the last, the accuracy hovered at under 28 percent (where 20 percent was chance, given the question setup).

Why is the illusion of control so persistent? Often, it can be quite beneficial for our health and success. It helps us deal with stress and keep going instead of giving up in frustration. Individuals who feel in control are more likely to recover quickly from illnesses and be healthier, both physically and mentally. Just like our other optimistic biases, this one comes with a dose of positive reinforcement.

Unfortunately, an unwarranted illusion of control can have the opposite effect: worse, more out-of-control performance. One study followed 107 traders in four London banks and found that those with the highest illusion of control performed the worst, as measured by managers' ratings of performance and the total compensation they received. In another, people pursued worse investment diversification strategies the higher their perceptions of control. In a third, the more illusory control a group of financial analysts experienced, the more overconfident— and wrong—they were in their market predictions.

And that notion that you can get out anytime you want? It's just as illusory. The more invested we are, the *less* likely we are to exit. The psychological promise of that possibility makes us think we can actually take it, long after we have ourselves cut off the route. We persist in thinking things are under control even when they aren't. That sense lends us confidence. And that confidence is misplaced.

If she'd ever seen a red flag, Freedman told me, she would have immediately called the whole thing off. She never felt—not once—that it was too late. Her commitment was to the art—and if the art came under question, well, she would never let that stand. Even after the lawsuits started coming in, though, she remained firm. There were no red flags. There was no reason to doubt. The paintings spoke for themselves, and the paintings were real.

The day that stands etched in her mind: the morning her lawyer called her to tell her that Glafira Rosales had confessed. The paintings were all forgeries. Stunned into silence, Freedman replaced the receiver. It couldn't be. The paintings were real. She knew it in her heart. She would have known. She would have sensed. She would have seen. But Rosales's confession was something she could not control. And in the end, it was unequivocal. All those years, all that work, all those masterpieces: it had all been a lie. The send and the touch had gone off without her knowing she was even in a game.

It was evening, the night before her birthday. Ann Freedman sat alone on a hotel bed in St. Louis. She was there for an alumni meeting at Washington University. As always, she was staying at the Ritz. She stared at her cell phone. Each year, since at least 1995, Glafira had never failed to wish her a happy birthday. She had never failed to get her a gift—something tasteful and restrained, nothing over the top, but always something with meaning. She knew she shouldn't dial. Her lawyers had warned her of that often enough. But she couldn't help herself. They needed to talk.

Glafira picked up on the first ring. Ann hadn't actually expected to hear her voice. She had, she knew, been warned to stay far away as well. They were in the middle of a criminal suit.

"You ruined my life." That was all Ann had wanted to say. "I hope you know, you've ruined my entire life. I trusted you, and you ruined me." Glafira didn't respond. She muttered something incoherent, something that sounded like an apology. Maybe. But Ann thought she detected a sob. The line went dead.

CHAPTER 9

THE BLOW-OFF
AND THE FIX

Regard your good name as the richest jewel you can possibly be
possessed of.

—SOCRATES

O ne hot summer afternoon in 1915, Sudie Whiteaker and Milo F.
Lewis approached a farm in rural Iowa. Madison County, just
southwest of Des Moines. Mrs. Hartzell saw them approaching
from afar. They were dressed modestly, with faces she at once deemed
earnest. But what were they doing in the middle of farm country? They
weren't from 'round those parts—that much was clear from the most
cursory glance.

Could Mrs. Hartzell spare a bit of water? They had come with a
proposition for her own benefit, you see, but they'd walked a long way
and it was mighty sweltering out there.

In a sparse living room, Mrs. Hartzell sat her guests down. She
called in her sons, Oscar and Canfield, who'd been working out back.
The family assembled, they sat down to listen to what the two strangers
had to say. They had a remarkable proposition. You see, they told her,
back in the late sixteenth century—January 28, 1596, to be precise—the
famous Sir Francis Drake died aboard his ship, the *Defiance*, just off the

coast of Nombre de Dios. This was *the* Sir Francis Drake, they helpfully pointed out. The famed buccaneer who'd raided the seas for Queen Elizabeth.

But they knew something most historians didn't. Drake may have perished, but one thing didn't die with him: his astonishing fortune, accumulated over years of buccaneering and careful collection. Its scope was so large that few could comprehend the enormity. But that's not all. Drake had an heir, they continued. His childlessness was a rumor started to protect the most devastating secret of all: that the commissioned pirate had an illegitimate son. That son was sired with none other than the queen herself.

Seeing the illegitimacy and potential scandal, naturally, the heir had never received his inheritance. But for centuries now, the fight to free the fortune had raged on. Any individual who helped provide the capital necessary for the legal fight—a fight that was to near its climax very soon—would make back his original investment multifold, as a thank-you from the current heir. For "every dollar you invest to help free this treasure," the couple continued, "a hundred will be returned to you." It would all be there the moment the bureaucratic red tape was cut, at long last.

Day turned into evening. The strangers showed no signs of slowing down, and the more details emerged, the more alluring the treasure became. Mrs. Hartzell looked at her sons. They nodded assent. Go to the attic, she told Oscar. There, take the tin box and bring it down. That box contained the entire family's life savings: $6,000. Everything went to the visitors—you couldn't skimp when great opportunity called. Milo wrote out a receipt, and the two departed with many a reassurance. As soon as there was any news of legal progress, they would be in touch.

There the story would have ended—just another iteration of one of the oldest running cons in history, the promise of a fabulous, nonexistent inheritance dangled in front of unsuspecting suckers—had Whiteaker and Lewis been just a bit more careful in their choice of victim. They'd failed, however, in that most fundamental stage of the con, the put-up. When they should have been reading all the signs and employing all their skills at assessing their would-be marks, they were too busy counting the money. And sure, they'd made off well with the lady of the house. But she wasn't alone. And as any good con artist will tell you, everyone who bears witness to the take must be equally taken.

Oscar Merrill Hartzell was a shrewd salesman. Heavy-jowled and slightly bug-eyed, he could nevertheless manage to ingratiate himself with most any client. Together with his brother, he'd been working the farm circuit for years, before quitting to join the sheriff's department, selling equipment and seed all over his native Iowa, into Illinois, Wisconsin, Nebraska, and the Dakotas. He knew a sell when he saw one. And the more he thought about it, the more something about the Drake fortune didn't sit quite right.

The next morning, Oscar made his way to Sioux City. It was a long trip, going on two hundred miles, but it was also the closest town with a library. And a library is what he was after. For hours on end, Oscar scoured the stacks. He was looking for any book, article, record that touched on Drake. He wanted to know what he was dealing with. Soon enough, his suspicions were confirmed. There was no direct heir, and no fortune to speak of. Drake had died without leaving much of an estate behind. The little he had had gone to a cousin. That's all Oscar needed to know.

He rounded up his law enforcement network. Working as deputy sheriff, he'd made a connection or two. He needed to find the duo who'd taken their money. It took no more than a few inquiries to zero in on Des Moines. There, he learned, was where Sudie and Milo made their home. Lucky. It was almost on his way home. Oscar was on the next train.

A question here. A tip there. A bit of luck. There were Ms. Whiteaker and Mr. Lewis in the flesh, intent on relating the story of the marvelous fortune to an enrapt hardware merchant. Then they saw Oscar. Surprise was quickly replaced by fast patter as the pair realized they were face-to-face with a past victim—something they tried to avoid as much as possible.

"We were about to send you a letter about the inheritance," Sudie gushed.

Oscar cut her off midstride. "I know all about *that* inheritance." He suggested the three of them retire somewhere private for a little chat.

It didn't take long for a full confession to come tumbling out. Over two months, the pair told Oscar, they'd taken Iowans for over $65,000. They meant no harm, they assured him. And if he would just—

That's when the story took another strange turn. Oscar started laughing. And then he did something else: he called them "rubes." He'd learned a thing or two about the history of the "Drake fortune," and Whiteaker and Lewis didn't know the half of it. "The field is untapped," he told them. "You took small pickin's." He didn't want his money back: "Why, my mother still believes your scheme will come through. So does everyone else I talked to who fell for your line." They'd been settling for thousands. The promise of the Drake fortune was a scheme worth millions, if only they played their cards right.

The Drake con wasn't new. It had been practiced in England since Drake's death, and in the United States since at least 1835. In the 1880s, Robert Todd Lincoln, the American ambassador to the Court of St. James, even issued a warning to would-be investors that the so-called shares in the fortune were worthless, and the treasure itself nonexistent. Its very resilience was proof of its genius. Warn all you will; the treasure was simply too alluring, and seemed all too plausible. Hartzell, however, would take it to the next level.

In short order, Oscar had established himself as head of the Sir Francis Drake Association. With the air of legitimacy, and the background knowledge to match, he was soon bringing in hundreds of thousands of dollars. For the next fifteen years, he inveigled over seventy thousand investors spanning multiple continents; for nine years, he operated out of London to be closer to the "action," as he put it to his investors. (Really, he just wanted a financed stint abroad.) Disposing of Whiteaker and Lewis early on—"a couple of crooks," he called them, "who have been reneging on donations and secretly lining their pockets with our honest collections"—he went on to earn over $2 million for the enterprise, more than half of that going into his own pocket. He took in entire towns, and many people invested multiple times over despite never seeing a dime in return. So convincing was his story that they were sure the *eventual* return would far outstrip the nonexistent one, even if they had to wait years.

What may be even more remarkable than the con itself, however, was how it ended: somehow, over years of deception, despite having received no return whatsoever on their investment, almost every last person he'd conned remained loyal to Oscar Hartzell. To the very end, hardly a one of those seventy thousand marks would go to the police— and most all would vocally deny that any deception had even taken place. When Hartzell was apprehended at last, he easily made his $78,000 bail and defense money: it was provided by the very people he had conned. During the long trial, they would pay $350,000 more in his defense, convinced as ever that he had been wronged.

* * *

Our reputation is the most important thing we have. It determines not only how we're seen by others, but also how they will act toward us. Will they trust us? Will they want to do business with us? Do they consider us responsible, reliable, likable, effective? In medieval Europe, *fama* meant two things: what people said about others' behaviors, and reputation. The fact that both ideas were represented in a single word signals a fundamental truth: our reputation, in effect, is what others say it is. Financial ruin is often the least part of the confidence game; in fact, many con artists aren't even after money. The deepest scars come to our reputations—to how we're seen by others and how that perception will, in turn, affect our future.

That is precisely what the confidence artist is counting on, even after, despite our best efforts at self-delusion, it becomes apparent that we've been taken for a ride: that our reputational motivation will be strong enough to keep us quiet. In the touch, we've finally been taken for all we've had: the grifter has gotten all that he's after, and is ready to disappear from our lives. But how to do that without getting caught, so that he can easily go on to play the same game he's just played with some new mark? In the blow-off, the confidence artist has one main goal: now that the touch has been taken, get the mark out of the way as quickly as possible. The last thing you want is for someone to complain and thus draw attention to the whole enterprise. The blow-off is often the final step of the con, the grifter's smooth disappearance after the game has played out. Sometimes, though, the mark may not be so complacent. If that happens, there's always one more step that can be taken: the fix, when a grifter puts off the involvement of law enforcement to prevent marks from making their complaints official.

Humans are members of the catarrhines: the intensely social primates that make up the Old World monkeys and the apes. Like our primate ancestors, we depend on living in groups for our basic survival; without one another for protection and sustenance, we wouldn't survive very long at all. But sociality comes at a cost. We fight. We displace others and are ourselves displaced in the relative food chain. We lie. We cheat. We steal. We quarrel. We betray. We backstab, literally and figuratively. As Thomas Hobbes put it best, life in its natural state would be nasty, brutish, and short. And so we must have ways of keeping one another in check to keep our social groups functional enough to successfully avoid predators and stay alive.

In the nonhuman primates, the task of group maintenance falls on a behavior known as grooming, a process in which monkeys physically touch, pet, and nitpick (in the best possible way) to signal to one another that they are invested in the relationships they have. Grooming is one of the most effective methods of bonding. The physical touch itself releases endorphins, and endorphins flood us with feelings of pleasure, warmth, and well-being. The time we invest in that touch signals that we have nothing more important to do than spend time maintaining our relationship. The more primates groom, in fact, the larger their possible social group. Robin Dunbar, an anthropologist and evolutionary psychologist at Oxford whose work for over four decades has centered on social bonding in primates, has found that grooming time along with the size of the neocortex (the part of our brain dedicated to higher-order functions) is a perfect proxy for how large our social groups can get.

That neocortical size, in turn, signals something very specific. The largest nonhuman social group tops out at about eighty connections. In humans, however, close connections have taken a qualitative jump, to almost double that, coming in at an average of 150—Dunbar's eponymous number. Presumably, such a leap in social group size would also signal a leap in grooming time. Our fellow catarrhines spend about a fifth of their waking hours engaged in grooming. Humans would theoretically need to spend proportionally more to get to their larger group size. But, Dunbar found, that doesn't happen. Instead, we spend roughly the same fifth engaged exclusively in grooming-like actions. So what changes?

In simple terms, language. We don't have to rely on grooming alone to maintain strong social bonds and forge large functional groups capable of withstanding the stresses of life. We have words. And just as grooming signals investment and trust, creating a sense of mutual obligation between groomer and groomee, so, too, can our words (combined, of course, with our actions) send very specific messages that guide how we are seen. When we speak, we not only groom—I'm invested in this conversation; here is what I can do for you and how I can help you—but share news about others—who did what, behaved how, said what. Language, in other words, allows us to establish our own reputation and share news about others that, in turn, establishes their reputation. That, in a very basic sense, is the entire premise of gossip. Gossip doesn't actually signal anything negative in itself. All it means is that we can use our interactions to share socially relevant information—information that can make society flow more smoothly. "In short, gossip is what makes human society as we know it possible," says Dunbar. It's also the reason the blow-off is usually the easiest part of the con—and the fix, so rarely necessary.

When we gossip, we establish how others behaved, even if we weren't there to witness it directly. We have, in a sense, access to the eyes and ears and experiences of our entire social network, making our functional network far vaster than the 150 people we call friends. We can say who behaved well and who behaved badly. Who was honorable and who was deceitful. Who is to be trusted, who to be feared, who to be avoided, who to be embraced. In establishing these basic facts, we become able to punish people who deviate from acceptable behavioral norms—like, for instance, those who would come forward against the Drake fortune and in so doing "jeopardize" the whole enterprise. Hartzell couldn't have been any clearer on this point in setting up his con; any press, and the whole fortune might vanish.

The whole world doesn't in fact lie, cheat, and steal, and life isn't nasty, brutish, and short, because we know that others will know how we act and that we can suffer for it. We care what they think—and what they think can impact how we fare later on. Without social information sharing, the ability to gossip and form consensus around acceptable behaviors and sanctions, society would devolve quickly into a mass of people who take advantage of one another.

In 1997, Dunbar and his colleagues did something we're taught from a young age to avoid: they eavesdropped. In university cafeterias, in bars, on trains, they discreetly (we hope) sat back as people went about their conversations. They focused specifically on those conversations that seemed to be between friends and that appeared relaxed and informal. Every thirty seconds, the eavesdropper would note the general topic of conversation, condensed into broad categories such as "technical/instructional" (someone explaining how, say, the election process functioned or a car engine works), "work/academic" (complaining about a class or pesky meeting), "sport/leisure" (that lousy Knicks game . . .), and so on.

When the researchers analyzed the topics that had been covered, they discovered a surprisingly consistent pattern. It didn't matter who was doing the talking or where it was taking place, whether you were younger or older, male or female, clearly in school or clearly not: over 65 percent of every conversation was taken up with social topics—for the most part, discussing others' behavior and analyzing your own relative merits, or how others acted and what kind of a person you are. That means that every other topic combined—work, school, sports, culture, art, music, and everything else—is only one third of our typical conversation. Everything else is, in one way or another, concerned with reputation, others' and our own. In some cultures, that percentage appears to be even higher. In one study of Zinacantán Indians in Mexico, social topics occupied 78 percent of nearly two thousand recorded conversations.

In 1994, economist (and future Nobel laureate) Elinor Ostrom had people make investments in two separate markets as they sat in front of their computer. As they made their bids, they could see what everyone else was doing as well—but not who those people actually were. One market promised a constant return no matter what. In the other, however, returns grew as a function of the number of investors. Which market would people choose to invest in, if they could choose only one?

It's a typical dilemma of the commons—the types of potential conflicts that Ostrom specialized in. (The name originally derives from the problem of sheep grazing on communal grass. If only one sheep grazes, all is well, but if everyone who owns a sheep lets it loose, the commons are depleted and there's nothing left for anyone.) If everyone invests in the second market, the group will reach its maximum payout and each person will go home richer. But if some people opt for the sure-thing steady payoff, that return ends up being higher than that of the no longer optimal second market. Ostrom found that, left completely to their own devices, people weren't all too certain of the anonymous others in the group. And so, many of them flocked to the first, steady market. As a result, everyone ended up making, on average, only one fifth of what they could have made had everyone joined market two. In other words, there were enough lone wolves who chose to bank on their own returns instead of trusting others that those who did trust in the collective good ended up doing worse.

But then Ostrom changed the rules. Now, in the middle of the game, she called everyone to stop playing and come join her for a quick refreshment break. There, they could all meet one another face-to-face. They would no longer be playing a bunch of anonymous bids; they could now put names to the numbers they'd seen flashing on their screens. As the players returned to their separate computers, the game became far more cooperative. Now the payoff was about 80 percent of the maximum possible amount. All it had taken was that brief moment of social exchange. In Ostrom's study, one final tweak brought performance to a new high: the ability to request that "defectors," that is, those who opted for market one, be punished by the experimenter with a fine.

Economist Robert Axelrod has found that one of the most successful strategies in games without communication—where we don't know who the players are and can't rely on what we know about them—is the tit-for-tat. You start off cooperating on your first turn. After that, you mirror what your partner did. If she cooperated, you reciprocate; if she defected, so do you. That way, if you both play nice at first, you establish a cooperative equilibrium early on. You are, in a sense, building your reputation as you go. That only works, of course, if you get to play repeatedly, as in Ostrom's games. Otherwise, you need to come in with a reputation to begin with—but for that to happen, anonymity cannot be the norm. Luckily, in the real world, it almost never is.

A reputation is a shortcut. It lets us know how someone will likely act and how we should respond to them even if we've never met or spent any time getting to know them. The famous prisoner's dilemma offers a useful example here: in this dilemma, if both prisoners cooperate—that is, stay quiet—they both get off; but if one defects and talks while the other doesn't, the one who stayed quiet gets the roughest end of the deal. One way to solve the problem would be to allow for communication—but the very essence of the dilemma is that communication is not permitted.

If you could agree not to tell on each other, you'd both get off. But you don't have that chance. What to do?

If we already have a certain reputation, it communicates for us. If we have never ratted someone out, chances are we won't do it now. If we've been known to be shaky, others are much less likely to trust us now. In one study, Catherine Tinsley and her colleagues found that groups in which one person was known for his competitiveness ended up faring worse overall in a negotiation than others. People knew the reputation, were wary, and ended up not being able to come to as good of an agreement. What people know about us affects how they act toward us.

Oscar Hartzell had effectively built the blow-off into the scheme from the start, making sure the fix wouldn't be necessary: part of buying into the idea of the Drake fortune was a commitment to staying quiet, lest the prize be blown. You didn't want to tell, because that would change how others would act: you wouldn't get your money. If you had a reputation of silence, you stayed in the game. If others thought you might talk, they could tell on you to the big boss, and you'd never get your payout.

But such a built-in forcing mechanism need not be the norm. Often, we don't even need external inducement; our own sense of self is the only blow-off and fix we need. We want people to think good things of us—and we fear the opposite. An Ann Freedman wants others to see her as a discerning doyenne of the art world, not as someone who falls for a scam, and so she persuades herself that there can't possibly be a scam even when it's staring her in the face. Chances are, were the whole case not to have been blown open quite so dramatically, many of the buyers who are now suing the former gallery and director for the forgeries would have stayed shtum and quietly asked for refunds. You don't want others to see you as an easy mark. (Indeed, not everyone who bought a Rosales painting has sued. And no one who has sued would speak to me; they did not want their names mentioned.)

Almost no one is immune to reputational slights, despite what they may want you to believe. We all say we don't care what other people think, but when it comes down to it, most of us really do. We ourselves are the grifter's best chance of a successful blow-off: we don't want anyone to know we've been duped. That's why the fix is so incredibly rare—why would it ever come to pressing charges, when usually all we want is for it all to quietly go away?

Our reputation is founded on how we act. We build it over time, by acting in ways that are consistent with the type of reputation we want. If we want to be feared, we punish, often and harshly. If we want to be loved, we reward, generously and frequently. If we want to be seen as fair dealers, we do the fair thing—like Victor Lustig, as he turned the fifty thou over to Mr. Capone.

Nicholas Emler, a social psychologist at the University of Surrey who studies reputational processes and gossip, argues that acting in ways consistent with a certain image is an important part of our social identity. "There are factual details of biography—in particular the history of their relationships with others—that people will piece together about one another and which draw on reports from third parties," he argues. "But reputations are also judgments, about vices and virtues, strengths and weaknesses, based on accumulating patterns of evidence which societies constantly process and reprocess."

We want to be seen as a certain type of person and so we act how that person would act. In her work on negotiation, NYU social psychologist Shelly Chaiken has repeatedly found that people employ tactics consistent with a particular reputation depending on how they want others to respond to them and what they hope to achieve. For instance, to get large concessions, they often act the part of the tough negotiator. In an unrelated study, researchers found that people often planned out how they would act in a situation in advance, so that they would convey a specific impression—and so develop a desired reputation. They would, for instance, follow rules like, "Be friendly so that he'll think I'm giving him a good deal." If he thinks that way, he'll tell others I'm fair. And then everyone will think better of me.

In all of these cases, however, something central is happening, regardless of the behavior: somebody else is watching. It doesn't matter if we act a certain way in private. What matters is that others see us acting in that way and pass it on to others—Dunbar's gossip pipeline in action. Anonymous charitable donors are relatively rare, and often the anonymity is thinly veiled. Someone already has a reputation for giving generously and anonymously to certain types of places, so by the venue and the amount, it becomes clear who that someone is. "Social identities," Emler writes, "are conferred or agreed by the collective, not merely assumed by the individual."

We don't just care about acting in certain ways. We care that others see us doing so. In one study, Emler and Julie Pehl asked a group of students to imagine that they'd been part of either good or bad events, for which they either were or weren't responsible. For instance, they'd won a competition through luck or a scholarship through hard work, had gotten into a driving accident, or been falsely accused of theft. Some people were told that an acquaintance had seen it happen; others weren't told anything. How much effort, if any, would they go to to share the event with others, from close friends to casual acquaintances?

In cases where seemingly no one was there to witness the event, people were likely to go to a lot of effort to share the news that cast them in a good light, and were slightly less enthusiastic about sharing the negative events. The negative, they would share only with close friends and family; the positive, with the world. But that changed if others had been there: now they would go to great lengths to share the negative—so that they could put their own spin on things. They expected their witnesses to talk, and to talk quickly. It was therefore crucial to outmaneuver them and do some damage control.

We may even go so far as to behave differently in public and private. In 2010, psychologist Mark Whatley and his colleagues recruited a group of students to participate in what they thought was an art evaluation study. They would arrive, soon be joined by another student (actually a confederate), and spend some time looking at and responding to slides of different paintings. After the sixth painting, the experimenter turned on the lights: there would be a three-minute break to let the students rest their eyes.

At the end of the break, both students returned to the room. In some cases, the confederate came back with two packets of M&M's. She'd picked them up from a vending machine, she explained, and decided to get some for the other student, too. In other cases, she would return empty-handed. The students then finished looking at the slides, and were taken to separate rooms for a private response questionnaire. A few minutes later, the experimenter would return, explaining that the other student (the confederate) had had to leave to go to work—she'd been dropping hints about being late for her job all evening. She did, however, leave behind some charity donation forms that she had asked to pass along. The experimenter then left the room, leaving the actual student with a fake questionnaire and a real charity donation form.

What Whatley found was that two factors were important in determining whether someone decided to donate, and if so, how much. Half the time, the pledges were private. That is, the contribution would be anonymous, sent directly to the charity, Run for the Kids. Half the time, the pledges were public. That is, the student had to list her name and address, and the envelope itself was addressed to the organization, attention of the confederate. That alone substantially changed behavior. Not only did more people donate in the public condition, but they gave a substantially higher amount: $3.98, as compared with the $1.87 average donation in the private condition.

The second factor that made a difference: the M&M's. People who'd gotten a favor became more likely to reciprocate by making a donation: $3.45, on average, compared with $2.32 for those who hadn't gotten any candy.

Public reputation, Whatley concluded, mattered a lot. We care how we're seen, and will act differently if we think someone is watching than if we think no one will notice. And we care about reciprocity: we expect others to treat us well if we've done them a good turn, so we'll do a good turn to those who've treated us well (i.e., fed us some delicious candies).

When I was in my early twenties, freshly moved to New York City, I went on a date with a young man who'd also recently graduated from the same college. At some point in the evening, we found ourselves walking through Washington Square Park.

"Excuse me!" An obviously upset man came up to us. He was dressed neatly, a light jacket over a button-down and slacks. "I'm sorry to bother you," he went on, a look of real consternation on his face, "but I need money for the train. I've forgotten my wallet and I can't get home to New Jersey. Please, my family's waiting. Anything at all you could spare would help." Ever the savvy New Yorker, I gave him a skeptical eyebrow. "I'll pay you back," he continued. "Just give me your address, and I'll send you the cash the moment I get home." I remained unconvinced. My date, however, pulled out his wallet and handed him a ten-dollar bill. "Don't worry about returning it," he told the man.

Our poor train-missing gentleman had assessed the situation perfectly. A date, probably an early one. The man still wants to make an impression. Approach him, make your plea—and he'll be generous. He doesn't want the girl to think he's cold or, god forbid, stingy. The story he told, too, was perfectly calibrated. He was a businessman commuting from New Jersey. He had a family. He just wanted a little help, not the whole train fare. And he was credible: he'd return it all. He wasn't begging, just asking for a moment's help. Who were we to refuse?

Actually, who *were* we to refuse? Later that evening, I was filled with guilt. Why was I so skeptical of the human race? Wouldn't I want someone to help me if I'd ever lost a wallet or found myself cashless without a phone or way of getting home? At the time, I lived just a few blocks from Washington Square. The next evening, I made my way back and sat on a bench just to see what might happen. Sure enough, I heard a familiar voice: "Excuse me, I'm sorry to bother you . . ." I got up and left, guilt fully assuaged.

Reputation is why so many frauds never come to light, why the blow-off is the easiest part of the game, and the fix a rare occurence indeed. The Drake fraud persisted for decades—centuries, in fact— because people were too sheepish about coming forward after all that time. Our friend Fred Demara was, time and time again, not actually prosecuted for his transgressions. People didn't even want to be associated with him, let alone show who they were publicly by suing him. The navy had only one thing to say: go quietly—leave, don't make a scene, and never come back. The monasteries went even further: they didn't want Robert Crichton to even write about Demara's time there. Some wrote incensed letters begging to be kept out of the whole thing. They didn't want the good men of God to be tarnished by association with that no-good son-of-a-bitch bit swindler.

Warren Buffett puts it this way: "It takes twenty years to build a reputation and five minutes to ruin it."

In some ways, public reputations bring out our best. Charities get more money. Worthy causes gain support. Reputation can even make people "cut off their nose to save their face," in the words of psychologist Bert Brown. In 1977, he found that, to impress an audience, people would incur huge personal costs: I will sacrifice myself—so long as it's publicly, of course—to prove to everyone else what a great person I am. In the grifter's hands, the same effect works to not-so-worthy ends, through no fault of our own. The sheepish man who lost his wallet gets his ten bucks; Hartzell lives to swindle another day.

Reputation comes with a dark side: the same public that rewards us can create vast amounts of pressure, sometimes very difficult to resist, for us to keep performing in ways that grow ever more difficult. Take a scientist making a research career or a journalist establishing his writing chops. You work your ass off, and there is the payoff. A paper in *Science*. A piece in *The New Yorker*. You are thrilled. You're making it. Suddenly, a broad vision of the future is swimming in front of you. The benefits this research will have. The breakthroughs your story has achieved. Prizes, awards, envy from colleagues: we allow all the potentially good things to come to overshadow any shortcomings or doubts we have about our ability to achieve them quickly.

But the glow quickly fades, and it's on to the next paper, the next story, the next book. Unless you can keep producing, you will fade from the public eye and that glorious vision will never come to pass. You not only have to keep producing; you have to do so quickly, before everyone has forgotten about you. And you have to do it at increasingly high levels. Something that was good for your first big break won't sustain you over the long haul. Then, you were a neophyte. Now you're more seasoned. In academia, it certainly doesn't help that the world is screaming "Publish or perish!" in increasingly harsh tones. Produce, produce, produce. Produce, or be eaten alive.

So what do you do? It took you so long to get that first masterpiece out into the world. But now that it's out there, you don't have the luxury of the same amount of time for the follow-up. To most people, it means taking a deep sigh and acknowledging that the glimpse of greatness was but that. You will have to keep slogging along and hope that, with effort and luck, you'll once more reach a comparable place. Yes, you'll be out of the spotlight. Yes, your colleague might get tenure faster. But you will do your best, and eventually you will get there.

Others, however, crack—under the pressure of performance, often from people who happen to be very important, coupled with the memory of the warm glow of adulation. And so, they begin to cut corners. One common explanation for Jonah Lehrer's dramatic fall—the one he gives himself, in fact—is that he was under too much pressure. So he started to borrow from himself rather than produce new work. Then he started to borrow from others. Then he started to change the facts themselves to better fit a nice story. The rest, of course, is history. Same for Marc Hauser or Diederik Stapel, two of the most high-profile perpetrators of academic fraud in recent years. First it's one small massaged data point. Then you have a reputation to sustain, and new, breaking research to publish. You cannot subsist on history alone. The rest, of course, is history.

The pressures of reputation that are so essential to the blow-off and fix can also, at their strongest, create con artists where there were none before: the same force that makes people loath to disclose they've been had can sometimes make those same people into grifters in their own right.

Academia has changed dramatically over the last few decades. Before, you needed only a few publications to get a job offer. The pace was slower. Some people were offered their first job on the strength of their dissertation research. No more. It's no longer uncommon for candidates for even entry-level positions to have CVs spanning pages upon pages, with dozens of publications, many of them first author, many in top journals. In a crowded field, it's increasingly difficult to stand out.

Something else has changed in recent years, too: academic retractions, a sign, often, of the con artist at play on the academic turf. Over 1.4 million papers are published each year. Five hundred or so—a quarter of 1 percent—get retracted. About two thirds of those are because people willingly misled or falsified. There are, however, more and more every year. In the last two years alone, according to *Retraction Watch*, over 170 (and rising) scientific papers have been retracted for a very specific reason: their authors rigged the system of peer review to push their papers through to the end, in at least six separate cases. Elsevier, Springer, Taylor & Francis, SAGE, Wiley: the affected publishers are a who's who of scientific research, the best of the best.

Starting in 2010, Peter Chen, an engineer at the National Pingtung University of Education in Taiwan, went on a publication spree. His research, it seemed, had finally borne fruit—and the *Journal of Vibration and Control* was seeing the result. Over the next four years, he submitted over sixty papers to the journal. The only problem: the e-mail addresses of the reviewers were fake. They were, in fact, all Chen himself—130 "assumed and fabricated" identities that, an investigation at SAGE found, was "a peer review and citation ring." And some of the papers didn't even list him as author. Chen had written papers under other names as well, likely to bolster his own citation count.

Chen almost got away with it. But in May 2013, an author who submitted a paper to the *Journal of Vibration and Control* received two e-mails from people claiming to be reviewers. In itself, that was remarkable: reviewers never contact authors directly. But the e-mail addresses themselves seemed suspect—they had been sent from Gmail accounts rather than academic institutions. Ali Nayfeh, the editor in chief, forwarded the tip to the publisher. The SAGE editors then e-mailed the reviewers—this time, at their academic posts. One scientist responded quickly. He'd never sent that e-mail and did not even work in a related field. The revelation prompted a fourteen-month investigation, spanning over twenty people in SAGE's editorial, legal, and production departments. Eventually, 130 suspect e-mail addresses were identified, and SAGE announced retractions for sixty papers—one of the largest retractions in scientific history.

It's a crime that permeates cyberspace. Take Orlando Figes, a prominent British historian, who admitted to writing fake book reviews on Amazon, praising his own books and attacking those of rivals, using false identities and accounts. And it's a crime that often speaks of a willingness to bend other rules, as well. Figes was later accused of "inaccuracies" and "factual errors" in his history of the Stalin era, *The Whisperers*. The Russian translation was subsequently canceled, and allegations of improprieties in past books surfaced soon after. Reputation can be a demanding mistress. It makes you a more pliable mark, willing to help the blow-off along any way you can—but it can also make you into a more ready fraudster of your own.

It's not that the confidence artist is inherently psychopathic, caring nothing about the fates of others. It's that, to him, we aren't worthy of consideration as human beings; we are targets, not unique people. We must forever be just another statistic—one in a stream of "jobs" rather than individuals in our own right. In something psychologists term the "identifiable-victim effect," people tend to be more generous toward unique individuals than statistics. If you're asked to donate money to, say, Doctors Without Borders, you will typically give less than if I were to ask you to support Annique, an eight-year-old from Ethiopia who has malaria. It makes no sense—the former needs more money than the latter, and you'd likely have more impact if you reversed your donation amounts—yet the emotional appeal of a victim we can seemingly touch, and certainly identify with, is strong. Baby Jessica, a girl who fell into a well in Texas in 1987, received more than $700,000 in donations. Ali Abbas, a boy caught in the Iraq conflict, commanded £275,000 for medical care within days. Even a dog stranded on a ship in the Pacific got nearly $50,000 in aid. We are more concerned, more emotionally distressed, more empathetic when we have a single, concrete name and face in front of us. And it's very difficult to resist. Even Mother Teresa once remarked, "If I look at the mass, I will never act. If I look at the one, I will." The con artist reverses that. He must see us as a homogeneous mass; that way, he will feel no compunction at all when it comes to blowing us off and putting in the fix—leaving us high and dry and the authorities none the wiser.

In 2005, psychologists Deborah Small, George Loewenstein, and Paul Slovic set out to determine whether they could break down the identifiable-victim effect through sheer force of logic. In a series of four field studies, they systematically explained to people what went on in their heads when they saw a single victim as opposed to a so-called statistical victim. Then they measured how much money each person gave to a charity or an individual. The results weren't quite what they had expected. People did indeed start giving less to individual victims—but they didn't re-channel their generosity to greater statistical causes. Instead, they were simply less generous overall. It didn't matter how the effect was framed: that people typically give more to individuals or less to statistical victims. And if the statistics were shown along with the victim—this is Annique, and she suffers from malaria, just like 67 percent of the population, or about 61.4 million people—the donations likewise fell.

One of the reasons Rosales was so successful for so long is that she cared nary a moment about the reputations she was savaging. One of the reasons Hartzell persisted for decades was that he conned tens of thousands—a sea, not individuals. It's easy to rationalize away conning someone—they were complicit, too. A truly honest mark, the saying goes, would never be conned. Of course, that's far from the truth, but the rationalization goes a long way. It allows the grifter to play the game to the end, disappearing into the night in a well-played blow-off, or after a well-timed fix, if it comes to that. And it allows him to keep the game going over and over, following each successful ending with a fresh beginning.

But we are not statistics to ourselves. And our view of the world is so egocentric, so intimately tied to the notion that we are just as important to everyone else as we are to ourselves, that we cannot fathom that everybody isn't caring nearly as much about our story as we ourselves do. So we cling to our reputation. We think everyone pays attention to the slightest thing we do, the slightest thing we say, the slightest deviation in our demeanor. And so, to the end, our concern for our reputation allows the confidence game to continue, over and over and over: the blow-off and the fix reach their intended end. We stay quiet. And the wheel turns again. The same players. The same victims. The same tricks. All sustained by our need to believe, not only in the best version of the world, but in the best version of ourselves.

CHAPTER 10

THE (REAL) OLDEST PROFESSION

Con men and tricksters run the world. Rascals rule.

—PAUL AUSTER

Bebe Patten looked resplendent: tall and elegant in her streaming white silk gown, roses adorning her hair. She had learned from the best. When she was a young girl, Bebe Harrison, she had studied with the great Sister Aimee at the International Institute of Four-Square Evangelism. Now, as she stood in front of the thousands-strong congregation, swaying back and forth, she could say she'd done her mentor one better. She was planting the tree, she said. "Amen," they replied. They'd be the ones harvesting the fruit, she called. "Amen," they replied. She was doing God's work. Saving the sinners. It didn't hurt if the saving came with a price tag.

Below, her husband was busy with the collections. She'd met Carl Thomas Patten—C. Thomas, he went by; the C, he joked, was short for "cash"—in Oakland, California. Patten was over six feet tall, 218 pounds. He dwarfed most men who came near, if not in length then at least in girth. He was a careful dresser. Bebe appreciated that in a man. Fond of handmade cowboy boots—only the best—and never without his Stetson, a silk tie ever at his throat, Patten had done well for himself. Another trait Bebe admired. His father had been a bootlegger back in Tennessee, and though Carl himself had never finished high school—he'd been expelled for operating a still out of the basement—he always somehow landed on his feet. He'd even gotten the judge to suspend a two-year sentence for transporting stolen cars across state lines. When he talked, people listened. The Tennessee cowboy, Bebe thought, would make a perfect evangelist.

In short order, Patten was ordained in the Fundamental Ministerial Association. And it only got better from there. Ten years of revival meetings had netted them a tidy sum, most going into their personal accounts rather than the myriad missions they claimed to uphold, and they were, at last, ready to settle down.

It had been six years since they'd first arrived in Elm Tabernacle, one of Oakland's less glamorous districts, in 1944. They'd started out in the tiny pulpit of the local church, their followers barely filling the front pews. But they were preaching the faith, good and true. Their followers had heard the call—that, or read the advertisements that Thomas placed in all the papers—a steady five thousand to six thousand dollars a week going toward reminders of "Green Palms! Choir Girls in White! Music! Miracles! Blessings! Healings!" Within weeks, the crowds were overflowing the church doors. They moved then to Oakland Women's City Club. That, too, soon overflowed. Next, the eight-thousand-seat Oakland Arena. Less than five months later, and $35,000 richer, they took up at the City Club. This town was as pious as they came. The Pattens liked it. Here, they would make their home.

Bebe's sermons stemmed from the Pentecostal traditions. As she and her flock survived "exhaustive and emotional bouts with the devil," there was Thomas, collecting away. He had close communion with the Lord, and his savior never failed to inform him of precisely what they would accomplish that day, down to the last cent. As Bernard Taper recalled, writing in The New Yorker in 1959, Patten's voice would ring through the vast space. "All right, now, brothers and sisters, God says there's five thousand two hundred and forty dollars and fifty-five cents that is here today that is to be taken up for His work, and God's word never fails," went the patter. "If God told me that money is here, it is *here*. That's a fact. How many say, Amen?" A chorus of Amens. "Hallelujah, to His glorious name. That's a lot of money, but believe it or not, brothers and sisters, there's three people here among you going to open their hearts to the Lord and pledge a thousand dollars each. Isn't that glorious? Everybody say Amen!" Amen. "How many people believe the Lord is telling the truth when He says there's three people here going to give a thousand dollars each? Raise your hand." A chorus. "Now, who'll be the first? Somebody in the back rows?" A timid hand. "Pray for him, brothers and sisters. He's got his hand up. It's brother Lilian. Bless you, Lord, and the angels sing! Isn't that wonderful? Now there's just two more going to feel the Holy Spirit on them today, just two more . . ." And on it went. If there was resistance, God's wrath wasn't long in coming. "God is going to slap you cock-eyed in about two minutes! This is where the fireworks start . . ."

Now they owned the whole place—just a quarter of a million dollars was all it had taken. Well, their congregation owned it, the Pattens told them. It was a people's church. "It will always belong to the people. It will be here until Jesus comes, until the hinges are rusted off the door," Bebe sang. The physical deeds, though, were—naturally—in the Pattens' names.

A school followed. A plan for a tabernacle (never actually built). Life was good. The congregants flocked. The Patten bank account held six figures, nearing $1 million. Bebe's dress: made by the dressmaker to the stars, Adrian of Hollywood. C. Thomas's boots: one of two hundred custom pairs, at $200 a pop. In the garage, four Cadillacs, two Packards, a Lincoln, a Chrysler, and an Oldsmobile. Preach the faith.

A month later, Bebe again stood in front of an audience. Gone was her white gown. She was in a blue skirt, pleated, and a tight blue collegiate sweater, the gold *P* of the Patten Academy for Religious Education emblazoned on the front, a gold cross prominently at her neck. And she wasn't preaching to her flock. She was instead addressing a courthouse—though that, too, was packed as tightly as could be, crowds spilling into the aisles. It was February 1950, and C. Thomas was being indicted for grand theft, fraud, embezzlement, and obtaining money under false pretenses. (For some reason, Bebe was not part of the indictment.) For four and a half months, the prosecution meticulously detailed how the Pattens had used their power to rob their congregation blind. Close to $700,000, the records showed, had gone to their own private use. Not just their lavish lifestyle. Turned out, C. Thomas also had a nasty gambling habit. "I made a little mistake," he shrugged when one casino owner testified against him, $4,000 debt in hand. They'd even sold the church they promised the congregants would always be there.

The Pattens were vocal in their own defense. "People give it to me," C. Thomas objected. "I'm the man who keeps the wheel lubricated to keep the spiritual machinery moving." He'd robbed no one, he insisted, echoing the refrain favored by clergy since the pre-Reformation heights of indulgence selling. Every cent was a willing donation. "We have God on our side!" Bebe echoed. "Glory Hallelujah! Amen!"

Even here, the answering chorus of "Amens!" dwarfed the courthouse. Their flock, or at least some of it, remained loyal.

C. Thomas hurled his curse in the direction of the jurors. "When you get your eyes off Jesus, you will always go down! How many say Amen?" Amen. Amen.

As the trial drew to a close, and the assistant DA read off her characterization of Bebe—"It was she who made the emotional appeal, she who set the stage . . ."—Bebe turned her wrath on the court. She held up a single rose. "This is just one of the many flowers that will come from the graves of those opposing us," she cried. "It came from the casket of that woman"—a woman who'd criticized the Patten church and quit in protest of its ways. "Now she has no power to change God's word. She is praying in hell tonight." She continued with a death wish on anyone who would dare question her legitimacy. "Lord, knock someone cold, no matter how unimportant, just as a sign You're on our side!" Strings of shouted "Amens" followed her exit. Her flock wouldn't desert her.

The justice system, however, wasn't quite as kind. The convictions came in. All of them.

* * *

C. Thomas and Bebe's loyal followers may seem like dupes of the highest kind. Suckers, pure and simple, who won't accept that they've been taken in even when the evidence is laid out in front of them. If they want to hold on to the Pattens' piousness even in light of all evidence to the contrary, so be it. In a way, it serves them right: if you willfully ignore evidence, you get what's coming to you. But the Patten con wasn't just any scam. It was the scam of all scams—the one that gets to the heart of why confidence games not only work but thrive the world over, no matter how many expert debunkers and vocal victims there may be. It was a scam of belief, the most profound yet simple belief we have: about the way the world works, why life is the way it is. We *want* to believe. Believe that things make sense. That an action leads to a result. That things don't just happen willy-nilly no matter what we do, but rather for a reason. That what we do makes a difference, however small. That we ourselves matter. That there is a grand story, a higher method to the seeming madness. And in the heart of that desire, we easily become blind. The eternal lure of the con is the same reason religions arise spontaneously in most any human society. People always want something to believe in.

"When people want to believe what they want to believe, they are very hard to dissuade." So David Sullivan—Sully, as he was known to friends—told his rapt Commonwealth Club audience one evening in July 2010. It was the first time he was speaking publicly about his unique profession: an infiltrator of cults. For two decades, Sullivan, a cultural anthropologist turned private investigator, had made it his business to get on the inside of cult-like organizations around the country, learning the groups' language, their customs and ways, their views on life. It was only as a "true believer" that he could hope to talk to any of the groups' members—and, potentially, persuade them to leave. He worked closely with law enforcement, following individuals at the behest of their families, trying to extract vulnerable victims or take down powerful organizations. He was remarkably successful, and where he couldn't go—many cults thrived on a very specific victim profile: young, female, vulnerable— he trained his colleague Jennifer Stalvey to go instead. In her three years working undercover alongside David, Jennifer told me, there was only ever one failure, a woman who to this day remains in the organization that had recruited her many years earlier. Over the years, Sullivan and Stalvey made their share of enemies.

The Pattens, of course, hadn't been running a cult. But in many ways, the type of faux evangelism they embodied was at the heart of what Sullivan hated most of all: individuals who exploit our need for belief for their own private gains—the hallmark of the confidence game. He would have understood perfectly the Patten flock's devotion. Indeed, he spoke about people just like them, people who claimed they were raising money to "finance building a new church, finance a new mission in Uganda, Guatemala," the precise sorts of projects, in short, that the Pattens pressed on their credulous congregants time and time again. That was always the way to hook the fish, be it into a congregation or a scheme or an organization of dubious nature. Appeal to their sense of goodness and make them feel they are making a difference in the world. Make them feel they are part of a greater, better whole, that their participation will make them into better people.

Stalvey remembers the approach well, those hope-filled early days of belonging, when you first feel yourself brought into a fold, a community, a group with a higher purpose that can, in turn, lend purpose to your own life. "The process of starting with just going to yoga and helping children in Africa, to giving up your money, your family—it's fascinating," she said as she thought back to those days, now a decade in the past. "It always starts out really wonderful. And there's some element of truth there—these are psychologists, theologians, really intelligent people who draw you in. And there is always some basis of love and support that is really there. There is a lot of giving." All cons, cults not least of all, rely on a basis of some sort of truth and reality. What sets them apart from their more legitimate counterparts is where and how that truth is then used. Manipulate it well enough, and no matter the evidence, people will continue to follow. To do otherwise would be to uproot an important, self-defining reality.

"They were usually so convinced," Sullivan said of cult followers, that he needed to go to extraordinary lengths to challenge their steadfast certainty in the rightness of their cause. "I have to show them that the money that went to the mission was actually spent on a second house, a mistress, a lavish lifestyle in LA. And the trip to visit the orphanage, well, here's the receipt: they were in Vegas, gambling." In other words, apart from the mistress, the exact same deceptions that the Pattens had been so fond of—and that their parishioners refused to acknowledge took place or signified much of anything. It's not surprising. But as Sullivan frequently pointed out, physical evidence often didn't even matter. Show it to those who'd already bought into the fiction, and many would say, "No, that's impossible. I know this man; he's a man of God. No way." And even though Sullivan had seen the same dynamic play out dozens of times, it didn't make it any less troubling or difficult to wrap his head around. "That still to this day sometimes stops me in my tracks." An expertly planted belief is a nearly impossible thing to shake.

Think back on some of the stories in these pages. There's Thierry Tilly, crafting an alternative world for an aristocratic family that fully replaced their reality for a decade. There's Oscar Hartzell, implanting a belief in the Drake fortune that was so strong no amount of legal challenges could undermine his followers' trust. There's the Cazique of Poyais, a country at the ready, hapless believers sailing off to their deaths under the sway of his new world. There's Glafira Rosales, creating a family, a history, a world that hoodwinked the art community for twenty years. Every confidence artist you've met is in the exact same business, using our deep-rooted need for belief, in all its guises, to advance an agenda all their own. The screaming evangelist or the grandstanding religious leader or the cult spiritual guru is simply the most extreme incarnation: he doesn't just go after small beliefs; he attacks the core of existence. "We're really adamant we have free will," Stalvey said. "But so often, that's simply not true. Everyone has a weakness. We want to connect to someone or something greater. I'm spiritually bent, and here is someone offering me a way to be a better person. The cult stuff just goes to a different level from your regular con."

Sullivan died suddenly in 2013, from a recurrence of liver cancer that caught everyone who knew him off guard. (Conspiracy theories, naturally, sprang up almost at once: had he fallen victim to an angry cult out for revenge?) In the months leading up to his death, he had been planning a memoir of sorts, to be cowritten with the journalist Joshua Jelly-Schapiro. Josh and I met in the winter of 2015, in a dimly lit bar on a quiet block in New York's West Village, to talk about David's work, his outlook, his take on beliefs and deception. "He would have loved to talk to you," Josh told me. "That's the exact way he looked at it: cults are the ultimate con game." The crux of the belief doesn't matter, Sullivan thought. "It doesn't matter if it's Vishnu, Jesus, or a new way to get rich quick. It's immaterial to me," he had said. The techniques and basic psychology remained the same. "They're being profoundly—subtly but profoundly—manipulated at their great expense, at the expense of their life in some cases."

And the reason it happens—and often happens to the most intelligent of people (note, Sullivan would say, the typical cult recruit: young, smart, sophisticated, savvy)—is that human nature is wired toward creating meaning out of meaninglessness, embracing belief over doubt. "There are certain essential things we all have in common," Sullivan said. "There's a deep desire for faith, there's a deep desire to feel there's someone up there who really cares about what's going on and intervenes in our life. There's a desire to have a coherent worldview: there's a rhyme and reason for everything we do, and all the terrible things that happen to people—people die, children get leukemia—there's some reason for it. And here's this guru who says, 'I know *exactly* the reason.'" It's the reason behind all cons, from the smallest to these, the deepest.

It is our need to hold on to belief, to meaning—logic be damned—that continues to fuel the great cons of the world, even as their contours shift with the times. Before, you could pick cults out like sore thumbs, Sullivan joked. Back in the heyday of sixties spiritualism, you could reliably follow the scent of spiritual awakening to the nearest guru. But in the modern world, it has all become more insidious. They wear suits and ties, host corporate retreats, look increasingly like the more legitimate self-help movements of modern corporate America. Like Landmark, an organization, Jelly-Schapiro told me, that Sully considered quite cult- and con-like, predicated on the same techniques, many of them "not very nice," that wear at your sense of self and slowly change the parameters of your world. "They are all founded on meaning, community: what everyone wants."

That's why Sullivan found cults to be a particularly enraging confidence game, more infuriating than most: it was a co-optation of a very legitimate quest for meaning. Everyone wants to believe, everyone wants meaning, everyone wants stories that make sense of incoherence. Everyone sees meaning in chaos, crafts narrative out of haphazardly floating geometric patterns. It's natural, and it's not only understandable but often laudable. Shouldn't we want to search for truth and discern the meaning of reality? Spiritual cons exploit us at our most vulnerable. And because the process is so natural and insidious, it is particularly difficult to resist. You become a sucker almost in spite of yourself.

In a sense, then, managing to survive the cult or spiritual con—the ultimate in confidence games—is the closest we can come to ever figuring out how to avoid falling for the lure of the con man more broadly.

Sullivan and Stalvey, after all, managed to infiltrate cult after cult and come out on the other side. They were, in a sense, con artists in their own right: doing the con artists one better, deceiving them into accepting that they were genuine marks who had been expertly suckered in. Sullivan was largely reticent about his specific approach—tricks of the trade, he called them—but there was one thing he stressed over and over: the key to resisting persuasion and manipulation was to have a strong, unshakeable, even, sense of self. Know who you are no matter what, and hold on to that no matter what. It isn't easy—it was years before Sullivan was able to find a suitable female infiltrator; Stalvey, he said, was an exception. "It's very rare to find someone to put into a cult. You have to have a very strong sense of your own identity," he said. "And it's not easy to do this. The psychological techniques that are now employed to coerce you are phenomenal."

When we spoke, Stalvey elaborated on the approach her mentor had taught her. One of the most important things, she said, was to maintain objectivity: logic to counteract feeling. You know your emotions will be manipulated—they always are, in any con, big or small. That's the whole point of the put-up and the play. And once you become emotional, your reasoning can easily become short-circuited. "Always pay attention to the details," she told me. That is one way to ensure that you are staying rooted in the physical, the objective, rather than the psychological, the subjective. The details themselves may be harrowing—Stalvey observed everything from physical abuse to kids banging their heads on walls to exercises in extreme shaming. "Through it all, you have to make sure you are observing as much as feeling."

Most con games, of course, don't involve such extreme manipulation, but they all depend on the mechanism of emotion to a significant extent. A large part of resistance, of making sure you don't start getting pulled in, is to know yourself well enough to recognize and control your emotional reactions. What kinds of things provoke what kinds of responses in me—and can I see it happening early enough to resist it, by staying grounded in details and logic? Stanford University psychologist

Roderick Kramer believes that one of the ways we can inoculate ourselves against false persuasion is through self-knowledge—one of the elements that forms what Sullivan called your "core self." Know what people you're likely to trust, what triggers are likely to catch you, whether positive or negative, and try to be aware enough of your own behavior that you won't get swept up in it. In short, hone your skills of observation and detail-noting, as Stalvey puts it, when it comes not just to others but to yourself.

Another key element in Stalvey and Sullivan's arsenal: set limits. "I'd decide before I went in what my limits were, the lines I wouldn't cross, physically or emotionally," Stalvey said. She made sure that trusted others knew those limits and were ready to step in if she was getting close to the edge. Of course, cons in real time aren't as clear-cut: you never know you're in a con game until it's over, and even then, not always. But the principle holds: always know the types of comfortable limits you have and the boundaries you won't cross. Think of how many cons work because they take you, in the emotional heat of the moment, beyond a comfortable boundary. Frank Norfleet borrowing money when he'd never done so before for that second chance at making a fortune. William Franklin Miller's victims investing even more money to recoup their losses from his ill-timed absence. Sylvia Mitchell's psychic marks handing over cash only to regret it moments later under the pressure of her steady gaze—but by the time the regret comes, it's too late. The moral is simple. Know yourself well enough, and ask the questions ahead of time, in any venture or interaction: How much am I willing to stake? How much am I willing to lose? How far am I willing to go? And then never let anyone tell you, "Just once more . . ."

Of course, the entire dynamic of limits is predicated on knowing not just when, but how, to get out: if you have a limit but have no mechanism to enforce it, the limit becomes meaningless, a car with its brakes broken. Stalvey always knew exactly how she would exit the situation. Whom she would call, or who would know to come get her after a certain time if she hadn't emerged on her own. When it comes to other potential cons, or situations where your comfort level is uncomfortably close, the same thing holds true. To avoid getting duped, Kramer stresses, have an escape clause, or a way of exiting any interaction with your dignity intact. We often are sucked up in cons because we don't quite know how to disengage—it feels like we're losing face, letting someone down. And by the time we realize that, no, we should have gotten out, it's too late.

The final mode of attack—one that is, in many ways, fundamental, says Stalvey—is knowledge, pure and simple. "Just knowing what you're going through can be immensely helpful," she says. "It's like boot camp. If you know you're going through fifteen hours of psychological hell, you can prepare yourself." Before going deep into a new cult, she would make sure to learn as much as she could about its history, purpose, and techniques early into her infiltration. That way, she wouldn't ever be caught completely off guard. Of course, her experience was unique, in the sense of having been planned. You can't learn about a scam you don't realize is happening. But what you can do is learn about cons more broadly: the types, the approaches, the methods, the techniques. Seniors who are taught about the grandparent scam, for instance, become far less likely to fall for it. And then, with any luck, you will be able to pick out a con game's contours before you've fallen prey to its approach.

Nothing, of course, is foolproof, and constant resistance takes a deep toll. Stalvey is now transitioning to being a full-time photographer. After three years, and one infiltration that lasted over eight months, she had had enough. "I couldn't take it. It's not the life I wanted to be living," she told me. And even Sullivan, the lifelong infiltrator, came close to calling it quits. "Everybody has a breaking point. I'm trained, I've been through this a zillion times," he said. "I use techniques to keep from being programmed." And even with all of that, he nearly broke.

He remembered that afternoon like it was yesterday. The cold ground, the rustling leaves, the faint echo of voices through the door to the training room, and he, lying in the earth, on his belly, covered by bushes, whispering urgently into a dying cell phone. On the other line: the lawyer who'd hired him for his latest infiltration. "A kind of triple-type-A attorney who knows exactly what he wants," Sullivan calls him. "He doesn't brook failure." And what he most desperately wants to convey to this man is one single, urgent message: he needs to get out. "I can't take it anymore. I think they're going to kill me. My cover is blown," he pleads. He has just come off several days without sleep or food; a session of extreme shaming where he was forced to stand in a corner without food, water, or bathroom access and answer to the name "Anal-Cranial Inversion"; a ransacking of his hotel room and sabotaging of his car; dehydration and exhaustion worse than any he can recall. And mixed with it all, the certainty that he is going to be killed, or at the least badly hurt, after his assigned partner somehow manages to escape from the program. (His fear is justified; he was the one who'd orchestrated her flight.) All he wants to do is make a run for it while he still can.

The attorney doesn't hesitate. "What do you mean your cover's blown? What are we paying you for? You get your ass back in there."

Sullivan insists. "You don't understand. I'm at the end of my limit. I don't think I can."

The lawyer insists more. "Listen to me. Sully, listen to me. You get back in there. You haven't even been reborn yet."

At that exact moment, the cell phone dies. And Sully gets ready to reenter the windowless room where he's certain his days as a cult infiltrator are doomed to a premature ending. "I knew I was in serious trouble."

But what he also knew, perhaps better than anyone there, cult leaders included, was precisely why these most powerful of confidence schemes are as powerful as they are—and he could manipulate belief along with the best of them. ("My fallback is starting my own cult," he would joke. "He understood these men. He was really forceful, charismatic, a good storyteller," Jelly-Schapiro recalled. "He understood the power personality.") And so, when Sully returned to the room, to the theme from *2001: A Space Odyssey*, the leader's chosen sound track, he returned with the beginnings of a plan.

The order of the day was as usual: a healthy dose of negative energy thrown at the outside world (today's theme: anger at parents), followed by a redemptive message from the leader. At the session, Sullivan went all out. He yelled, he punched, he cried. By the end, his hands were bruised and swollen—he'd eventually need to be hospitalized for injuries—his voice hoarse. And then it came time for the redemption. Atop the stage at the front of the room, the leader took the microphone. No matter how low you were, he told his audience, there was a way out—through him, through this program, through its training. All you needed to do was take his hand, and, together, walk forward into a new life. "It was very moving," Sullivan remembered. Not to mention the story about the throat cancer survivor who would never sing again—and then, miracle of all miracles, was once more able to sing.

It was then that Sullivan jumped out of his seat. "Yes, yes, I know—I know what you mean—I feel it!" he screamed. "Oh, sir, can I just try to express what's inside me?" The leader looked down benignly. "Sure, Anal-Cranial Inversion," he acquiesced. With that, Sullivan grabbed the microphone and, before anyone could stop him, jumped on the stage. With all his might, every life-loving fiber of his body, he began to sing—"belt out," as he preferred to call it—a song that seemed to encapsulate the moment: "The Impossible Dream." "There wasn't a dry eye in the house. To dream the impossible dream. To fight the unbeatable foe. To bear with unbearable sorrow—I built it right to the last. They were weeping," Sullivan remembered. "The head embraced me with tears in his eyes. And we all sang together, louder and louder, all off-key and screaming. And I was redeemed. I was suddenly solid. I graduated. I got to be reborn. I got my new name. It was nice, not to be Anal-Cranial Inversion anymore." And he didn't just redeem himself. He surpassed redemption. At the end of the program, the leader and his helpers, the "angels" (the Gestapo, Sullivan silently called them), asked him to join them in a private room. And there they informed him that he had been chosen not only to graduate, but to graduate to the training for trainers. "I was deemed worthy to come and brainwash the next crowd coming through."

Sullivan was able to take the game of belief to the next level. He knew precisely how the game worked, and he mirrored the leader's own techniques back at him, amplified several times over. He knew the power of the story, and how to tell it well. How could he not be a true believer when his words were coming right from the depths of his soul?

* * *

David Sullivan was never a true believer. That term he reserved for those he was trying to help. But he was, in Jelly-Schapiro's words, a true seeker. He was spiritual. He wanted truth. He had lived with the Sioux Indians and studied with their medicine men, practiced Buddhism, roamed the political communes of the sixties. He wanted always to explore the depths and possibilities that spirituality could offer. "He was drawn to it," Jelly-Schapiro explained. "He wasn't a cynical secular guy. And he took it personally when people used spirituality for perverse ends. He resented it." That, in a way, was why he would become enraged at the false promises of the spiritual con. He knew just how powerful a thing belief could be. Something so fundamental to our sense of the world should not be tampered with for personal gain.

Meaninglessness is, well, meaningless. It's dispiriting, depressing, and discouraging, not to mention profoundly disorienting and disturbing. Nobody wants their reality to resemble Kafka. And in those moments when it does, when we can't make out what or why or how, we nevertheless try our best, as soon as we recover from shock, to explain it all once more and fit it into any sort of schema. Even Joseph K. can't stand the apparent meaninglessness of his arrest and trial. He knows he must have done something, and tries his best to impose a semblance of meaning on the things that seem to keep happening through no doing of his own.

Before humans learned how to make tools, how to farm, how to write, already they were telling one another stories—and not just any stories. Stories with a deeper purpose. The man who caught the beast wasn't just strong. The signs were on his side. The spirit of the hunt was smiling at him. The rivers were plentiful not because of the weather or some natural cycle. It was because the spirit or ruler or god or king of the river was in a benevolent mood. In society after society, group after group, religious belief, in one form or another, has arisen spontaneously throughout history. Anything that cannot immediately be explained must be explained all the same. It cannot just *be*. And the explanation often lies in something bigger than oneself—a bigger force, an unexplainable one that can, in turn, explain everything else.

The often expressed view of modern science is that God resides in the cracks. That is, as more and more of the world is explained through understandable phenomena, and ends up being not so divine after all, the cracks in knowledge—the remaining gaps that we have no explanation for—are where the force that needs no explanation resides. Its home may have shrunk, but it will always exist. As long as there is something to explain, and no easy way to explain it, belief will rise up.

It's little wonder that so many cons flourish in the world of religious experience—and, indeed, that religiosity is one of the few factors that consistently predicts susceptibility to fraud. It's a thin line between belief in one miracle and belief in another. The Bebe and C. Thomas Pattens of the world have their work cut out for them: religion is the natural breeding ground of the confidence game. The threshold for belief has long been surpassed. Now you need only the right preacher to give it just the right revelatory meaning.

When he died in 1887, Adam Lord Gifford left an unusual bequest. He wanted his legacy to be used to found a series of lectures throughout the universities of Scotland that would "promote and diffuse the study of Natural Theology in the widest sense of the term—in other words, the knowledge of God." From the start, the lectures were considered a great honor, so when the news came that he had been selected, William James readily accepted.

In 1901 and 1902, James gave one of the most famous tours in the Gifford Lectures' history. It was a draining experience. After the first series of talks, he succumbed to a nervous breakdown, postponing the second tour by close to a year, and trying (unsuccessfully) to cancel it altogether. The result, however, became the basis of one of the most important books of his career, *The Varieties of Religious Experience: A Study in Human Nature.*

In its pages, James didn't just visit the origins of religion. Into the same family, he placed phenomena that to the religious and scientific men of the day alike were absolutely unthinkable: the psychic, the superstitious, the mystical. To him, it was all of the same vein. James was not an atheist—not by a long shot. He was, like David Sullivan, a seeker and a believer. But he was also a man of science. And to him, the parallel was clear. If you believed, you didn't just believe in religion. You believed in all mystical phenomena—if the facts were there to support it. You didn't just believe what was convenient. You believed where you were led by the evidence. If you were someone willing to embrace religion, you should also by right examine the rest of the unexaminable.

People balked. Religion was pure. *That* was worthy belief. Psychics were garbage. True religion did not admit any of that. Despite James's stature, James Ward, the British philosopher and psychologist who had earlier left the ministry for his overly liberal views of religious doctrine (and had given the Gifford Lectures before James), refused to review *Varieties* flat out. It was, he said, "tainted" with psychical research. He was as open-minded as the next person, but James had crossed a line.

To James, though, there *was* no line. "Everybody knows," he wrote to Elizabeth Glendower Evans, one of his former students at Harvard who later assisted him in psychical research, "that the real life of religion springs from what may be called the mystical stratum of human nature." That mystical stratum underpinned all belief. The question was, which beliefs were considered acceptable, and which dismissed?

That was, more often than not, a judgment call—a judgment call that could be legitimate or could well be exploited by the ethically dubious.

Every man, James said in his final lecture, is entitled to—and most certainly has—his own "over-beliefs," which were "the most interesting and valuable things" about him. The tendency toward over-belief was inevitable, and it was ubiquitous. "That the God with whom, starting from the hither side of our own extra-marginal self, we come at its remoter margin into commerce should be the absolute world-ruler, is of course a very considerable over-belief. Over-belief as it is, though, it is an article of almost every one's religion," James wrote. "Most of us pretend in some way to prop it upon our philosophy, but the philosophy itself is really propped upon this faith."

Everything was a matter of faith. The extent of the faith was the question. "I state the matter thus bluntly, because the current of thought in academic circles runs against me, and I feel like a man who must set his back against an open door quickly if he does not wish to see it closed and locked," he continued. "In spite of its being so shocking to the reigning intellectual tastes, I believe that a candid consideration of piecemeal supernaturalism and a complete discussion of all its metaphysical bearings will show it to be the hypothesis by which the largest number of legitimate requirements are met."

In other words, all of us believe, intrinsically and instinctively. We just differ on where we draw the line between "legitimate" and "illegitimate." One man's confidence artist is another man's spiritual leader.

And that isn't something to worry about. It is perfectly natural, and it is, indeed, to be desired. "No fact in human nature is more characteristic than its willingness to live on a chance," James concluded. "The existence of the chance makes the difference, as Edmund Gurney says, between a life of which the keynote is resignation and a life of which the keynote is hope."

Nobody joins a cult, Sullivan repeated often and emphatically. People join something that will give them meaning. "They join a group that's going to promote peace and freedom throughout the world or that's going to save animals, or they're going to help orphans or something. But nobody joins a cult." Nobody embraces false beliefs: we embrace something we think is as true as it gets. Nobody sets out to be conned: we set out to become, in some way, better than we were before.

Con artists, at their best and worst, give us meaning. We fall for them because it would make our lives better if the reality they proposed were indeed true. They give us a sense of purpose, of value, of direction.

That, in the end, is the true power of belief. It gives us hope. If we are endlessly skeptical, endlessly miserly with our trust, endlessly unwilling to accept the possibilities of the world, we despair. To live a good life we must, almost by definition, be open to belief, of one form or another. And that is why the confidence game is both the oldest there is and the last one that will still be standing when all other professions have faded away.

Ultimately, what a confidence artist sells is hope. Hope that you'll be happier, healthier, richer, loved, accepted, better looking, younger, smarter, a deeper, more fulfilled human being—hope that the you that will emerge on the other side will be somehow superior to the you that came in.

ACKNOWLEDGMENTS

This book was born one fall evening as I settled in to watch David Mamet's *House of Games*. Mamet's continuing fascination with cons got me thinking: why hasn't anyone written anything about why they work the way they do, and why even the smartest of us are endlessly vulnerable to the wiles of the confidence man? This book is the result. So, a thank-you to Mamet for the inspiration—if you ever want to talk cons, let me know.

Too many people to count helped make *The Confidence Game* a reality. I owe a tremendous debt to all those who so generously gave their time and emotional energy to share their con experiences with me. Not every story, alas, made it into the final book, but each one helped make it what it is. To the sources who chose to remain anonymous: thank you; I won't out you here, but I'm grateful to all of you. And to those who didn't: Tyler Alterman, Christie Aschwanden, Peter Blau, Moran Cerf, Michael Egan, Ribina Madan Fillion, Sharon Flescher, Adam Grant, Nancy Hall-Duncan, Kevin Hartnett, Jason Hernandez, Wilf Jaeger, David Kwong, Jim Ledbetter, Robin Lloyd, Sandip Madan, Josh Mann, Ed Mosher, Ivan Oransky, Ken Perenyi, Renee, Michael Shermer, Brenda Simonson-Mohle, Bryan Skarlatos, Jennifer Stalvey, Christine Suppes, Carl Zimmer. A few special thanks: Sarah and Jen Crichton, for sharing so many decades' worth of material on the Great Impostor and regaling me with childhood tales of his deceptions; Preet Bharara, for taking the time to help me understand the world of fraud; Ann Freedman, for being so open and gracious in letting me into her life; Apollo Robbins, for teaching me about the world of magical deception; Josh Jelly-Schapiro, for sharing memories of his time with David Sullivan; Luke Nikas, for his never-ending willingness to help me navigate the legal minefields of deception. Thanks, as well, to everyone who took the time to send in tips and leads; each one was greatly appreciated.

I'm so grateful to have an amazing editorial team behind me. Thank you, as always, to my wonderful agent, Seth Fishman, an ever support-ive friend who always senses the right moment to motivate a hungry writer with DKAs. Rebecca Gardner, Will Roberts, Andy Kifer, and the rest of the team at the Gernert Company: you guys are incredible. Wendy Wolf, my patient and tireless editor, whose always insightful sugges-tions shaped the book into what it is. Georgia Bodnar, Kate Griggs, Nicholas LoVecchio, Daniel Lagin, Jason Ramirez, Kristin Matzen, and the countless others at Viking who have worked to make this a reality. The lovely Jenny Lord, my editor at Canongate, whose suggestions were always spot-on. The entire Canongate team, for believing in this project from its inception, and especially Jamie Byng, Jenny Todd, and Anna Frame. And none of this would even be possible without the many won-derful editors who have helped me grow along the way, especially Elea-nor Barkhorn, Trish Hall, Jim Ledbetter, and Aaron Retica.

As I scrambled to finish the manuscript by some semblance of a deadline, I was very fortunate to have tremendous support from every-one at The New Yorker, who helped navigate deadlines and offered end-less invaluable editing and writing advice. A huge thank-you to Nick Thompson and John Bennet for the countless hours you've spent mak-ing me a better writer. Thank you to Josh Rothman, to the indispensable fact checkers and copy editors who have worked to make my pieces what they are, and, of course, to David Remnick, for believing in my future as a writer.

I've been lucky to have a number of incredible mentors, but I want to thank especially Katherine Vaz, who believed in me from the moment I stepped into her writing class as a confused eighteen-year-old; Steven Pinker, who has taught me so much of what I know and has been a constant source of inspiration; and Walter Mischel, for hours of wisdom, beautiful art, and always thought-provoking conversation.

And a final, most heartfelt thank-you to the people who've had to put up with me the longest, and somehow still decided to stick around. The friends who listened to me moan over countless meals and bottles of wine—and despite my often less-than-stellar company still offered in-person deliveries of tea when I shut myself in for weeks at a time. I am very lucky to have you all in my life. My amazing family, who have always supported everything I do. And, of course, my husband, Geoff, without whose love and support none of this would be possible. I love you.

NOTES

INTRODUCTION

The introductory chapter, as well as all future references to the story of Ferdinand Waldo Demara, "The Great Impostor," relies on four major sources: Robert Crichton's *The Great Impostor* and *The Rascal and the Road*, personal interviews with the Crichton family, and several boxes full of carefully organized letters, clippings, and notes courteously provided by the Crichton family. These include correspondence from Demara, correspondence with victims of his frauds, and hundreds of original historical records, spanning the 1950s, 1960s, and 1970s, many of which never made it into Crichton's books.

The cited fraud and con statistics come from several surveys administered by the AARP and the FTC from 2011 to 2014. Information on historical cons is provided by an 1898 article in the *New York Times*, "An Old Swindle Revived," as well as the excellent *The Big Con*, David Maurer's account of the language and customs of con men. Maurer's book will be revisited throughout the narrative.

CHAPTER 1: THE GRIFTER AND THE MARK

Apart from Demara's story, Chapter 1, as well as all subsequent chapters, includes numerous original psychological studies, most easily located by author and subject. All specific references, here and in future chapters, are available at www.mariakonnikova.com/books. The plight of the *Slate* author is taken from his first-person account. The accounts and statistics relating to psychopaths come from Robert Hare's research, as well as his popular books *Without Conscience: The Disturbing World of the Psychopaths Among Us* and *Snakes in*

Suits: When Psychopaths Go to Work. James Fallon's account comes from his book *The Psychopath Inside* and a 2014 article in *The Atlantic*, "Life as a Nonviolent Psychopath." Survey data comes from the AARP, FTC, and the Investor Protection Trust.

The chapter also mentions cons taken from original interviews conducted by the author between 2013 and 2015, with Michael Shermer, Preet Bharara, Jason Hernandez, Robin Lloyd, Renée, Leanne ten Brinke, and several anonymous sources. All other con accounts come from assorted news stories.

CHAPTER 2: THE PUT-UP

The account of Sylvia Mitchell's exploits draws on a number of sources: court transcripts and documents, in addition to contemporary news coverage. Demara's stories continue to draw on the original sources listed in the introductory chapter. Additional con accounts come from original interviews conducted by the author between 2013 and 2015, including anonymous interviews, as well as conversations with Sandip Madan and Moran Cerf. The rest of the con stories rely on extensive news coverage.

CHAPTER 3: THE PLAY

Samantha Azzopardi's story has been compiled from international news sources over a number of years. The stories of Joan and Alexis rely on original interviews conducted by the author in 2014. The rest of the cons are drawn from news accounts.

CHAPTER 4: THE ROPE

The story of Matthew Brown derives from news sources, along with two interviews conducted by the author in 2015 with individuals purporting to know Brown from childhood—but with shady enough backstories that the author suspects them of being Brown himself, on one occasion hidden behind sunglasses in Skype video, and on another in a series of e-mails that never quite added up. The Cazique of Poyais appears courtesy of several books and news stories, and the Nigerian prince and Cassie Chadwick come, as do many of the older cons in this book, from Jay Robert Nash's *Hustlers and Con Men*, an important older account of many original con games. All information about Glafira Rosales relies on interviews with Ann Freedman, Rosales's defense attorney, Freedman's attorney, and multiple court documents. The story of Rudy Kurniawan is based on original interviews with Wilf Jaeger, Michael Egan, and Jason Hernandez, conducted by the author in 2014, alongside court records and transcripts. The chapter also includes cons based on original interviews with Apollo Robbins and Tyler Alterman, conducted by the author in

2013 and 2014. The rest of the cons derive from news accounts, including Herbert Brean's exposé of Marvin Hewitt in *Life*, from April 12, 1954, "Marvin Hewitt, Ph(ony) D."

CHAPTER 5: THE TALE

Paul Frampton's story is based on a collection of contemporaneous news accounts from the UK, the United States, and Spanish-language sources in Buenos Aires, as well as documents from UNC Chapel Hill. Thierry Tilly's story is compiled from English and French news sources. Dave and Debbie's tale stems from original interviews conducted by the author in 2013. And the caper in the *Sun* comes from contemporaneous news sources, as well as Matthew Goodman's *The Sun and the Moon*.

CHAPTER 6: THE CONVINCER

The account of William Franklin Miller's escapades was compiled from several years' worth of contemporaneous newspapers, mainly the *New York Times*. The rest of the cons in the chapter were taken from news sources, and the story of Lustig and Capone from *Hustlers and Con Men*. This chapter also references Simon Lovell's account of his gambling and con techniques as well as Charles Mackay's *Extraordinary Popular Delusions and the Madness of Crowds*.

CHAPTER 7: THE BREAKDOWN

Frank Norfleet's story is based largely on his 1924 autobiography, *Norfleet*. The rest of the cons derive from news sources.

CHAPTER 8: THE SEND AND THE TOUCH

The story of Glafira Rosales and Ann Freedman was compiled through an extensive series of original interviews conducted by the author over the course of 2014 and 2015, with Ann Freedman, her lawyer Luke Nikas, the lawyers for Glafira Rosales and Jimmy Andrade, and a number of art experts, including the head of IFAR, Sharon Flescher, along with close readings of relevant transcripts and court documents. The Teton Dam account is taken from the congressional and official reports on the disaster.

CHAPTER 9: THE BLOW-OFF AND THE FIX

Oscar Hartzell's story is based on both *Hustlers and Con Men* and news accounts. The stories of fraud derive from a combination of news accounts and original interviews with Ivan Oransky conducted by the author in 2014. The psychological studies in this chapter are supplemented by original interviews with Robin Dunbar, conducted by the author in 2014.

CHAPTER 10: THE (REAL) OLDEST PROFESSION

The story of Bebe and C. Thomas Patten relies on historical documents combined with Bernard Taper's account in *The New Yorker*, from January 17, 1959, "Somebody Is Going to Get It," as well as *Hustlers and Con Men*. David Sullivan's story relies on his 2010 talk at the Commonwealth Club, as well as multiple original interviews conducted by the author in 2015, with Joshua Jelly-Schapiro and Jennifer Stalvey. This chapter also owes a debt to William James's *The Varieties of Religious Experience*.

INDEX

HOW TO THINK LIKE
SHERLOCK HOLMES

MASTERMIND

MARIA KONNIKOVA

CANON ‖ GATE

MIND
OVER
MONEY

The
Psychology
of Money
and
How to Use
It Better

Claudia Hammond

Presenter of BBC Radio 4's *All in the Mind*

CANON▌GATE